SCREEN

TIME

SCREEN TIME:

HOW TO MAKE

PEACE WITH

YOUR DEVICES

AND FIND YOUR

TECHQUILIBRIUM

BECCA CADDY

First published in the UK by Blink Publishing
An imprint of Bonnier Books UK
80–81 Wimpole Street, London, W1G 9RE
Owned by Bonnier Books
Sveavägen 56, Stockholm, Sweden

facebook.com/blinkpublishing
twitter.com/blinkpublishing

Trade Paperback – 9781788704212
Ebook – 9781788704229

A CIP catalogue of this book is available from the British Library.
Typeset by IDSUK (Data Connection) Ltd
Printed and bound by Clays Ltd, Elcograf S.p.A

1 3 5 7 9 10 8 6 4 2

Blink Publishing is an imprint of Bonnier Books UK
www.bonnierbooks.co.uk

For Mum and Dad,
for always being interested and making sure I have enough
batteries and pens

CONTENTS

INTRODUCTION

Ever since I was small, I've been mesmerised by anything with a screen. Long before touchscreen technology became commonplace, I would stare, moon-eyed, at all the televisions, flip phones, desktops, laptops and speaker systems on display at the big Currys my dad took me to at weekends. Everything had a flashy display or interface that told me things or gave me control over the device. I was desperate to know how all these flat, shiny surfaces could do so much.

That's ultimately why, for more than a decade, I've made a living writing, reviewing and thinking about tech. It's given me endless opportunities to get hands-on with new tech, trial incoming products at conventions, quiz the people who make it all, and figure out what it adds to our daily lives. By doing all this, I've learned that the many screens in our modern lives – the phones, tablets, wearables and smart home gadgets – can be as much a source of stress as a source of joy.

I've sometimes had the feeling that my screens were more in control of what was going on than I was, and tried all kinds of things to get that control back. I went on a meditation retreat, I switched out my smartphone for a 'dumb' one; I even tried an electroshock device designed to break bad habits. None of these things worked. Why?

Because for all the downsides, my devices also provide me with plenty of good things that I don't want to give up. The truth is, I don't need to detox, delete or downgrade, I just want more balance.

I know people who, at the start of 2020, made resolutions to cut down on the amount of time they spend on their screens. To help themselves, they downloaded browser extensions that limit access to time-wasting websites. They deleted Instagram and Twitter from their phones and shut down their Facebook accounts. Then Covid-19 happened and priorities changed for everyone.

Because of social distancing and more people working from home than ever before, our screens suddenly became the most reliable – in fact, the only – way to stay connected with our friends, family and the people we work with. Accessories turned into necessities and our relationships with tech became ever more deeply symbiotic. Which is why now, more than ever, I believe we need to know how we strike a healthier balance with our devices.

Before we start, I think it's helpful to be super-clear about what we even mean by the word 'technology'. Because even though it's a word everyone uses all the time, it can sometimes be a bit broad and nonspecific, leaving room for doubt in people's minds as to what is or isn't being covered.

The definition of technology is: 'Machinery and equipment developed from the application of scientific knowledge'. By definition, then, the glasses I'm wearing as I type these words are classed as technology. As is the biro next to my keyboard that I'm using to jot down notes every so often. Is this a book about fixing our unhealthy relationships with eyewear and stationery? No, of course it isn't. So we need to be more specific.

We're going to focus on 'connected' technology. Devices that connect to the internet to send and receive information, to play video games online, to share photos and videos with friends and strangers. Smartphones, tablets, smart TVs, fitness wearables. Things with screens and all the things you can do on them. You don't need to own all of these things to get something out of this book. The main points will apply whether your tech use is minimal or maniacal. You don't have to be a card-carrying tech lover to read this book. Just ready and willing to find your best tech/life balance.

I have in the past, like many others, tried to make the case that tech is neutral. That technology in and of itself can neither be good nor bad and that it depends entirely on how we as individuals use it that determines whether the value it creates is positive or negative. But with so many technologies now being designed to actively filter and affect our attention in real time – social media, especially – the case for tech neutrality is becoming that much harder to make.

Technology companies used to make money by creating and selling new products and services. Now, though, there's a considerable amount of money to be made from gathering, analysing and, sometimes, selling information about you. How do you think Facebook became a billion-dollar company when not a single one of its billion-plus users pays a membership fee to use it?

As the saying goes, if you're not paying for the product, you are the product.
Everything that everyone does online is tracked and measured to help businesses gain a deeper understanding of how we all behave. Throughout the coronavirus lockdown, whole galaxies of data were generated by our doing everything online while we stayed away from people and places. Country-sized portraits were painted of what people do with their tech time when they're under extreme stress.

The goal for all of the online service providers using this data is to find more effective ways to encourage us to continue scrolling, clicking and buying. To find smarter ways to nudge each of us down the purchasing path to whichever advertiser is paying for the space on your screen.

This is probably why I often get asked things like: 'Should I delete my Facebook?', 'Should I get rid of my smartphone?' and 'Should I go on a tech detox?' Now, I'm all for recommending the things that nourish each of us, and if any of those things feel right for you, go ahead and do them. But I genuinely don't believe they're what most of us truly need. Drastic measures rarely work. Pick any of your New Year's resolutions and ask yourself: how many have ever made it past spring?

Just as the practice of detoxing our bodies with extreme fasting and lots of lemon juice has been called into question by researchers, the notion of a tech detox is simply not helpful to the greater majority of us. We'll be doing ourselves a favour if we can agree to retire the word 'detox' from our tech vocabulary for good and keep it in its proper context – for when someone is in the process of expelling hard drugs from their system or getting treatment for a snake bite.

Why does this matter? Because words matter. The language we use about any given subject affects the way we think about and react to that subject. Many of us rely on technology for work, for entertainment and for connection with other people. Admittedly, the tech we use every day isn't flawless and in some instances, as we'll learn, has been designed to influence and monetise our attention. But by implying tech is toxic, well, we turn it into something to be only distrustful of, and being suspicious about new things is a very human reaction.

In 1926, a charity group in the US asked: 'Does the telephone break up home life and the old practice of visiting friends?' Don't be fooled by the calm and objective tone of the question. The implied answer was a loud and concerned 'yes'. Telegrams, television, mobile phones and, more recently, video games and virtual reality have all provoked near-identical responses. These are examples of what experts call moral panic. It's a particular type of reaction people have to changes in society that appear to threaten their familiar values or traditions.

I think it's important to recognise that a knee-jerk response to new technologies is entirely expected, but it's not entirely helpful. Focusing our concern on the amount of time children spend on screens, for a very current example, risks overlooking the under-lying factors that drive this behaviour and misses out on the more meaningful conversations we could all be having instead.

Moral panic has its place, but alarmism, which leads to needless bans and restrictions, gets in the way of clear-eyed understand-ing and healthy progress. That's why this book isn't a sermon on logging off from social media permanently. I'm not going to try and convince you to downgrade your smartphone to something less clever. Instead, we're going to explore practical ways to make peace with the screens in our lives by getting to the heart of how our device usage makes us feel better and worse about ourselves.

I've dived into all of the research I could lay my hands on – some of it brand new, some which has been around for years – to show us that the behaviours which drive many of our problems with tech are, for the most part, normal and well documented. We'll see that a lot of our issues aren't caused by our devices – but they can certainly be exacerbated by them.

For example, why aren't we better at knowing when we've had enough? Well, a 2005 study was conducted to see if people knew when they'd had enough soup. Researchers gave half of the group a regular bowl of soup, while the other half were given bowls with a hidden tube that continually added more soup. We'd all like to think we'd notice an infinite bowl of soup, but the findings of this study suggest we'd likely keep supping away until the cows came home.

Granted, the way we eat and the way we 'consume' updates, photos, videos and news on our phones isn't exactly the same. But I think this is a good visualisation to keep in mind as we look at the ways certain technologies are engineered to be near-impossible to turn away from. How there's no 'end' to our social media streams and how our poor brains are looking for the cue to step away from the virtual soup bowl and do other things.

Many of the individual topics we look at could fill entire books all of their own, so think of this as a guidebook that brings together all of the current best thinking about topics like time management, regaining focus, using tech to entertain and de-stress, handling social comparison and how algorithms influence us.

We live in a world powered by tech and have, in our lifetimes, witnessed technological leaps forward that changed the world several times over. The Generation Z kids have never known life without Facebook and touchscreens. The thing is, it's fine to be a fan of your phone, your apps, your social media platforms and all the tech in your life. I am.

There's more than enough worst-case-scenario digital fear-mongering out there, as well as plenty of brand-worshipping tech evangelism. Both have their place, but both can also be deeply unhelpful. I want us to take the time now to find our happy balance – our 'techquilibrium' – and think about the ways we can adjust our relationships with our devices so we get more benefit than bother out of them. To give ourselves control of our screen time.

Five things to remember:

- **Tech changes fast**

  I've done my best to make the advice and information as current as possible and a lot of the research represented here is broadly applicable – a Facebook-centric study can still give you helpful insight into the other social platforms that you use.

- **Research isn't gospel**

  All the research represented in this book is valid and accredited, but never assume that the findings of one study apply to all of us equally. Use the information here to expand your understanding and think more critically as you engage with tech day to day.

- **Share the advice**

  Body image, mental health, echo chambers – there are many ways tech can trigger problems and even make them worse. Don't take on other people's problems, but do share any of the advice you find here that might be helpful to others.

- **Tech companies should be held accountable**

  This book is about us and what we can do for ourselves, but that doesn't mean we're giving the big tech companies a free pass. They can and must do more from an ethical and sociological standpoint. We can all do better for ourselves and each other.

- **Go easy on yourself**

  Change doesn't happen overnight – it's all about incremental gains. Start at the beginning and read all the way through, or dip in and out of the subjects that interest you the most. Learn more about technology, people and yourself and do what feels good.

ADDICTION

UNDERSTANDING THE KNOWNS AND UNKNOWNS OF WHY WE CAN'T PUT DOWN OUR PHONES

Hi, I'm Becca, and I might be a tech addict.

My addiction began with an off-brand Tamagotchi – the 'digital pet' that every child had to have in the late 1990s that looked like a big key ring with an LCD screen. Mine worked just as well as the real thing (that's what my mum convinced me, anyway). I was 11 when the Tamagotchi craze hit the UK, and everyone at my school had one too. My friends and I would all sit together, silently feeding our little pocket pets, playing games with them, cleaning up after them and giving them medicine when they got sick. Don't tell anyone, but sometimes I even spoke to mine. Not ironically, but as if it could actually hear me. For a few stressful months, my sole purpose was to keep my knock-off bundle of pixels 'alive'. But, like all primary school trends (see also: mood rings and gummy bracelets), the puppies, kittens and baby dinosaurs in our pockets got boring fast. In the playground, they were swiftly replaced by futuristic-looking yo-yos fitted with lights – the less said about my complete lack of yo-yoing skills, the better.

Fast-forward a few years, and Lara Croft replaced my needy virtual pet. My brother and I shared a first-generation PlayStation, and when I got the Tomb Raider game for my birthday, I became obsessed. I bought gaming magazines to get my hands on the latest cheats and, when I was meant to be paying attention at school, I was drawing level maps to help me plan the best routes around traps and enemies. My Tamagotchi would at least go to sleep every so often. Lara Croft was *always* ready for an adventure, and I was frequently up until the early hours of the morning, raiding tombs.

I signed up for Myspace in my mid-teens, and it felt like a portal into a world that was a million miles from the seaside town I grew up in (which was, to my adolescent mind, beyond boring by that point). Myspace helped me to discover new music, new friends and chat with boys who appeared to be infinitely cooler than the assortment we had at my school. I spent hours honing my selfie skills before anyone called them selfies and customising my profile page using rudimentary web design know-how that I still use today.

My first Fitbit was a tiny device that clipped onto my clothes. Although its data-collecting abilities were very basic, I found it endlessly fascinating. As a tech journalist, I've had the chance to try dozens of fitness trackers, smartwatches and other wearable gadgets, which were able to collect all kinds of information about how I slept, moved and ate. I added this data to spreadsheets, analysed my performance and evaluated every night out, walk to work and mouthful of food based on whether it moved me further towards or away from my goals.

Each of these tech obsessions might seem vastly different. But combined, the gadgets, apps, games, social media platforms and websites that have punctuated my life have helped me to connect to other people, escape from the world, calm my nerves, have fun, learn new skills, become more creative, express myself and distract myself. But technology has also taken up a huge amount of time, affected relationships, caused stress, disrupted my sleep, made me miss plans, made me cancel plans, exacerbated problems with eating and cost me a lot of money.

Your history with technology is likely just as complicated. Especially if you're a millennial and can (almost) remember what the world was like before smartphones. Did you carry around a bright pink Dear Diary with you everywhere you went? Maybe you spent more time talking to people on MSN Messenger than you did in real life? When you first got Facebook, did you feel a curious pull to check what your friends were up to on the one hand and a little icky about peering in on their lives on the other? How about your drive to become a Super Mario Kart champion or how often you played Solitaire on your phone during meetings at your first job? Have you noticed Instagram can turn from fun and friendly to fake envy fuel within seconds? Do you spend hours and hours at a time 'doomscrolling', continually feeling like you need to keep up with a despairing news cycle yet unable to peel yourself away from it?

There's no doubt that we love our apps, games, social networks, smartwatches and devices, but is there a chance that our love has crossed an invisible line and become an addiction? That's what this chapter is all about: how best to talk and think about our dependence on devices and how we can take control over how we use them.

ALL THE TECH, ALL THE TIME

Ask the parent of any teenager, and they will no doubt think that theirs is 'addicted' to the latest app or new video game. Take a quick glance around any cafe, bus or train, and you'll see most people with their heads bowed, engrossed in a high-definition screen, which they rarely look up from. Think back to any time recently when you had a few minutes to kill. I bet you spent it looking at your phone, on social media, playing a game or checking your email, right?

Don't worry, most of us do. One 2018 study found that, on average, people check their phones within five to ten minutes of waking up – 27 per cent even check within 60 seconds of opening their eyes. Stats from 2019 suggest that we will continue to check our smartphones at least another 58 times throughout the day and we'll clock up about 3 hours and 29 minutes of time online.

If these numbers sound high to you it's because every time new stats like this are released, they keep getting higher. Higher still since the Covid-19 social distancing measures were announced and made us all even more reliant on device-based interaction than we were already. In April 2020, the amount of time we spent online rose to an average of 4 hours 2 minutes each day. I couldn't find official numbers about how many times that means we touched our phones, but I'm guessing it's way up in the hundreds – at least. Throughout 2020 it's a safe bet that even the most tech-averse found themselves reaching for any nearby device with an internet connection as a lifeline to work, friends, family and the non-stop news cycle.

To be clear, though, I'm not saying there's anything wrong with spending time on your phone. Losing an hour or two during the week to social media scrolling isn't the reason to take stock of your relationship with technology. Instead, it's about how using technology makes you feel.

Research suggests there could be a link between technology use and depression, anxiety, loneliness, relationship issues and poor sleep – all issues we'll cover in depth throughout this book. Many of us probably don't need a study to confirm what we already know: that the way we use tech doesn't always seem good for us.

Many of the people I spoke to while writing this book told me they can feel reliant on technology one minute and pestered and drained by it the next. Clearly, this isn't a healthy state to be in. When we have friends in our lives who make us feel this way, we either confront the issue or reconsider the friendship. Tablets and smartphones are now as much a part of our everyday lives as our friends and family, but they shouldn't be making us feel exhausted, under pressure or miserable.

Another feeling people have talked to me about countless times is a loss of control. It sounds dramatic to say that we feel 'controlled' by our smartphones, but this could be why so many of us, rightly or wrongly, describe our reliance on devices as a kind of addiction. We need them, sometimes we feel like we love them, but it can certainly seem like we have no autonomy over what we look at, how we spend our time and where our attention goes.

This sentiment was very neatly summed up by the American stand-up comedian Jerry Seinfeld in his 2020 Netflix special *23 Hours to Kill*: 'I don't know what the purpose of people is any more. I think the only reason people still exist is phones need pockets to ride around in.'

If we're to make sense of the negative effects that technology can have, and what we can do to remedy them, there are two questions that we need to answer – what are our devices doing to make us feel powerless, and is technology addiction even possible?

UNDERSTANDING (AND MISUNDERSTANDING) ADDICTION

I've heard people say they're 'addicted' to Netflix, knitting and the green triangles in tins of Quality Street. But addiction is a serious disorder with a serious definition:

'A person with an addiction uses a substance, or engages in a behaviour, for which the rewarding effects provide a compelling incentive to repeat the activity, despite detrimental consequences.'

It's the nature of these consequences that sets an addiction apart from some of the preoccupations I described above – in most cases we use the word colloquially to describe liking something a lot and wanting a bit too much of it. For example, if someone is addicted to a substance or behaviour, then everyday activities, such as their work, leisure time and relationships, are all negatively affected.

Using this definition, can we identify technology addiction as something real and, therefore, treatable? Possibly, but it depends who you ask. Dr Mark Griffiths, a psychologist and Professor of Behavioural Addiction at Nottingham Trent University, offers one of the most widely accepted and easy-to-grasp explanations of technology's relationship to addiction.

Griffiths suggests that technology addiction should be considered a subset of behavioural addictions, and that all behavioural addictions have recognisable core components. I've listed those components here, along with my own tech-related examples:

- **Salience** e.g. you think about the internet all the time.
- **Mood modification** e.g. gaming makes you feel a 'buzz' of excitement.
- **Tolerance** e.g. you need more and more time on social media for it to have the same effect.
- **Withdrawal symptoms** e.g. you feel sad and irritable when you can't get online.
- **Conflict** e.g. you've had arguments with your boss and your partner about how much time you spend online.

o **Relapse** e.g. you've stopped going online for days or weeks at a time, but when you log back in again your usage reverts back to being sky-high.

It's important to note that even the word addiction is controversial. Dr Carlton K. Erickson, an author and research scientist, says it's 'vague' and writes that, because it's used so widely and often misunderstood, it proves that it's ill-defined to begin with. This goes some way to explaining why the idea that the existence of any addiction to technology, the internet or Facebook is so hotly debated.

INTRODUCING INTERNET ADDICTION

In 1995, psychiatrist Ivan Goldberg published one of the first tests designed to help people find out if they had internet addiction disorder (IAD).

His test listed seven symptoms, which included being 'online for longer periods of time than was intended', 'important social or occupational activities that are given up or reduced because of internet use', and 'voluntary or involuntary typing movements of the fingers'. He then published the test on an online psychiatry bulletin board.

Unfortunately, Goldberg's test for IAD had one major flaw: IAD didn't exist.

Goldberg wanted to make a point about how the processes used to diagnose disorders can be manipulated to arrive at almost any conclusion. He created the prank test by taking criteria from the 'bible' of diagnosing mental disorders, the American Psychiatric Association's *Diagnostic and Statistical*

Manual of Mental Disorders (DSM), which is used to diagnose problems, like pathological gambling. But people were already worrying about the amount of time they were spending on the internet and took Goldberg's test in good faith, only to find out they could have IAD. Goldberg may have designed his test as an illustrative hoax, but it inadvertently hit upon a genuine concern.

THE CASE FOR INTERNET ADDICTION

Dr Kimberly Young took internet addiction more seriously than Goldberg did and was a pioneering voice in its research, diagnosis and treatment. Young began diagnosing and treating patients for internet addiction in 1995 – the same year Goldberg posted his bogus diagnosing test. She created the Internet Addiction Test (IAT), which many other researchers and clinicians have since used as a template to create their own.

Young believed that better understanding and treating internet addiction was important because, just like an addiction to a substance, lives could be badly affected by it. In her research she found instances of relationships breaking down and jobs being lost due to online affairs, chat-room use and bills spiralling out of control.

She's just one of many who have advocated over the years for internet addiction to be taken seriously. From private hospitals through to boot camps, there are now treatment centres all over the world dedicated to helping people overcome addictions to the internet, to their smartphones, to video games and to social media. However, it's impossible to say for sure whether the addictions that are being treated should even be considered addictions in the first place.

THE PROBLEMS WITH INTERNET ADDICTION

Let's take a look at why some experts believe 'internet addiction' as a term in itself is problematic. And why saying we're addicted to the internet, our smartphones and our apps is much more complicated than we think.

1. It's not officially official

Internet addiction isn't listed in the American Psychiatric Association's *Diagnostic and Statistical Manual of Mental Disorders* (DSM). A doctor wouldn't be able to diagnose anyone as having a technology or internet addiction, at least not officially. Many psychologists and specialists diagnose and treat it anyway, but there exists no validated or standardised test to diagnose people or treatment to help people.

The only tech-related addiction which the DSM officially recognises is internet gaming disorder. Even then, it's included in part of the manual that recommends it needs more research and exploration to be better understood. For gaming activity to be considered a possible case of internet gaming disorder it needs to result in a 'significant impairment or distress' across different aspects of someone's life. Some of the signs of internet gaming disorder are similar to the components of behavioural addictions, including an increased tolerance, which means you need to spend more time gaming to feel satisfied, as well as withdrawal symptoms, including sadness and irritability, when gaming is taken away or not possible right now.

Gaming disorder is also included in the World Health Organization's International Classification of Diseases (ICD), which is a similar guide to the DSM. This has caused some controversy. Critics believe its inclusion pathologises gaming behaviour and ignores the positive benefits of playing video games.

2. What does 'internet' really mean?

My biggest complaint with the term internet addiction is that the word 'internet' is broad. Are we talking about social media or phones? Porn or games? Gambling or just screen time generally?

Young devised the Internet Addiction Test to include all contact you might have with any screen, device, phone or connected tech that could go online. It even covers websites, online games, social media and online entertainment.

I don't know about you, but I use all of these things completely differently. I need to spend huge amounts of time online reading websites and journals for my job. Yes, I might fall down a research rabbit hole regularly, but that's all part and parcel of what I do. My social media habits are a different story. I can lose way too much time scrolling or watching Instagram stories for no good reason. And online entertainment is just that: entertainment. I do spend a lot of time catching up on Netflix shows, but I don't think this is something I'd ever need help with – it's a source of necessary relaxation. Trying to bundle all of these platforms, activities and different uses together would be confusing and unhelpful.

Some researchers have suggested separating internet addiction into distinct areas based instead on the platforms: internet addiction, internet gaming disorder, smartphone addiction and Facebook addiction, whereas others believe the focus shouldn't be on technology at all, but instead on behaviour. One study proposed that we should replace the term internet addiction with specific behaviours whether they take place online or offline, like gaming, gambling and sexual activity.

Here's an important question for you to consider: are we addicted to the internet or is that just a convenient space for us to indulge our addictive behaviours?

3. It's not an addiction

Some people believe the word addiction isn't right in this context. In a 2018 TED Talk, neurobiologist Dr Cyrus McCandless explained that we shouldn't use the word 'addiction' about technology because it's making it harder to have conversations and find solutions for drug addiction. 'Marketers, app developers and most of all, journalists need to stop using the word when they're talking about iPhones, Candy Crush Saga or cheeseburgers,' he says.

4. There are lots of different tests

If you type 'internet addiction test' or 'tech addiction test' into Google, you'll find hundreds of them. Not all of these tests have been created by academic researchers or accredited psychologists working to diagnose internet addiction, but there are still a great many nonetheless.

A lot of them share similar themes. They want to know if you lose track of time when you use technology, if you feel that you need to use it more and more to feel satisfied, if you use it to feel better or less stressed out, and whether you feel unhappy or agitated if you stop using it.

However, without an official, medically recognised diagnosis for internet addiction, there exists no authoritative method for assessment. This immediately creates problems for anyone with cause for concern about their own internet reliance, because they could take one test that says they're addicted, and then take another which, after asking a different set of questions, tells them they're not.

Without an agreed-upon method for recognising and diagnosing internet addiction, understanding the true nature and scope of it as a potential illness is extremely difficult. It also makes it challenging to better gauge the health of your own use of the internet and technology – which test should you trust?

Take a test

As you read this chapter, you may very well have asked yourself, 'Am I addicted to being online?' I think that's casting the net pretty wide. So instead, let's take a look at your relationship with your smartphone specifically.

The Center for Internet and Technology Addiction, run by Dr David Greenfield (an Assistant Clinical Professor of Psychiatry at the University of Connecticut School of Medicine) has created a Smartphone Compulsion Test. It asks 15 yes or no questions, and here are five of them to get you started:

1. Do you find yourself spending more time on your smartphone than you realise?
2. Do you find yourself mindlessly passing time on a regular basis by staring at your smartphone?
3. Do you seem to lose track of time when on your smartphone?
4. Do you find yourself spending more time texting, tweeting or emailing as opposed to talking to people in person?
5. Has the amount of time you spend on your smartphone been increasing?

If you answered yes to more than half of these, you may have a smartphone addiction. I don't know about you, but I answered yes to all five. I'm pretty sure that most people with a smartphone would find themselves at the 'addict' end of the scale if they were to take this test purely at face value, along with the many others like it.

5. People might have other problems

Imagine someone finds face-to-face interactions stressful, so they use the internet more than the average person for talking to other people. Would that mean they have an internet addiction or social anxiety? Is it possible to even separate the two?

This is another problem when it comes to understanding internet addiction, as well as our relationship to technology more generally. For example, it's extremely difficult for researchers to determine whether a person feels depressed because they spend so much time online, or they're spending more time online because they feel depressed.

This subtle difference is significant because it means someone who needs treatment for depression could potentially be diagnosed with an internet addiction and end up receiving the wrong kind of help.

6. The case for fun

Many of the internet addiction tests I found while researching this chapter mentioned 'loss of time' as a key factor in defining addiction. But we all know that 'time flies when you're having fun' – so what about when you're simply enjoying your time online?

I know that I've completely lost all sense of time when I'm perusing pins on Pinterest, when I'm trying out different colour palettes for a new website I'm working on, when I'm researching a subject that deeply fascinates me, and I've been following link after link after link. Does this mean I'm addicted?

How I feel doing these activities is similar to what psychologist and author Mihaly Csikszentmihalyi describes as 'the state in which people are so involved in an activity that nothing else seems to matter; the experience itself is so enjoyable that people will do it even at great cost, for the sheer sake of doing it.' In other words, experiencing a state of 'flow'.

I'm not suggesting we all experience flow every time we pick up our devices. I know I certainly don't when I'm scrolling through

Twitter aimlessly or watching the 58th Instagram Story of the morning. But maybe if internet addiction is one day considered an official, valid disorder it could stigmatise some of our favourite tech-based pastimes – and that would be a shame.

The many debates and discussions around tech addiction, and what it is and isn't, can be a lot to process, but they show us that there is no cleanly defined problem and solution to any of these issues. It also shows us that we each need to question when we hear or read terms like 'tech addiction' or 'internet addiction' being used – whether it's in conversation with friends and family, in a news article or on a TV panel debate show. More than anything, we need to remember that just because internet addiction may not be recognised as an illness, it doesn't mean there aren't problems we can resolve by trying to better understand the time we spend online through our smartphones and other devices.

HERE'S WHY YOU LIKE, SWIPE AND CHECK

Our brains are chock-full of so-called 'happy chemicals', some of which you may already have heard of, like serotonin, oxytocin and endorphins. To understand why some people can end up overdoing the time they spend on screens and the dependence they have on their devices, we're going to look at one of the most important of these chemicals: the hormone and neurotransmitter dopamine.

The way dopamine works is really complex. So, for now, we're going to focus on just a few of the reasons why it's important in relation to tech. Dopamine crops up again and again throughout this book, so keep an eye out for it.

I've tried to distil what dopamine is for you myself, but the best, most straightforward explanation comes from Dr Loretta Graziano Breuning in her book, *Habits of a Happy Brain*. She writes: 'Dopamine is the excitement you feel when you expect a reward.' The reason you feel this excitement is because your brain wants you to meet an important need – whether that's food, water, sex, connection or anything else your body has to have to survive. Dopamine motivates you to seek and find these all-important things.

Let's first consider how this works in relation to one of our most basic needs: food. To understand dopamine's role in our lives, Breuning suggests we consider how it helped our ancestors when they needed to forage for food.

So, let's imagine that. Transport yourself back more than 10,000 years (or thereabouts) and imagine you're foraging for food. You can't rely on Deliveroo or Uber Eats when your stomach rumbles as an early human. So, instead, you need to continually be on the lookout for something to eat. Dopamine plays a big role in making this process easier so you don't go hungry.

You're looking around and scanning your environment for a tasty treat. Then you see it, a piece of fruit hanging on the tree above you. Dopamine signals that you've found something – something that you've likely tried before that you know satisfied your need for food in the past. Dopamine then makes you feel good about getting it. There's a misconception sometimes that dopamine's job is just to make you feel great, but using this example we can see there are a couple of purposes. As Breuning puts it: 'Dopamine unleashes a reserve tank of energy when you see a way to meet a need.' You feel good so you can, often literally, go and grab what you need.

Another reason you feel good is to reinforce what just happened so you're likely to do it again. This helps to create something called a neural template. You can't spend all your time hunting for brand new food every single time you need it. To save time, push you in the right direction and help you find the best rewards, dopamine circuits have developed to steer you where you need to go – this worked and felt good before, so let's seek it out again is roughly what's going on here.

With the help of dopamine you, a forager, have found a piece of fruit you know was great the last time you ate it. It gave you the motivation to find it, the buzz of anticipation when you spotted it, the energy to reach up and snatch it from the tree above you and the positive feeling as you ate it so you're more likely to remember to do it all over again.

It's time to leave the past and fast-forward to the present day. The big question is, how is this fruit-finding neurotransmitter relevant to right now? Well, there are a bunch of reasons.

I think one of the most important is that we might associate checking messages and social media with our need for social connection. Sure, it doesn't always feel like a sad scroll is ticking our need for a deep relationship with someone else, but you might have a neural template that links looking at Facebook with feeling socially fulfilled. What that means is when you think about Facebook or see there's a notification from Facebook, dopamine is activated – just like you've seen a nice juicy fruit. You're motivated to check and you feel good about it.

What's more, one review explained that the social goodness we consider rewarding, things like seeing faces and getting positive feedback, can activate dopamine. When you experience similar kinds of social goodness online – think notifications, text messages, likes, WhatsApp messages and pictures of loved ones – you might expect to experience the same kind of dopamine influx, so just the very nature of what you see when you unlock your phone might be linked to ticking off social connection from your checklist of needs too.

Another important part of the dopamine and tech connection is the seeking and finding function of dopamine. What does the always foraging mindset of looking around and hoping to find a new reward that might make you feel good remind you of? Granted, it might be a bit of a leap for everyone, but that feeling of wandering round searching for fruit (and getting increasingly hangry when you don't find it) made me think of the way I pick up my phone and check my apps, hoping to find some kind of virtual piece of fruit – a new email, a nice message from a friend, a bunch of likes on my new Instagram post. Things that make me feel good.

This example is still driven by social connection, but I think it's also about rewards and finding new things more generally and how, over time, we've associated hunting for online validation – likes, emails, messages, comments, friend requests – as a way to feel good. We've developed a neural template that looks something like: your phone made you feel good that time you got a lovely message. Check it again, just to see what's there. It might be another lovely message. Something new to reward you. Even if there isn't a notification, the anticipation builds based on the times we remembered there was one – the times when we *did* get a reward. That's why it's so hard *not* to look at your phone when you already feel compelled to.

I know what you're thinking: what about all the times when we *didn't* get a reward? Why doesn't the experience of no notifications, angry emails and doomscrolling teach us anything? Let's take how I feel right now as an example. I know there won't be anything exciting waiting for me on Twitter – at least nothing interesting enough to justify turning my attention away from writing. I'd bet money on it. So why do I feel compelled to check Twitter as soon as my next break kicks in anyway?

The reason we still check and feel a little buzz of excitement that something new *might* be waiting for us isn't solely to do with the feel-good anticipation of dopamine, but it's also likely due to the unpredictability of the rewards we receive. We'll look at this in more depth soon, but the idea is that, sure, there's probably nothing exciting waiting for you. However, the promise that there might be – because there's no sure-fire way to predict when good or bad things happen on social media platforms – is appealing enough as it is. It's a similar reason why people become hooked on games and even gambling. What if the next one is the one? What if I've had ten new notifications? What if there's some good or urgent news I'm missing out on?

It doesn't matter if there's rarely a reward waiting for us in our inboxes or DMs or anywhere else. It's both the unpredictability *and* the anticipation of a possible reward that activates dopamine. As one study succinctly puts it: 'arousal is more highly correlated with reward anticipation than with the reward itself'.

However, that doesn't mean we feel rewarded when we open up Twitter to see zero notifications. Dopamine makes us feel good every time we seek a reward. But when we find no rewards are waiting for us, we experience what's known as dopamine disappointment. This is a deflated feeling that can then lead to even more checking and seeking as a means to feel better about ourselves. The more we carry out this loop of checking and expecting a reward, finding nothing and feeling bad, checking and expecting a reward, and so on, the more habitual it becomes. I hope your own tech-checking is starting to make a bit more sense.

There are more reasons why we check our tech so often, and we'll look at some of them over the next few pages, but dopamine gets a lot of attention in articles and research papers, and it's often misunderstood, which is why I wanted to dedicate space to it here.

Drugs, phones and cheeseburgers are not the same

I said it before, but I think it's worth reiterating: dopamine is complicated. That's why experts get uptight whenever it gets boiled down to a one word catch-all. You might spot this in news articles that say things like 'dopamine is love' and 'dopamine is addiction'. You'll also notice this in articles about how one thing, such as eating sweets or looking at Facebook, is being compared to taking drugs. An article in the *Sun* once asked, without irony: 'Are cupcakes as addictive as cocaine?'

Despite there being a lot that science still doesn't know about recreational drug use (as well as our brains generally), most experts agree that addictive drugs don't affect the dopamine in our brains in the same way that food and technology does – or at least if it does the evidence is far from conclusive.

Yes, they make people feel good and yes, this is partly to do with dopamine. But that's where the similarities end. Most drugs trigger artificial surges of dopamine – far greater than any amount our body would produce in response to any regular activity. Our brains act as though the drug is a huge surprise and a signal of great success.

So, in short, yes, plenty of different things trigger a dopamine response, including drugs and checking Twitter, but what's going on in our brains isn't the same. 'Addicts want their drugs far more than you could ever even conceive of wanting your iPhone or Facebook or anything else,' McCandless says.

This means comparing our phones to hard drugs is a fallacy and a waste of time. The truth is, there isn't just one thing our tech use can be comfortably compared to. Nothing else affects us and our brains in quite the same way or encompasses the full range of uses, dangers and pleasures that our devices can bring us.

PLAYING THE ATTENTION GAME

At an event in 2017, Sean Parker, the creator of Napster and founding president of Facebook, said this about the thinking behind Facebook: 'How do we consume as much of your time and conscious attention as possible?'

The answer: '. . . we need to sort of give you a little dopamine hit every once in a while, because someone liked or commented on a photo or a post or whatever.' And why do they want this? '. . . that's going to get you to contribute more content, and that's going to get you more likes and comments.'

There's a common misconception that, as the users of Facebook, we are its customers. That the nice (free) comfy space online where we can share news and photos with friends and family is all for us and we have a say in how it works and what it does. This is simply not correct. Technology companies – whether that's Facebook, Twitter, Instagram and many of your other favourite apps – make money by collecting highly informative data about everyone who uses them and selling space to advertisers. What this means is that it's not solely about growing the number of people who've signed up to use their service that matters. Instead, it's about how long you stick around. That way, you'll see more adverts. That way, there'll be more chances to collect data about what you like, what you look at and how you respond to what you see. All of these things turn into profit for the platform you're doing these things on.

All of this obviously sounds a bit creepy, but it helps to explain why so much effort goes into making sure that every app has the appeal of a virtual Disneyland – a place you'll never want to leave.

The technology companies behind all the most successful apps, social networks, messaging services and devices know how dopamine works and how to take advantage of it. It's no secret how much time and money they've all invested in figuring out how to make unputdownable products. Many of the tactics they use have been lifted from other industries built on keeping your attention for as long as possible, such as gambling and advertising.

Many of these tactics are well known to us now. Ex-employees of companies like Google and Facebook have spoken out about some of the methods used to get – and hold onto – our attention. This is great for us because it means we can get better at spotting them and, by doing so, take back more of the control it feels like we've lost.

The never-ending (Instagram) story

Remember the bottomless soups from the Introduction? This is one of the most effective tactics, and it's everywhere. So let's make sure we know how to spot it.

How many times have you been watching an episode of your new favourite show on Netflix and the next episode starts playing before you've had a chance to decide whether you want to keep watching? Have you ever felt that you could, if you didn't have to work or eat or sleep, carry on scrolling through Instagram forever? How many swipes up on TikTok would it take for you to lose all sense of reality? What about how many times you could browse through Tinder before you've swiped left on all the single people on the planet? Do you think there's a prize at the end? Many of the apps and services we use the most are, intentionally, bottomless.

Other types of media offer us clear moments to end an activity and focus our attention elsewhere. For example, you get to the end of a chapter in a book. You finish a magazine. These are stopping cues. Before on-demand viewing came along, you'd watch one episode of a TV show and have to wait a whole week before you could see the next one. Now, the social media apps, streaming platforms and websites we view content on give us no signal to stop and move on. They actively do the opposite and make it very easy to keep going.

We know dopamine keeps us alert to new ways we can meet our needs and find rewards. That means if we get the opportunity to endlessly scroll, swipe and watch, then many of us will.

The slot machine in your smartphone

Many of the 'bottomless' apps have a function in common: the 'pull to refresh' action. This is when you 'pull' the screen down with your fingertips to make it spring back up with fresh content. The thinking behind this action is very intentional and is one of many design features that tech experts have likened to the way slot machines work.

Instead of pulling down a lever on a slot machine, you pull down the screen to refresh the photos, updates, videos and news. By mimicking the action and experience of a slot machine – there's even a tiny delay between the pull and the refresh – anticipation builds, dopamine starts flowing and we unconsciously find ourselves waiting for a new reward.

And, just like a slot machine, you don't know what you're going to get next. Will you find a job offer in your inbox? A viral tweet with tens of thousands of likes? A juicy piece of gossip that your favourite celeb just put up on Instagram? Maybe nothing at all? It's the built-in unpredictability that many of us find so compelling.

It might seem like this is giving you control over your content stream, but it isn't. Because something we never find ourselves saying is, 'Wait, how many times have I pulled down the screen to refresh?' but we absolutely should.

That's because we never know what's coming next – and this is by design. It's called a 'variable ratio schedule'. The variable bit refers to the fact we don't get an expected amount of good things at a scheduled time – it varies. One notification when you look at your phone. Two notifications and a message and a new photo update from your friend the next time. An email the third time. Nothing else the fourth time. As we explored earlier, the unpredictability of these rewards is what keeps us interested and what keeps activating dopamine to seek out more and more chances to get something, to 'win'.

Throughout the 1940s and 1950s, behavioural psychologists B.F. Skinner and Charles Ferster studied ways to influence behaviour by determining when and how to give rewards. Although Skinner most famously studied the behaviour of animals, we can still apply the same thinking to people. Skinner discovered that there are numerous kinds of reward schedules. For example, you can give a reward every time someone completes a task, every other time they try or never at all. These different schedules result in different behaviours.

But both Skinner and Ferster, and researchers since, believe the variable ratio schedule is the one that makes both people (and rats) come back for more the most often – even when rewards aren't given out regularly. It's also the one that's hardest to step away from. That's why it should come as no surprise that slot machines use this kind of schedule – as do many of the apps in your phone.

The social animal

We already know social connection plays a role in how our dopamine reward system works – we're always looking for new ways to connect and feel connected to others, even when we may feel like we're sick of everyone. One study has even suggested that checking our phones is driven by our need to see what others are doing and to be seen ourselves. Head to the Mental Health chapter for more on how and why we compare ourselves to other people.

On the surface, social media apps offer a way to connect with other people. But buried beneath that surface, many tactics are being used to encourage us to interact more than we may want or need to.

For example, 'presence features' tell you who's available right now. Think of the little 'online' indicator on WhatsApp and the two ticks to show your message has been received and seen. Or the chat sidebar on Facebook, which places a little green dot next to whoever is online right now. These small features can put pressure on you to respond quickly and to talk to whoever is available.

That's because these 'I'm available' markers mimic real-life conversation. Think about it: you probably wouldn't stay silent if a person was standing in front of you ready to talk. Presence features might also be effective due to our Fear of Missing Out (FOMO), which is 'the desire to stay continually connected with what others are doing' and researchers believe it's a huge driver of social media use. We want to feel connected, in the know and like we're part of what's going on at all times.

Notifications play a critical role in ensuring you continue to check in on everyone, and feeds are designed to be full of the kinds of content you've already displayed a measurable interest in. This is part of the reason why newsfeed algorithms exist. They're designed to favour the content you're most likely to care about and place it at the top of your feed, where you're more likely to like, click, comment or share.

It might also be one of the reasons why the 'like' came into being. It's a shortcut to feeling a sense of approval from other people, and for giving our approval to others. This presents a problem if your self-worth becomes tied up in how many other people give you a virtual thumbs-up. However, social media platforms actively encourage likes for a whole host of reasons, mostly because they drive you to check in on how many you have continually, increasing your time on the platform. But also because what you like provides them with more information about you and the ads you might want to see.

There are so many more tactics and features. Think of all the design choices on your favourite apps. The bright red notification badge that makes you feel panicked, excited and a little bullied by Facebook? That's intentional. The notification noise you hear when a new message arrives if you're not always on silent? Composed to make you want to check what's going on. The pop-it-in-your-pocket design of your smartphone? So you'll never be without it. A lot of thought goes into keeping you on the hook.

Finding out about some of these tactics changes the shape of enquiry into whether you can have an addiction to technology. It starts to become less a case of: 'Oh no, how did I become an addict?' and instead becomes more a case of: 'Well, what chance did I have of *not* becoming an addict?'

Try this labelling trick

Next time you open up an app, see if you can spot and label any of these tactics. This is a mindfulness meditation technique designed to lessen the effects of strong emotions and, in neuroimaging studies, has been found to diminish emotional reactivity.

All you have to do is notice when you're feeling something and label it. For example, if you feel angry, you say 'anger'. Simple. Try it for the techniques above. If you realise you've been scrolling on Instagram for you can't remember how long, say 'the never-ending Instagram Story'. (You can sing it to the theme tune of the movie *The NeverEnding Story* if you grew up in the 1980s like me.)

> Do this often enough and it can have a disarming effect on the tricks being used to 'consume as much of your time and conscious attention as possible'.

WAIT, SO AM I ADDICTED?

Despite the very brightest minds having studied, thought and written about the ways we all use technology, no one can agree on whether technology addiction – whether it's your smartphone, the internet or social media – truly exists. If it does, what do we even call it? An addiction to technology? Dependence on digital? A smartphone compulsion? Nomophobia (the fear of being without your phone)?

Let's imagine for a minute that internet addiction simply *does* exist. If this were the case, I'm sure that most of us would not qualify as addicts. The time many of us spend on our smartphones, messaging apps, using social media and playing games is, admittedly, problematic. But true addiction causes severe disruption to an addict's life and that simply isn't the case for the majority of people who spend a lot of their time on their phones.

Perhaps, then, the question of whether or not we're all helpless tech addicts isn't as urgent as so many panic-inducing headlines would have us believe. Instead, what's more important and valuable to us is being able to look through the tests and measures for internet addiction and see if we can recognise where our own tech use steps over the line into unhealthy areas.

Do you:

- Think about the internet and social media regularly?
- Use your phone to help you deal with emotions?

- Use your phone a lot?
- Feel irritated when you can't check your notifications?

You may not answer yes to all of these questions all the time, but enough of them often enough might give you pause for thought.

What this all boils down to is even though tech or internet addiction isn't officially recognised as a disorder, there are plenty of reasons to take stock of our everyday use and reliance on tech.

One of the main reasons, for me, is that a lot of the technology we currently use is still relatively new. While many tech-related concerns could easily be written off as technophobic alarmism, the truth is that very little has been around long enough for anyone to measure the long-term effects accurately.

This doesn't mean we need to give anything up to be on the safe side or settle into a constant low-grade panic about what we don't know about our devices. It means we simply need to do what we can to find a better balance for ourselves.

Let's start by replacing the word 'addiction' in this context. I've been searching for different words we might use to help us better talk about and understand our relationship with tech where it is problematic. It isn't easy. Even the people who aren't so sure about labelling these issues an addiction have found it challenging to arrive at an alternative.

I've started to think of my technology dependence as a bundle of habits. Some are good habits and others not so good. I agree, 'habit' doesn't give it the same note of urgency or empathy that addiction inspires, but that's a good thing if we are truly going to get to grips with what's going on.

We can begin to see how things start to pile up and have an effect on us when we break a suspected tech problem down into a list of habits: you find out what's new in the world by reaching for your phone when you wake up in the morning; you measure today's health developments by strapping on your fitness tracker; you check in with your nearest and dearest through a bunch of WhatsApp messaging groups; you check Twitter when you're waiting for the kettle to boil; you visit Facebook when you're bored. And so on.

Let's now look at ways you can start to change your technology habits. Our ultimate aim here is control – getting more of it back and giving less of it to your smartphone.

MANAGE YOUR TIME, MANAGE YOUR TECH

There are plenty of steps (some big, some small) you can take to start changing your tech habits. Many of them are here in the pages of this book. One which I've repeatedly come across during my research is: take control of your time. You can do this by adding some schedules, stopping cues and rules to your day, so you have a greater say over how you spend your time. The good news is it doesn't have to be strict to make a difference.

The notion that you have to hide your phone away forever, plunge yourself into an unforgiving tech detox or attempt to permanently log off weren't the answers offered by any of the studies I looked at about dealing with tech habits and overuse. Instead, like this book, people are encouraged to reduce time spent online – not eliminate it.

The steps towards achieving this are clear and much easier to put into practice than anything vague and unhelpful like 'just do it less'.

A lesson in awareness

We can't change our habits if we don't know what they look like, so let's start by finding out where our time is going right now. By tracking the time we spend working, on our phones, using apps and playing games, we start to get a clearer picture of how we're currently using our tech.

Research shows that we're all (surprise, surprise) really bad at estimating how much time we spend on our phones. One study found the actual amount of time that participants spent on their smartphones was double what they had initially estimated. As we found out earlier, this is no accident. The most successful apps have been deliberately designed by tech companies to occupy our attention and hoover up hours of our time.

If you want to put this to the test right now, write down how much time you think you'll spend on your phone tomorrow. Then use any of the following time-checking methods to see how much time you actually spend on it. Your estimate is likely to be way off the truth.

There are timekeeping apps you can download to keep tabs on your phone use throughout the day. I particularly like Moment. But most phones and tablets now have automatic time-on-phone tracking capabilities built in. You'll need to make sure these settings are switched on and then, this is the tricky bit, you'll need to look at them. And no, you can't wince and look away. You need to commit to properly understanding how often you use your device and the apps, games and social networks you spend most of your time on. Remember: many of us underestimate.

Although this is an exercise in awareness more than it is about making changes, you might notice something interesting start to happen when you begin seeing those stats. When I first started to keep track of the time I was spending on my smartphone, I noticed that I was spending a shocking amount of time playing a game where the object is to rearrange coloured tiles to create a perfect gradient (I know, I know). I cut back on this straight away. While it didn't make as big a difference to some of my other time-suck activities on my phone (including the much longer time I was spending on Instagram), it turns out that adding a little awareness was enough to spark some positive change.

One 2018 study found that people who were asked to actively monitor the time they spent on their phones for four weeks experienced a decline in their fear of missing out (FOMO) and general anxiety at the end of the study. The researchers who conducted this study observed that this could be a direct result of the self-monitoring aspect of the study – because even people who didn't change any of their behaviours as a result were more aware of how they were using tech and simply felt better for it. Maybe all we need to feel more in control is a clearer sense of where all our time is going.

Add the important stuff into your day

One study suggested that the reason some people notice their mood gets worse after using tech (Facebook, in this case) could be because they feel like they haven't done anything meaningful with their time. I can certainly relate to this. Sometimes I don't think there's anything especially wrong with the way I'm using tech – it's more about what it stops me from getting done in other aspects of my life in the meantime.

This is why it's important to figure out where you fit the things that matter most into your day. Tech time should, of course, be included, but work and other essential tasks also have to be given time too. But how do you prioritise?

One way is to eat the frog. Wait, come back! To 'eat the frog' means simply to get the worst, most difficult things you need to do out of the way first. This is one of many productivity hacks you can find online, and I've tried many of them with varying degrees of success. Another which has really worked for me is the Pomodoro Technique.

This is where you work in 25-minute chunks with five-minute breaks in between. You repeat this four times; then you give yourself a longer break of 20 or 30 minutes. You can do what I do and use the timer on your phone to keep track. You can download an app, like Focus Keeper for your phone or get an extension for your browser, like the Marinara Pomodoro Assistant. You can also get an actual Pomodoro kitchen timer, which looks like a little tomato and is where Francesco Cirillo got the idea for this technique when he was a student.

You've probably heard of this method before, but I'm suggesting that you use it to schedule your work time *and* your tech time. How do our phones fit in? In those five-minute breaks, I write out a list of everything I can do in a chunk of work and everything I can do in a break. Checking my phone is always allowed.

Would the time be better spent taking a walk? Doing push-ups? Reading? Maybe, but I want to check my phone; I like doing that, it relaxes me. I'm not judging myself on the worthiness of my breaks. I just want to get things done, and knowing there's an allotted time to check my phone helps me to do that without having to feel bad about it.

Head to the Work chapter for more time management and scheduling tips – as well as some of the common traps we all fall into when trying to create the perfect to-do list.

Take tech out of your day

Sticking to a schedule laid out by something like the Pomodoro Technique can work well for focused time spent on work and break time spent on anything else. As well as scheduling in work and tech, it's also worth scheduling *out* time spent with technology too – or you might spend *all* of your downtime scrolling.

A common recommendation is to have a specific time of day or activity when you don't look at your phone – it can be a short and easy period, but you set this rule in stone.

Dr Kimberly Young recommends dinner with your family. She calls it 'disconnect to reconnect'. This is a good suggestion because saying 6:00pm every day doesn't work. You might be doing different things each day. Dinner time, on the other hand, gives you more flexibility.

If dinner sounds too long or doesn't suit you for whatever reason, choose something else. I have a phone-free, game-free, social media-free first coffee of the day. For me, that's a pause to write a job list and get ready to write.

Over time, this small phone-free coffee might lead you to a phone-free lunch, a phone-free dinner, a phone-free morning or a phone-free working day. To begin with, though, the important point is to pick something short and achievable.

Create your own stopping cues

One way to combat the tactics of big tech companies? Reverse them.

If you've got a bottomless app, like Instagram, give yourself a stopping cue. You can do this by setting a timer every time you open your favourite app. I sometimes like to do this with a traditional alarm clock, a smartwatch or, if I'm feeling deeply pretentious, an hourglass. That way I'm not relying on my phone to let me know when I can stop looking at it.

But, let's be honest here. I only remember to do this once or twice a day at best. The rest of the time, tech is actually the best thing to stop me from getting carried away with tech.

There are some great apps you can get for your phone, tablet or laptop that help you to stay away from time-eating activities online. Some of them work by cutting you off from the internet entirely, while others limit your access to specific apps. I like Freedom, Forest and LeechBlock.

You'll need to put some thought into setting limits initially and choosing which apps you need to blacklist. Then, when you're up and running, you'll have your stopping cues and a time-release padlock on the bottomless biscuit barrel of social media.

How much is too much?

I already mix and match a bunch of different time management strategies. The big question I still have when tracking my time, reading the studies and thinking about how deep my own tech dependence is, is, 'How much is too much?' Like many of the questions in this chapter, there appears to be no clear answer.

In her TED Talk about internet addiction, Dr Young says this is 'like trying to diagnose alcoholism by counting the number of drinks one consumes' because this is about behaviours, not numbers. Fortunately, research into tech dependence and addiction offers a few insights that could be useful in helping you to find your own balance between healthy and unhealthy tech use.

One study suggests that reducing time spent checking your phone to 30 minutes a day – or ten minutes on each platform – could have a significant positive impact on your well-being. Another study found that people who engage with digital media for less than an hour a day score higher for psychological well-being than people who clocked up more than five hours a day. These results are helpful but restrictive.

There's evidence to suggest we can start by cutting down on tech time rather than setting a strict limit. One 2020 study that looked into the problem of Facebook addiction found that reducing time spent on the app ended up also reducing symptoms of depression. The interesting point of this finding is that the participants only reduced Facebook use by 20 minutes each day – regardless of how long they spent on the app in total.

From looking at the research, it's clear that there's definitely a middle ground to tech use. People who don't use digital media at all score lower in overall well-being than light tech users. (In case you needed further proof that logging off for good might not be as beneficial as you think it will.) Decreasing our tech use can make us happier, but we shouldn't assume that the answer is to give it up completely, because this can have the opposite effect to what we were hoping for.

REWIRE YOUR HABITS

There are innumerable books, plans, theories and methods to help you build better habits and get rid of old ones. I've read about (and tried) many in the process of writing this book to help you find the best ones to suit you. Many of them are not simple, and the last thing my burned-out, tired-of-tech mind needs right now is complicated.

The good news is I came across a method which I've found to be both straightforward and transformative (and I don't use that word lightly). Not only has it helped me to radically reduce the time I spend every day looking at screens, but it's also helped me stop biting my nails. It's called The Golden Rule of Habit Change.

Learn the Golden Rule

Every habit has three stages, and these stages make up a 'habit loop'. First, there's **the cue** – this is what triggers your habit. It can be an emotion or situation that tells part of your brain to go into 'automatic mode' and pick a habit to use. Next up, there's **the routine**. This can be physical, emotional or mental. And finally, there's **the**

reward. This is what helps your brain to decide if this loop is worth remembering to use again.

Habit loops gradually become more automatic and less conscious over time. This means they just happen without you thinking about them. This is good news if it's a good habit. But if it's one that doesn't serve you well, it makes it a real challenge to stop.

Charles Duhigg, an investigative reporter and author, explains in his book *The Power of Habit* that The Golden Rule of Habit Change is: you can't get rid of a bad habit, you can only change it. To do this successfully, we need to keep the cue and the reward in the habit loop the same, but come up with a new routine.

I'm going to be using two of my habits as examples throughout this section. Instagram scrolling with no purpose and checking Twitter.

Let's take a look at one of my Instagram habit loops:

Cue: I'm bored and a bit lonely
Routine: Scroll through Instagram for 20 minutes
Reward: I feel as if I've done something and I'm a little less lonely

Duhigg stresses that, before you decide on a new routine, you need to get really clear about what the cue for your habit is. Otherwise, it just won't work. Many people struggle to recognise what the cues for their behaviours are because their habits have become so automatic.

Identify your cues

If something is driving you to do something, but you don't know what that drive is, you have to investigate it.

Over the next week, I encourage you to commit to paying more attention to the ways you use your devices. What you're looking for is the moment *before* you open an app, start a game or check Facebook. It's a slippery moment to catch, but it's there if you look for it. And when you do, you need to ask yourself how you're feeling and what might be motivating you in that moment.

You can carry on then, and do whatever it is you were about to do, but keep a list in a notebook or a note-taking app to keep track of how you feel before you start every tech-based activity. Just a single word will do, as long as it makes sense to you. At the end of the week, you should have a map of the emotions you're experiencing when you feel the need to reach for your smartphone, or games console, or whatever else. This map will start to show you the cues that drive your habits.

The challenge is remembering to pause and question yourself. One suggestion I've found helpful is using prompts. A prompt is what Stanford University behavioural scientist and author BJ Fogg suggests people use to trigger new habits in his book *Tiny Habits*. A prompt can be a Post-it note. An Alexa reminder. A calendar invite.

In this case, I needed a prompt that would remind me to ask myself how I feel when I pick up my phone. I tried a Post-it, but it fell off. So I've changed the lock screen on my phone to a big question mark. You can change it to say 'How do I feel?' or some other symbol or question that'll remind you. Just try to avoid being judgemental with your phrasing. 'Just what the hell do you think you're doing?' isn't the way to go.

Create new habit loops

Knowing how to home in on your cues is the first piece of the habit loop puzzle. From identifying the cue, you can start to figure out what the reward might be. For example, if your cue is 'I'm feeling agitated', your reward might be 'to feel calmer'. If your cue is 'I feel lonely', your reward could be 'feeling more connected to people'.

We can work on these some more in a bit, but first, let's talk about the final step – experimenting with different routines to see if they achieve the same effect.

Here are some suggestions from my own Instagram scrolling habit:

Message a friend
Send my boyfriend a funny GIF
Ring someone I work with

These would all, in theory, fulfil the 'I feel lonely' cue and my need to feel more connected. They'd give me the same reward too. I could even combine these new routines with something that gives me the same reward for the 'I feel bored' cue. How about:

Go for a short walk
Do a quick yoga stretch
Read a few pages of a book

I've created a table below that you can fill in. Start with the cue, the old routine and the reward. Take your time defining the new routine.

Cue	Old routine	New routine	Reward
Feeling creative – I want to engage with colour	Go on Pinterest	Draw	Satisfied, creative, more myself
Stressed – I want a distraction	Go on Twitter	Go for a walk	Something to do
Lonely – I want to connect with people	Go on Instagram	Message a friend	Connected, content

I've deliberately made all of these sound quite good because they're going to end up in a book. Please do feel free to add anything you would much rather do instead.

Make it easy

Once you've decided on a new habit loop, you need to do everything you can think of to make it easy for yourself. I know I can't rely on my motivation (or even my memory) to think back to what my new habit loops are and why they matter next time I'm feeling sad or lonely. So let's give future-you a helping hand.

When I worked on these new habits the first time around, I added a lot of prompts to my day to remind me to carry out my new routines and mostly failed at them.

Let me give you an example for my Twitter checking habit. I put my comfiest walking shoes next to my desk. They might have worked as a prompt all on their own, but I wanted to add another, so I wrote WALK on a Post-it note and stuck it on my monitor. This one worked well to stop me checking Twitter quite so often, which I mostly look at on my laptop. I'd put the Post-it in the perfect place.

But the one that worked the best was the prompt for my Instagram scrolling habit. After taking a close look at my phone usage apps and Screen Time on my iPhone, I realised that I often turn to Instagram at 3:00pm when I feel a mid-afternoon energy lull. I'd need a prompt specifically for that time and that feeling. I didn't think a Post-it would cut it because I know I look at Instagram on my phone. Instead, I set the alarm on my phone for just before 3:00pm – another success. I managed to catch myself with the prompt before I opened Instagram and made myself a cup of tea with a biscuit instead.

What prompt will you choose to add to each new habit loop? Make it simple. Make it noticeable. Make it hard to ignore. The prompts and preparations we're putting in place may seem small, but they could have a big reward. At the very least, you might be able to reduce the time you spend staring at various screens by a few minutes every day.

Remember: Go easy on yourself. Many of the habit loops we're trying to change here are well established. We've been checking the same apps for years. What's more, we've learned that smart people are working hard to make our favourite apps, social networks and games as compelling as possible to check – regardless of how great your prompt is.

Checklist

We can't know if we have an internet, phone or tech addiction. Even though tech or internet addiction isn't officially recognised as a disorder, many of us have good reasons to take stock of our everyday use and reliance on tech.

Tech is designed to keep us coming back for more. Likes, comments, sharing, 'endless' scrolling. These are a few of the tactics used to get us to check our devices, apps and social media accounts regularly.

Reframe your tech 'addiction' as a bundle of habits. This will give us language to describe how we use our devices, as well as some tried-and-tested methods, like The Golden Rule of Habit Change.

Notice when you use tech, what tactics are at play and how you feel. Awareness is key. Understanding how we use tech and what we rely on it for can be a solid first step in the right direction for gaining more control.

Manage your time. Add schedules to your day, stopping cues to your app use and rules to your home life so you have a greater say over how you spend your time.

You can't get rid of a bad habit, you can only change it. You can learn how to change your habit loops. This way, you can replace your dependency on devices with behaviours that will serve you better.

Important: If you feel like your tech use is taking up a lot of time and affecting your work, relationships or mental health, you might need some professional help. Go to the resources on page 333 for further reading about mental health.

MENTAL HEALTH

THE TECH TRUTH ABOUT CATCHING, FIGHTING AND DEALING WITH FEELINGS

Every smartphone should come with this warning:

UNLOCKING THIS WILL MAKE YOU FEEL FANTASTIC, TERRIBLE AND EVERYTHING IN BETWEEN BEFORE YOU EVEN GET OUT OF BED THIS MORNING.

Within moments of tapping our phones awake, we can expect a roller-coaster ride of emotional provocations – full of soaring highs, swooping lows, boring lulls and the occasional vomit-inducing loop the loop. Here's what I went through this morning when I looked at Twitter on my phone: delight when I saw that I'd received a direct message from a writer I admire; despair at the response given by a politician to recent climate change news; sadness, reading about a close friend's ongoing experience with grief; awe, watching a time-lapse video of the Sun; envy, looking at pictures of someone's new house by the sea; excitement at the announcement of a new movie adaptation of one of my favourite books; elation, watching a video of foxes laughing (seriously, look that one up). Every one of these occurred within seconds of each other and all before I'd even had my first cup of tea of the day. All of these emotions, all felt in under five minutes.

And of course, this experience isn't exclusive to Twitter. Opening up your email inbox, playing a video game, checking the news, logging on to any social media platform, watching your favourite YouTuber's newest video. Each of these seemingly trivial, habitual actions is in fact a loaded roll of the dice on how you're going to feel after you're done with it, with next to no thought given as to how it's going to affect you for the rest of the day.

We've already seen that, by design, some of our favourite apps share similarities with slot machines. The most obvious of these is the scroll to refresh followed by a short wait for a reward. Our attention span might not be the only casualty of these casinos in our pockets – our mental health could be suffering too.

Ding-ding-ding! Three matching symbols, you've 'won'! These could be anything: a DM from a friend that makes you happy, news that turns your sadness into excitement and a message that connects you to other people – go you!

But with another turn, uh oh, nothing matches. You're served an announcement that makes you feel sad, you scroll on to a news headline that breaks your happy mood, and an email notification ends up making you feel isolated and alone – bad luck.

Even though each of these emotions can be very short-lived, they're well worth paying close attention to, because each of them leaves a mark.

We now spend so long on each of our many devices that we're losing track of how our emotional experiences are stacking up throughout the day and affecting our overall outlook. What's more, our devices have become the first thing we reach for when we have to deal with difficult emotions. We are getting lost in emotional loops driven by devices. It's no wonder we feel so exhausted.

I'd like you to think of this chapter as your opportunity to pause. To step off the roller coaster and away from the slot machine. Take this time to consider how the tech you use has both a positive and negative effect on your feelings – and find out what you can do to bring more balance to your day.

DOES OUR TECH HAVE THE POWER TO ALTER OUR MOOD?

Mental health is the condition of your psychological and emotional well-being and, according to the mental health charity Mind, good mental health is defined as: 'being generally able to think, feel and react in the ways that you need and want to live your life'. Poor mental health means 'you might find the ways you're frequently thinking, feeling or reacting become difficult, or even impossible, to cope with. This can feel just as bad as a physical illness, or even worse.'

Identifying the origins of mental health disorders is an ongoing field of study, but what is fairly well established right now is that no one single thing tends to be the cause. Instead, your mental health is influenced by a range of factors, including your life experiences, upbringing, physical health and your genetic make-up.

As technology has grown to become a part of all our lives, more and more research has been carried out to determine the effects on our mental health. The main goal is to discover whether the time we spend on our digital devices could bring about mental health problems, such as anxiety and depression.

Having read a dizzying number of these studies to help me write this chapter, there is one thing I can say with absolute confidence: we're not there yet.

Researchers have measured, examined and analysed both the positive impacts and the adverse effects of tech on our mental health, but a definitive conclusion has yet to be reached. Which means that anyone you encounter who claims that smartphones, social media, video games and the like are the ultimate causes of people's mental health problems has an agenda that sits outside the sum total of scientific research on this topic.

Here, then, are some key points you should keep in mind:

- **The relationship between internet-connected devices and mental health is a hot topic.** This is why you'll have seen many (often panic-inducing) headlines on this subject over the years, and will continue to as more new research gets commissioned.
- **Tech use has been linked to a rise in mental health problems in young people.** Research has shown a correlation between the amount of time young people spend on their devices and increased cases of depression, anxiety and sleep problems. It remains unclear, though, whether tech use is the cause of these problems or a symptom. Similar studies have cast doubt on the 'cause' argument and shown that the rise in mental health issues is pretty small.
- **Much of the research is focused on teens, and Facebook use.** Naturally, this limits us in terms of being able to see the broader picture of tech and mental health as it applies to different age groups and social media platforms.
- **Frequent device use may increase the chances that our mental health is affected.** Even researchers who don't believe tech use can take the blame for mental health issues say that spending more time in front of screens could lead to an (albeit small) rise in certain problems, such as decreased general well-being.

- **Most of the existing research is based on self-reporting.** This means a lot of the research is informed by teens and parents estimating how much they use their smart devices. This is a common way to measure time spent in front of screens, but if you're thinking, 'This doesn't sound like the most reliable way of measuring it,' you'd be right – especially when you take into account what we've learned about how great people aren't at judging the time they spend online.

- **Chicken or egg?** One point which keeps cropping up in the research is that it's still unclear whether spending a lot of time on devices causes poor mental health, or if people spend their time staring at their device screens because they have poor mental health. The jury is therefore very much still out on this, but that doesn't mean we can't consider ways to improve our day-to-day well-being through more balanced tech use.

We're going to focus now on three topics I think are central to understanding the relationship between tech and mental health. First, how we use our smart devices to help us manage difficult emotions. Second, how feelings can, in fact, be transmitted through our online networks faster than a cute panda video. And third, how social media platforms, apps and games could be engineered to make us feel certain emotions by design.

YOUR PHONE IS A COMFORT BLANKET

Many of the choices we make every day tend to be driven by our hearts, not our heads. We turn to our tech when we need help dealing with difficult emotions, and we often do this without even realising that's what we're doing.

We chase away sadness by streaming a stand-up comedian on Netflix. We unpack a stressful day at work with a zombie shoot-'em-up in the evening. We settle our nerves before a hospital appointment by playing a trivia game on our phones. If tech can affect how we feel, it can also influence how we behave.

Taking active steps towards dealing with our emotions is called emotional regulation. I very much like how Dr Leanne Rowlands, a researcher in neuropsychology, describes what this looks like day to day in 'The Conversation': '[emotional regulation] can enable us to be positive in the face of difficult situations, or fake joy at opening a terrible birthday present. It can stop grief from crushing us and fear from stopping us in our tracks.'

Emotional regulation is central to good mental health because it means giving ourselves the power to pick ways we can enjoy and focus on our positive emotions, and engage less with the negative ones. On the flip side, people who find it challenging to regulate their emotions are less able to influence how they feel. This can play a significant role in mental health disorders, such as depression and anxiety.

Dr James J. Gross, a Professor of Psychology at Stanford University, has outlined five different types of emotional regulation, which he calls 'processes':

The first of the five is **situation selection**. This is about moving towards or away from people, places or objects to make yourself feel better. This could mean muting someone you disagree with on Twitter. Step away from the stress and enjoy your day.

The second is **situation modification**. This is about taking action to change the course of something to make the most of a not-so-great situation. This could mean asking your boss to take a heated conversation you're having via email to a Zoom chat so you can defuse the tension. Or vice versa. You might tell a colleague who is frustrating you by delegating task after task via a video call to please just write it up in an email.

The third is **attentional deployment**, which means deliberately putting your attention to work on something else to feel better. Distraction is one form of attentional deployment, like playing my go-to favourite game on my phone. Another is concentration, so paying close attention to a little photo editing before uploading to Instagram. And then there's rumination, or really digging into how you feel and thinking about the same thing over and over. Rumination can sometimes become a problem and lead to symptoms of depression if you're focusing heavily on negative feelings and not finding ways out of them.

Cognitive change, the fourth process, aims to improve the way you feel about something by adjusting how you think about it – instead of trying to change the thing itself. So if you lose an eBay auction to a last-minute bidder, instead of being angry about it, you focus on feeling grateful for the money you've saved. That type of thing.

And finally, the fifth of Dr Gross' processes is **response modulation**. This one addresses how you manage your reactions after they've happened and change your state so that whatever you feel in the moment doesn't dictate how you feel for the rest of the day. You might open up a meditation app and listen to a soothing guided meditation, which would work to decrease the physiological aspects of negative emotions, like a tight chest and wobbly arms because you've been feeling anxious after a stressful work-related Zoom call.

We are aware of some of these processes when we're doing them, while others occur without us noticing – this is similar to what we learned about habits in the Addiction chapter. For example, the cue might be stress, your routine might be playing Solitaire on your phone, and the reward is stress relief. Because this form of emotional regulation has become a habit loop, it may well kick in without you thinking, 'I'm feeling stressed, so I'm going to play Solitaire and feel better.' You just do it.

Our devices offer various ways to help us manage how we're feeling – our phones especially because we can take them out and use them in any place, at any time. That's why some researchers refer specifically to digital emotional regulation. But here's the issue: there's no established 'right way' to steer your feelings with your phone. For instance, I can't say for a fact if you should open up Pinterest when you feel sad and spend one hour pinning pictures of 'good dogs'. This could be the perfect remedy for some people, but for others it makes them feel sad because they don't have a dog and would really like one or maybe they're just more of a cat person. We all have to take stock of our needs as individuals and be honest about whether the things we think help really do – and if they don't, it's time to make some changes.

One of the things we need to look out for are choices that have only short-term benefits but could lead to long-term harm. These could be impulsive decisions, like dropping a couple of hundred quid you can't afford on an online shopping spree because you're feeling sad and really want a pick-me-up. Or blowing through your work deadlines watching vlogs on YouTube because you're anxious about your annual review.

These are helpful and entertaining activities now and again, but they can fast become counter-productive to our mental well-being if we rely on them regularly.

To get to grips with how we use tech to find day-to-day happiness, settle our nerves, add some excitement – to generally manage our difficult emotions – let's take a closer look at the four emotional cues that make you reach for the nearest digital device the most often: boredom, stress, sadness and loneliness.

To help you get the most out of this chapter, I want you to start the habit right now of checking in with how you're really feeling. Start by closing your eyes and taking a few deep breaths. Then simply notice whatever emotion you're feeling now. 'Reading a book' doesn't count. Whatever happened in your day will have left a mark on how you're feeling, so just take note of what that feeling is.

> **Tip:** I like 'box breathing' as a way to slow down and check in with how I'm feeling. This is when you breathe in for four seconds, hold the breath for four seconds, breathe out for four seconds, wait for four seconds then repeat the whole process again, four times over.

Boredom

None of us likes being bored, but it might surprise you to learn just how much people dislike it. In a series of studies carried out in 2014, a team of psychologists found that two-thirds of men and a quarter of women would prefer to give themselves an electric shock than have to sit quietly with their thoughts for 15 minutes.

And this isn't the only study into boredom that features electrocution. In a different study, researchers showed three groups of volunteers one of three film clips that were either boring, sad or neutral. As the volunteers watched the clips, they had the option to give themselves electric shocks. Can you guess what happened? The group watching the boring clip shocked themselves more often (and with more intensity) than the groups watching the sad and neutral clips.

These were all very mild electric shocks – none of the participants were writhing in agony to escape their boredom – but they were undoubtedly unpleasant, so why would anyone *choose* pain? The researchers from the first study perhaps summed it up best when they wrote: 'Most people seem to prefer to be doing something rather than nothing, even if that something is negative.'

If you find yourself feeling unconvinced that people can't handle being bored even for a few moments, take a look around next time you're in a queue, on a bus or in a waiting room. I'll bet that almost everyone is using their smartphones instead of sitting alone with their thoughts. Because feeling bored simply isn't something that anyone *needs* to feel any more. There's always an instant remedy, waiting in our pockets – something to check, read, like and swipe. But is there anything inherently wrong with using our phones to swipe away the boredom?

The short answer is: not really. For many of us, tech is a reliable and accessible way to make boredom more bearable, even if it means we're not doing anything other than scrolling mindlessly and shifting our lack of focus to our screens.

It should be noted, though, that turning to tech when you're bored can enable impulsive actions. While impulsivity in itself isn't necessarily a bad thing, a 2019 study carried out by researchers in Sweden found that young people who buy clothes online are often motivated by boredom. Interestingly, their findings also showed that when people are bored they more easily fall for sales tactics designed to lure them into spending more, like price reductions and free delivery.

The researchers acknowledged that this is a coping mechanism to help replace boredom with positive emotions – emotional regulation in action. Which sounds good in theory, but it depends how often you're relying on it. If you feel bored daily, you could quickly find yourself in debt.

Another study from 2015, carried out among university students in the US, suggests that because we now have easy access to the internet through our phones, people's boredom thresholds may have become lower. In other words, our reliance on tech to remedy feelings of boredom may be making us more bored more quickly. The researchers believed this might be why some of the students had difficulty concentrating on important tasks.

Psychologists James Danckert and John D. Eastwood, co-authors of *Out of My Skull: the Psychology of Boredom*, believe this is because we're all stuck in a cycle of looking to things with which to 'solve' our boredom problem, and every time we find some relief, we lose a little bit of our own inventiveness. They write:

'In our attempts to outrun boredom we rob ourselves of the chance to learn how to be in the moment and redirect our energies in positive ways.'

Instead of trying to banish boredom from our lives entirely, there is evidence to suggest that letting ourselves be bored more often could help us to become more productive and creative.

In one study, participants were asked to carry out tedious tasks, such as copying out the numbers from a telephone directory. They then completed creative thinking tests, which included coming up with as many uses for polystyrene cups as possible. The group that completed the boring task first came up with significantly more answers than the group that didn't. A certain amount of boredom might be beneficial. So rather than try to distract ourselves from boredom (attentional deployment), the answer is to change how we feel about it (cognitive change).

I've had plenty of opportunities to observe the power of boredom. Once, I was struggling with an intense writing assignment and had to go to the post office the day before my deadline. I'd been so wrapped up in my work that I hadn't realised I'd let my phone's battery dwindle to nothing, so I was forced to stand in the post office queue with only my thoughts to occupy me. And you know what? I came up with plenty of solutions to all of the problems I'd had with my assignment. Who knew that all I had to do was stare at some padded envelopes and the backs of people's heads for an hour instead of my phone screen?

Permitting ourselves to feel boredom, to sit with our thoughts and daydream also lets us pay real attention to how we're feeling, both physically and mentally. I like this quote from Maria Popova, writer and creator of the blog Brain Pickings: 'To be bored is to be unafraid of our interior lives – a form of moral courage central to being fully human.'

But even after my breakthrough experience in the post office queue, I'm still trying to break out of my 'in queue, phone out' reflex and only manage to catch myself doing it half of the time. When reaching for a digital distraction has become a habit, how do we go about making boredom feel welcome?

- **Put nothing in your diary.** You can ease yourself in by actually scheduling time in your day to do nothing. Start small; just ten minutes will do. You can combine it with a task too, if it helps: take a walk around the block, drink a cup of coffee, people-watch out of the window – whatever it is, just do it without looking at your phone.

The best case scenario you can get from this is you can end up feeling more in charge of your day and even find creative solutions to some niggling problems. The worst case scenario? You've given yourself a few moments of quiet in a noisy world. I call that a win-win.

- **Make time for mindfulness.** Studies have shown that practising mindfulness can enhance our abilities to cope with boredom. Not only that, but it might also be helpful in lowering our boredom levels in general. This is because the whole purpose of mind-fulness is to encourage a closer connection to the moment, and being able to let idle thoughts come and go without getting hung up on them.

I've used several different meditation apps over the years and can highly recommend them – especially if you're dealing with anxious thoughts. They're not a miracle cure, but studies have shown meditation apps to be effective at calming anxiety and improving mental health more generally.

There are plenty of apps for you to choose from; check out my recommendations at the back of the book, so if you try one and it doesn't particularly gel (an annoying voice can really put me off), then try another. Most of them have courses created for beginners to help anyone get started. You can kick off your day with a guided meditation or listen to soothing sounds before bed.

Stress

In 2018, a study conducted by YouGov found that nearly three-quarters of people had experienced stress during the previous year and reported feeling overwhelmed and unable to cope at least once. Numerous similar studies showed that throughout 2020 stress and anxiety levels were running at an all-time high due to worries about the pandemic, work concerns, childcare problems and a general sense of unease about what the future might hold.

For me, technology can often be a source of stress. There are always emails to reply to, tweets to send, WhatsApp groups to respond to and video calls with family to fit in. All of these are things I need, and often want, to do. But the pressure to get all of them done can sometimes be a bit too much. Especially when more emails, alerts and notifications start popping up just as I start to cross some of these off my job list. On days like this, reaching for my phone feels like the opposite of stress relief.

This was even more pronounced during Covid-19 restrictions when stress-induced scrolling became an hourly occurrence – and that was on a restrained day. Many of us felt a continual pressure to stay up to date with the news cycle, watching conflicting pandemic-related advice roll in and case numbers rise – which many referred to as 'doomscrolling'. Brian Chen, a technology writer for the *New York Times*, defined this as: 'sinking into emotional quicksand while bingeing on doom-and-gloom news' and I felt that throughout much of 2020 on a deep, cellular level. The feeling that fuelled doomscrolling for me was a mixture of stress and despair fuelled by a need to look for reassurance that just never materialised.

However, it's almost too easy to get caught up in these stress-inducing aspects of tech that we overlook that there are plenty of times when our devices can really come through for us.

Back in 2019, during a period of high work stress for both my partner and I, we got the Oculus Quest virtual reality system. I credit this magical piece of techno-wizardry (it's a VR headset that doesn't need to be connected to a computer or console so that you can run around anywhere with it) with getting us both through our respective workloads without burning out completely and, in particular, a game called Beat Saber.

If you haven't heard of it, it's basically the same as those machines you see at seafront arcades that people have to dance on. But instead of hitting floor panels with your feet, you wield two glowing laser swords and have to slice flying cubes in time to the beat (it's hard to put into words, but you'll be able to find a trailer on YouTube that does it justice).

Suppose we think back to the emotional regulation processes at the start of this chapter. In that case, our Beat Saber sessions are a type of response modulation, using a high energy VR experience to change our physiological states. And wow, was it effective. After just a few minutes of slicing up those flying boxes to ribbons, I felt like I'd loosened all the knots that had been bunching up in my shoulders.

But it doesn't have to be a virtual reality dance-destruction game for it to be effective for you. There's a lot of evidence to suggest video games, in general, can relieve stress and help you to relax. What's more, one study suggested that playing video games can help you to transform negative feelings into more positive ones.

Researchers divided participants into three groups to look at the effects of break-time activities during a regular day at work. The first group spent their break in silent rest and later reported that they felt less engaged with their work and more worried in general. The second group participated in a guided relaxation activity and later reported feeling fewer negative feelings and less distress. The third group spent the time playing video games and later reported feeling better than before their break, which continued for the rest of the day.

Why should gaming have such a positive effect? It's fun, it's distracting, it gives us a feeling of having control, but perhaps most importantly, it allows us to experience *flow*.

As a quick refresher, psychologist and author Mihaly Csikszentmihalyi writes: '"Flow" is the way people describe their state of mind when consciousness is harmoniously ordered, and they want to pursue whatever they are doing for its own sake.'

One study of the relationship between flow and video games mapped how you can create the key elements of flow in games. For example, flow requires a task to have clear goals. Games contain 'survival, collection of points, gathering of objects and artefacts, solving the puzzle'. Flow also requires immediate feedback. In games we can 'shoot people and they die. Find a clue, and you can put it in your bag.' And so on.

This naturally all sounds very positive and enriching. Still, if something is getting in the way of benefiting from all the rewards of video games and indeed any other relaxing activities, it is ourselves.

During my research, I learnt that some people feel guilty about relieving stress. They find out that something helps them to relax, but then feel guilty about indulging in 'time-wasting' activities. Could this be a by-product of the pressures of an 'always on' work culture?

Researchers have observed this feeling and called it ego depletion. When we're always 'on' all day – making decisions, avoiding mistakes, engaging in small talk – we become exhausted as our ego is gradually depleted, leaving us feeling as though we have insufficient willpower left. When we're in a state of ego depletion, we need fun and relaxation, but instead we interpret stress relief as procrastination. This means not only do we feel guilty about it, but we also don't feel the same rejuvenating recovery from stress. If this sounds familiar to you, understanding what's happening is essential to challenging and changing it. It can be tricky to unpick these feelings of guilt and figure out whether they're valid (spoiler alert: they're probably not). Ask yourself: do activities you know you enjoy sometimes cause stress and guilt? Does this tend to be worse after a long day or a stressful period at work?

Give yourself permission to take time off doing things you know (deep down) feel good. This might not be easy at first; many of us have become used to the constant nagging guilt. But trust me, you don't need ego depletion guilt. You need to engage the power of situation selection, step away from stress and recharge with video games, funny viral videos and your favourite series on Netflix.

- **Flow for non-gamers.** If gaming isn't your pastime of choice, we need to find something that brings you the same kinds of benefits we just found out video games can provide. You may already have a strong sense of what gets you into that flow state – compiling playlists, calligraphic design, coding websites, combing through recipe blogs – or you may have to do a bit of digging to find it.

Focusing, flexing your skills, hitting goals, getting feedback, altering your sense of time in positive ways. These are the ingredients for flow and, while it can occur out of the blue, more often than not we have to cultivate our flow within an activity we enjoy. There's no 'one size fits all' either. Someone else's sure-fire plan for finding flow might fall flat on its face when you try it out for yourself.

- **Plan your breaks.** Researchers have discovered video games can be an effective and fun way to recover from demanding and stressful tasks. But one of the main things I've learnt from my reading into the benefits of gaming is: what you do in your breaks matters.

Whether you play a video game or not appears to be less important than actually *choosing* something to do with your downtime. If you treat it as an afterthought, you're more likely to feel bored, unfocused and, inevitably, go to your default time-filler and scroll the minutes away, doing little to relieve your stress.

Try creating a daily break schedule for yourself, and plan non-work activities into it. That way, you can use your time throughout the day to refresh your mind instead of spending your free time after a busy day simply recovering from the mental exhaustion of non-stop work.

Sadness

When you're feeling at a low ebb, it's super-easy to go online looking for a distraction from your thoughts. What happens, though, is you fall for all the tactics tech companies have developed to keep you looking at the profiles of people you envy, reading doom-and-gloom updates from news outlets and following links to scaremongering articles. So then you end up thinking the same sad, reflective thoughts that made you feel low to begin with. This is a type of rumination.

Rumination is a response to feelings of distress that's pretty unhealthy. When you ruminate, you focus on the thing you're distressed about instead of focusing on what you could do to feel differently. You stay fixed on a problem and how that problem makes you feel, which is why it's no real surprise that rumination can come hand in hand with anxiety and depression.

Studies have found that one of the leading causes of increased rumination online is 'social comparison'. If we look at the origins of social comparison, we see that it's both normal and that, as a species, we've been doing it for a very long time. Researchers believe social comparison likely comes from our need to evaluate ourselves and see how we're doing, and one of the best ways to do this is to compare ourselves to others. This helps us to feel more confident in our opinions, our abilities and our place in the world, and we do this all of the time when we have information about what other people are up to. The big difference now, though, is that we can see what people are doing wherever and whenever we feel like it, but what we're getting is a filtered, colour-corrected and selectively edited version of the truth.

While being able to peer in on the lives of others is the bread and butter of being on social media, we are aware what we see online is essentially everyone else's 'highlight reel' and every photo might have been manipulated. Despite this knowledge, though, seeing what other people share of their lives online can often make us feel sad, jealous or unfulfilled. Why is it so easy to forget we're looking at an illusion when we are in the middle of a sad scroll?

To better understand why this happens, we need to look at two types of comparison: upward and downward. Upward comparison is all about the people you think are superior to you in some way or another. Maybe they have something you want, or you admire their achievements or envy their looks. Downward comparison is to do with anyone you see as inferior to you somehow. You might pity them for something unfortunate that happened, or perhaps you experience a bit of *Schadenfreude* after something bad happens that (you think) they deserved.

Taking the time to contrast yourself with people who feel in one way or another high above you or far beneath you sounds like an icky way to spend your time online, right? On the one hand, stop making yourself feel bad looking at people who live very different lives to you, and also: who are you to judge?

But remember, social comparison is normal human behaviour, and there can be positive outcomes (sometimes) to upward and downward comparison, such as feeling inspired by someone else's achievements or reassured at having made different choices yourself. Online social comparison, though, is far too often a fast track to feelings of envy and resentment. One study found that negative social comparison on Facebook predicted an increase in rumination and symptoms of depression a whole three weeks later. To combat rumination, we need to take action and nudge our attention into another direction deliberately.

- **Engage more, scroll less.** Research has shown us that not all time with tech is spent equally. If you're the type of person who scrolls a bit passively through people's uploads and updates without commenting on them or liking them, you might be what's known as a 'lurker'. This type of passive engagement is linked to feelings of loneliness, anxiety and low mood more than someone who actively joins in or starts conversations with others on social media.

Of course, you shouldn't just go and post random comments under every photo you see on Instagram. I'm saying that by being a little more proactive about creating interactions with people through their posts, you experience more of an authentic social experience. This gives our minds a healthy reminder that there's a real person with a real life on the other side of all those squares on our screens.

- **Create an escape hatch.** Here's something I haven't told anyone before – whenever I feel low, I open up a note which I've saved in my Evernote app. At the top of the note is an animated GIF of a dancing blueberry (this is just to make me laugh). Underneath the berry, I've compiled a list of things I've achieved and compliments people have given me. Underneath that list, there's an action plan filled with steps I can take to improve my mood. Here are a few of the steps:
  o   Drink a glass of water
  o   Eat a snack
  o   Take five deep breaths
  o   Get some fresh air (sticking your head out of the window counts)
  o   Stretch your arms up into the air for ten seconds
  o   Make a list of five things you're grateful for (the simpler, the better)

I've relied on this emotional escape hatch to break me out of negative thought loops and give myself a few simple tasks I can focus on instead. They might sound simple, but they're the building blocks I need to feel calm, focused and able to move forwards with whatever I'm meant to be doing.

I highly recommend you create your own escape hatch. It could be a note with a dancing fruit of your choice – please do share your funny GIF choices with me – a folder full of beautiful things on your phone, a Pinterest board covered in poetry, an Instagram bookmark folder packed with art and colour. Create a way to soothe yourself today – future-you will be very grateful.

- **Track moods with an app.** There are many apps aimed at helping you manage your mental health, and the ones with built-in tools designed to track your moods can be the most useful. As well as providing you with a reminder to stop and check in with how you're doing, you can use them to home in on what it is that might be triggering any feelings of sadness. For example, you might notice that you always experience a drop in mood after catching up with certain friends or colleagues, or engaging in a specific online activity. I like Daylio for tracking my moods, but I've added a longer list of suggestions on page 333.

Loneliness

The Covid-19 pandemic proved to anyone who was still on the fence that digital devices are no longer simply nice-to-haves – they're necessities. They helped us to cope during lockdown: watch Netflix shows back to back (to back to back), play games when we'd usually be on a commute and tweet about the loaves of bread we'd learnt to bake. All these things offered a very welcome respite from the news cycle. And the most valuable thing tech allowed us to do was to build a digital bridge between ourselves and the loved ones it wasn't safe to see in person.

In 2016, a study found that social media platforms (the focus was on Facebook, but I feel the findings are completely applicable across others) can give us positive experiences and positively affect our well-being because they meet what's called our 'relatedness' needs: belongingness, connectedness and intimacy. Evidence shows that, for many people, opening up their favourite social media app can make them feel happy, connected and gives them the rewarding feeling of bonding with others.

Why, then, is social media able to increase feelings of connection for some while others experience a growing sense of disconnection? To find out, we need to understand 'emotional bids'.

An emotional bid is when we turn to others for attention, affection or support. In social media terms, a status update on Facebook, a direct message on Twitter or a photo on Instagram could all be examples of emotional bids. There are then three ways other people can respond to an emotional bid: 1) they can turn towards it with a positive response, 2) they can turn against it with a negative response or 3) they can turn away from it and ignore it.

Dr John Gottman is a relationship researcher, therapist and author who uses emotional bids as a way to encourage couples to communicate more effectively with one another. But we can apply the same principles to many different kinds of relationships. It is also an effective way of understanding how seemingly small actions on platforms like Facebook and Instagram can have a significant impact on the way we feel.

Gottman explains that we can think of this like filling up or withdrawing from an emotional bank account. Imagine this in the context of a couple. Every time someone turns towards their partner when they've made a bid, it's the emotional equivalent of popping a pound coin into their shared bank account. This can build up over time and, if it does, it helps them to stay positive when things get difficult – because they have a nest egg that makes them feel secure and connected. However, like your real-life bank account, if you've got nothing in it or you're overdrawn continually, that's bad news.

Although Gottman was talking in relationship terms, the emotional bank account metaphor works for social media activity because likes, shares, indeed any numbers we collect online, are all adding to our emotional bank accounts. We can quickly see how much other people turn towards our bids – as well as when they don't.

When people turn against, or away from the emotional bids we make online, it can have a negative effect on how we feel – and this can build up over time. One study found that when someone feels as though others have turned away from their updates, photos and online bids, they can feel disconnected from people. If someone feels others have turned against their emotional bids, they might withdraw – and this can lead to symptoms of depression.

The catch-22 of this is that feelings of disconnection caused by interactions – or rather a lack of them – on social media can make us want to get online even more in an attempt to try and feel more connected. But if we're not finding ways to meet our relatedness needs, loneliness online can become a slippery slope for our mental well-being. There are a number of Dr Gross' emotional regulation processes we could employ to deal with loneliness, but I believe situation selection is the best – intentionally choosing to do some-thing else with our time and attention.

- **Limit your time online.** The best piece of advice when it comes to reducing feelings of loneliness online is the same best practice we've covered already: be mindful about the amount of time you spend on apps and social media platforms. It can be challenging to keep track of just how much time we are spending in front of screens, so I've put together some recommendations for time management apps on page 333.

- **Give CBT a try.** CBT is cognitive behavioural therapy, and it teaches various techniques to help you cope with a range of different problems. Many apps use these techniques to get you into the habit of questioning your thinking and noticing any patterns that emerge. It can be difficult to pin down feelings of loneliness and isolation and find their root cause. By putting them under a CBT spotlight you may find it easier to uncover what your needs are – a sense of community, opportunities for romance, closer friendships, reconnect with family – and have a better chance of getting the help and support you need. Head to page 333 for mood-tracking and CBT apps.

Create your emotional toolkit

One of the reasons many of us don't choose the most rewarding or positive ways to deal with our feelings of boredom, stress, sadness or loneliness is because we're simply not prepared for them. The last thing I want to do when I'm feeling low is comb through my apps and try to figure out which is the best one to distract me.

There are steps you can take right now to start organising your digital life and give your future self a helping hand. These will help you quickly and easily pick what's important when you need it most:

- **Build themed playlists.** If you use a music streaming service, like Spotify or Apple Music, you have endless choices for creating personalised playlists. I have lots of different playlists to suit my moods and have taken a bit of time to label them, which helps me find what I need right away. The great thing about most music streaming platforms is they're excellent at learning about your tastes. After a while you won't need to create your own playlists – it will have lots of recommendations for you. Skip to the Identity chapter for a primer on the pros and cons of these tailored suggestions.

- **Organise your apps.** Instead of leaving your apps randomly spread across your screens, most smartphones will let you group them into folders or create themed pages to help you find what you need more quickly. Group yours together under themes based on what you need, so alongside things like 'work apps' and 'entertainment' you could also have 'productivity' or 'relaxation'. Help yourself to find the things you need most, so they're always close to hand any time you're feeling under the weather.

You could also make sure the apps that don't make you feel so good take a few extra steps to find. Those additional couple of seconds spent looking for them give you a chance to consider something more emotionally satisfying to do instead.

- **Find go-to podcasts for different moods.** Podcasts are an excellent way to occupy your mind, regardless of how you're feeling. They encourage you to listen and focus for sustained periods, which is a scarcity in these highly distracted days.

My podcast appetites change dramatically depending on how I'm feeling. I like listening to podcasts about the future, space and science when I'm awake and alert, and chatty podcasts with inspiring guests when I want to relax. Try a few out and find the right podcast for different moods, different activities and different times of the day. Subscribe to the ones that work for you and make sure they're set to auto-download, so you never have to wait around for your next episode.

- **Make a soothing watch list.** Throughout the coronavirus pandemic, my boyfriend and I rewatched (technically re-re-re-watched) old episodes of *The Office* (US series), and it was unbelievably soothing. Lots of people I spoke with during this time were also watching TV shows and movies from years ago as a way to revisit favourite characters and stories and possibly find reassurance and comfort during all the stress. Create a watch list for yourself (this could just be a note on your phone) full of the movies and TV shows you can quickly turn to when you need a pick-me-up. It'll save you from the decision paralysis that's common when you're scrolling through the endless content libraries of your favourite Video On Demand service.

> **Tip:** For more apps specifically designed for managing your mental health, check the resources in the back of the book on page 333.

HOOKED ON A FEELING

Imagine you're sitting opposite a close friend at a cafe you both love. You know she has big news to share – she told you as much in an instant message earlier in the day – and with a massive smile on her face, she tells you she's got the dream job she's been working towards for years now. How are you feeling in that moment?

You're probably thrilled too, right? If I were to ask you to pay close attention, you might also find your expression, voice and body language all mirror hers. This is normal, but there might also be more to it than simply being happy for her – you might have 'caught' her emotions. This is called emotional contagion.

Now I know the word 'contagion' isn't necessarily the most comfortable or appealing (trust me, I get it). The term is self-consciously borrowed from biology because it does the best job of explaining how feelings can be passed unconsciously from person to person quickly, and across a range of environments.

Social psychologist Dr Elaine Hatfield is a Professor of Psychology at the University of Hawaii and co-author of the book *Emotional Contagion*. She started studying the way we 'catch' emotions when she and Dr Richard L. Rapson were both working as therapists. They noticed they often 'caught' the emotions their clients were feeling. Hatfield writes:

'Often, as we talk through the sessions over dinner, we are struck by how easy it is to catch the rhythms of our clients' feelings from moment to moment and, in consequence, how profoundly our moods can shift from hour to hour.'

This is how emotional contagion works. Simply put, we see and hear what someone else is going through and then find ourselves feeling the same way. The important part is that most of the time we don't even realise we're doing it.

So as easily as you can catch a good mood, like excitement or joy, you can also catch a bad mood and feelings like anger or sadness. These different experiences may bring you closer to the person you're catching the emotion from. This is why the people who study emotional contagion believe it's rooted in connection. Hatfield and other researchers explain that emotional contagion is 'a basic building block of human interaction' as it allows people to understand others and share their thoughts and feelings.

In that way, emotional contagion is similar to experiencing empathy, which is when you can see a situation from another person's point of view and understand what they're feeling. Emotional contagion is believed to be a key component of empathy, the idea being that we can't fully understand what someone else is going through without sharing in their feelings too. In his book, *The Age of Empathy*, biologist and ethologist Frans de Waal describes emotional contagion as 'the first step on the road towards full-blown empathy.'

There are three steps required to catch someone else's emotion – familiarise yourself with these, so you have a better chance of noticing it when it's happening to you. The first is mimicry. This is when you copy someone's non-verbal cues, like their posture, body language or facial expression. If your friend is sitting up straight and smiling, you sit up straight and smile too. The second stage is feedback. The feeling you get from mimicking your friend. So, because you're sitting up straight and smiling, you start to feel happier. The final stage is full contagion – you now feel the same emotion as the person you're talking to, and you're showing the same non-verbal cues as well. You've caught the feeling.

A different kind of computer virus

Researchers used to believe that emotional contagion could only occur through face-to-face interaction because mimicry of facial expressions and body language is such a crucial first part of the process. Recent studies, however, suggest that emotions can be passed on through email, instant messages and, as we're about to see, social media status updates as well.

Many of us now spend a lot of time online, at least four hours a day according to one study, which means we're exposed to many different emotions of many different people as we encounter them virtually throughout the day. Research suggests you don't even need to be reading an email or text that's addressed to you to 'catch' an emotion – anything shared or posted publicly may have the same effect.

This was one of the findings from a controversial Facebook study carried out in 2012. Facebook data scientist Adam Kramer teamed up with researchers Jamie Guillory and Jeff Hancock from the Department of Communication and Information Science at Cornell University to find out whether emotional contagion can happen on Facebook.

Similar studies had already looked into the possibility of emotional contagion online. However, Kramer, Guillory and Hancock's was the first to manipulate the News Feed on Facebook of more than 689,000 Facebook users to test their theory – now you see why I said this study was controversial. The team analysed the language used in more than 3 million Facebook updates, which contained more than 122 million words. Using linguistic analysis software, they found 4 million were positive and 1.8 million were negative.

They divided users into two groups. One group had the amount of positive emotional content on their News Feed reduced. The other had the negative emotional content on their News Feed reduced (a control group within each also had random updates filtered out of their News Feed to compare results). Each group saw the same number of posts for one week, and researchers then analysed new status updates written by the users of both groups to work out the percentage of positive and negative words they used during the testing period.

The results showed that exposure to emotions expressed by others on Facebook could influence our own, or at least how we express our emotions in our updates.

They found that when they reduced positive posts in people's News Feeds, the percentage of positive words in their status updates decreased, and the percentage of negative words increased. Equally, when negative posts were reduced, the opposite was true.

They also observed 'a withdrawal effect' – people who saw fewer emotional posts (both positive and negative) were less likely to express emotions during the days after (we'll be coming back to this a bit later).

This study was significant because it showed that emotional contagion is possible even when there's no direct interaction between two people. Given how many updates, tweets, comments and captions we see daily, these results matter.

The researchers make the point that even though they observed a difference, the difference was, in fact, very small. But because the scale of social networks today is vast, small changes could potentially have big consequences.

Researchers have found similar results on Twitter. For a week in September 2014, more than 3,800 users were included in a study which attempted to reconstruct and then measure the emotions expressed in tweets that the users were most likely to have seen before they posted their own. The results showed that, on average, a person writes a negative tweet after overexposure to negative content, and positive posts appear after overexposure to positive content. While the researchers couldn't know exactly what people had seen before they tweeted – some may have been on Twitter for hours, others may have only just logged on and tweeted – the findings indicate that emotional contagion on Twitter is possible.

It may also be possible to catch emotions from videos too. One 2019 study looked at the emotional content of videos on YouTube, then analysed the comments that were written underneath them to see if the emotions matched up. Surprise, surprise, they did.

When you think about it, video content could be the most effective medium for passive emotional contagion, given what we initially learnt about the need for facial expression and body language to be involved. But how many of us are actively on guard against catching a feeling we don't want to have when we're disappearing down a YouTube rabbit hole?

Considering the ways emotional contagion can work via video also makes me wonder how much we might (unknowingly) use the psychology of emotional contagion to cheer ourselves up. Remember earlier when I told you about watching *The Office*? That was a way to regulate my emotions, a way to cope. But it might have also been to soak up some of that familiar, feel-good comedy too. What I'm reminding you is that emotional contagion, though it sounds disconcerting, could be useful for us if we can learn to differentiate when it's working for us and when it's working against us.

Find out if you're susceptible to emotional contagion

How vulnerable are you to catching other people's emotions? Researchers have found a lot of variety in people, with some showing a strong tendency towards spreading emotions, others for catching emotions, while some seem barely affected. Luckily, for those of us who are curious, there's a scale.

This emotional contagion scale was designed to assess your susceptibility to catching a range of emotions. It won't give you a definitive answer or 'contagion type' like a personality test. Still, it will show you if you're more or less likely to catch emotions – the higher the score, the more susceptible to emotional contagion you might be.

The scale is long, so I've picked out just a few key statements about negative emotions – anger, fear and sadness – so we can find out if we need to be more aware of our susceptibility.

Here are the numbers you need to use and what they mean:

1. Never = Never true for me.
2. Rarely = Rarely true for me.
3. Often = Often true for me.
4. Always = Always true for me.

Depending on your answer, add 1, 2, 3 or 4 next to each of these statements:

1. Watching the fearful faces of victims on the news makes me try to imagine how they might be feeling.
2. I notice myself getting tense when I'm around people who are stressed out.
3. I clench my jaws and my shoulders get tight when I see the angry faces on the news.
4. I tense when overhearing an angry quarrel.
5. If someone I'm talking with begins to cry, I get teary-eyed.
6. I get filled with sorrow when people talk about the death of their loved ones.

If your final tally is over 18 points, you should be taking more care online.

Remember: This scale isn't scientifically watertight, and there is no official measure for emotional contagion susceptibility. But it's helpful to have an indication – even a common sense one – of how much care we need to take with our feelings when we go online.

Finding an antidote

You don't need to stop 'catching' emotions – that could turn you into an unfeeling robot person, and that's no way for a healthy person to be either. But is there a way to become less susceptible to them and have more control over when it happens?

The challenge is that we are often unaware of it when it's happening, and of the negative effect that it has on our own feelings. A study conducted by Dr Sigal Barsade, a leading researcher in emotional contagion, discovered that many people couldn't identify where their 'caught' emotions had come from – even when they were big or had a positive effect on them. Instead, they experienced the emotion as if it was their own.

Fortunately, becoming aware that emotional contagion even exists can help you to be more aware of it happening, so reading this right now might switch you on to your own emotions and where they came from a little more. Since I started researching emotional contagion I've been noticing instances of it across all areas of my life and, hopefully, I'm getting better at spotting some of the more unwelcome ones.

Imagine that one of your colleagues is draining your enthusiasm each day. Or a friend who is frequently in contact through WhatsApp keeps bringing up a lot of sadness from your past. It's easy to see how emotional contagion can quickly add extra stress to your life and have a lasting impact on your outlook if it happens often.

In an interview with The Wharton School of the University of Pennsylvania about emotional contagion during the coronavirus pandemic, Dr Barsade revealed: 'The good news is that you can be inoculated, to a certain degree, against emotional contagion.' She offered three steps to achieve this: awareness, reducing feedback, and being purposeful and alert. Use these as your basis for better protecting the way you feel.

1. **Increase awareness.** You won't always know when you've 'caught' an emotion, but you *can* be on the lookout. Are there particular apps, people or activities that always seem to make you feel low, angry or stressed afterwards? If you think something (or someone) might be influencing your emotions, create a note on your phone where you can keep track of how you feel, or use a mood-tracking app like Moodily or Daylio. You might start to pick up on some patterns.

2. **Reduce feedback.** One sure-fire way to stop finding yourself at the whim of other people's emotions online is simply to reduce the time you spend online and see less of them. Or you can choose activities and apps less likely to trigger unpleasant emotions – growing my boards on Pinterest is a favourite of mine. You can also mute or unfollow people who make you feel a certain way. Establish boundaries with any friends and family who are continually bringing you down by messaging you with all of their problems (of course, if you know anyone in serious mental distress you can encourage them to seek professional care). Most of these are things you should already be doing, but now you know about emotional contagion it might give you the nudge to put more of them into practice.

3. **Be purposeful.** As well as catching other people's emotions, other people can catch yours too. So in addition to becoming more aware of the experience you're receiving from others, be mindful of what you're putting out into the world. That doesn't mean censoring yourself. Just consider whether a rant needs to be tweeted to all your followers, or whether it should stay in your WhatsApp group. Maybe Twitter, or Instagram, or even LinkedIn, is the perfect place for it because it could lead to change and positive outcomes. Just make sure you're acting with purpose and not on auto-pilot.

WHEN YOU'RE EMOTIONAL, YOU'RE PROFITABLE

We've seen that it's not by accident that certain apps, games, sites and social media platforms can seem irresistible to us. They're designed that way through rigorous testing and meticulous planning. This same attention to detail could be used to drive emotional contagion, so people post more updates and even create experiences built around emotional regulation, so that they turn to tech in times of need. By focusing on Facebook, let's now take a closer look at what we know about how – and why – tech companies make decisions about what we're meant to feel.

The truth about manipulation

When the researchers first published the Facebook emotional contagion study in 2014, it caused a stir. Many felt that manipulating News Feeds without users' awareness or consent was simply unethical – especially when we consider that the researchers had no prior knowledge of their test subjects' mental health before the study. Imagine if someone who was already struggling mentally was unwittingly part of a test pool to see if News Feed content could make them feel more negative.

The truth, though, is that social media platforms already do this all the time. In a 2016 essay examining the Facebook study and users' reactions to it, researcher danah boyd writes: 'This manipulation is not a stand-alone research act.' She continues, 'Facebook algorithmically determines which content to offer to people every day. If we believe the results of this study, the ongoing psychological costs of negative content on Facebook every week prior to that one week experiment must be more costly.'

When we sign up to a social media platform, we are effectively agreeing to be manipulated in a variety of different ways, and the emotional aspect of this manipulation is potentially the most dangerous.

What is an algorithm?

You've probably come across the word algorithm a lot, especially in relation to Facebook and Instagram, but what does it actually mean? Well, an algorithm is a mathematical model that makes decisions based on data about us, how we behave and other factors. I like to think of an algorithm as a recipe. Step-by-step instructions that work behind the scenes of all of your favourite apps, social media platforms and news sites to determine what you see when you open them up.

In her book *Hello World*, mathematician and author Dr Hannah Fry writes that there are several key algorithm types baked into the tech we use every day. Some algorithms *prioritise* content by using a mathematical process to put all of the choices in the best order for you, like when Netflix suggests what you probably want to watch next. Other algorithms *classify* content, like showing you ads for things that a person like you might be interested in based on the sites you visit and the type of person you probably are. There are also *association* algorithms, which find connections between things, such as how Amazon 'guesses' what you might want to buy next based on what other, similar customers have purchased. Finally, some algorithms filter *out* what's likely not very important to you. A good example of this is how Twitter identifies tweets or news stories you're more likely to find interesting and pushes everything else further down your feed. A similar example is the way speech recognition algorithms filter out sounds to help Siri and Alexa hear you better.

Most social media platforms, search engines, shopping sites, entertainment apps and dating apps use combinations of these kinds of algorithms. Now you know a bit more about what they are and what they're up to, you may find that you're able to spot the results of their handiwork.

Algorithms are used to show you things you're going to care about, whether that means music on Spotify, tents on Amazon, ads for barbecue equipment on Facebook, people you might like to date or updates you want to comment on the most.

Why? Because they help you. They make your favourite sites and apps more useful and easier to use so you can find what you're looking for. But there's another big reason they exist. The more you see things you're likely to like, the more chance there is you will click links, watch shows and buy products.

Remember: The types of algorithms above are mostly what's known as rule-based algorithms. Humans have decided on the different steps they should follow. Fry distils this simply as: 'Step one: do this. Step two: if this, then that.' For a really simple example, let's imagine someone buys a book about space from an online retailer. That means a recommendation algorithm, or association algorithm, works to recommend another book from a similar category next time, like astronaut training or star formation. But there's another type of algorithm, which will crop up later in the book. That's a machine learning algorithm. As Fry explains, this kind of algorithm 'is inspired by how living creatures learn'. These don't follow the rules. Instead, you give the algorithm information and a goal, then let it figure out the best way to achieve it – providing feedback along the way. You could refer to this type as artificial intelligence (AI). We'll see an example of this type of algorithm on page 233, when we take a closer look at facial recognition technology.

A flaw in the machine

Algorithms may power many of the most popular sites and apps in the world, but they remain far from perfect. You might have noticed this yourself when you're browsing a streaming site, and one of the recommendations it offers couldn't be less you.

Back in 2016, Instagram introduced a new algorithm which promised to prioritise 'the moments you care about' instead of showing you a chronological feed that put the most recent posts from people you're following at the top of your feed. Many users and businesses immediately voiced their disapproval of this change, saying they preferred to see new posts first, instead of whatever the Instagram algorithm decided they should see instead.

There are many, many examples of algorithms getting things wrong and causing a stir. But problems with algorithms can have much more serious and far-reaching implications. In her book, *Algorithms of Oppression: How Search Engines Reinforce Racism*, Associate

Professor at the University of California, Los Angeles (UCLA) Dr Safiya U. Noble writes:

'We often think of terms such as "big data" and "algorithms" as being benign, neutral or objective; they are anything but. The people who make these decisions hold all types of values, many of which openly promote racism, sexism and false notions of meritocracy, which is well documented in studies of Silicon Valley and other tech corridors.'

This is vitally important. Tech companies may constantly be working to iron out the flaws in their algorithms, but they are not flaw*less*. After all, they are created by people. People can be biased and, without even knowing it, they can pass their biases on to the algorithms they make. What's more, algorithms are 'trained' on big collections of information, called data sets. But no matter how big they might be, can we ever give an algorithm *everything* it needs to know? I like how this problem is worded in a Pew Research report about algorithms: 'Even data sets with billions of pieces of information do not capture the fullness of people's lives and the diversity of their experiences.'

When algorithms are the engine behind everything we see online every day, shaping our thinking, our behaviour and our views – these baked-in biases affect our whole world.

Bias in tech is a huge topic and there are plenty of researchers, engineers and activists who have studied and written about the problems and possible solutions for years. I've put together a list of further reading resources on page 334 if you'd like to find out more.

The most important lesson for us right now, though, is to have an appreciation for how algorithms, the mathematical recipes that fuel many of the most popular tech apps and platforms, can be simultaneously useful, profitable, irritating and also deeply flawed.

The more you feel, the more you post

The emotional contagion through Facebook study presented several relevant and surprising findings, including what the researchers called 'a withdrawal effect'. They found that people in the study who were exposed to fewer emotional updates in their News Feeds then didn't post as much in the days that followed.

This may seem like a small observation, but it highlights something that's important to how this information guides the decisions made behind the scenes: emotional content keeps people engaged, leading to more posts, more photos and more updates. It's therefore in the best interests of social media platforms to 'favour' more emotionally driven content when it comes to choosing what goes into your feed.

There are also incentives built in to encourage you to post more emotional content. Likes, shares and follower counts can make us feel more connected, and they can be used to push our emotional buttons. There's evidence to suggest that the more emotionally intense a tweet is, the more likes and retweets it would get on Twitter. This means people get a sense of reward for expressing more emotion. The more emotion they express, the more this could lead to increased emotional contagion. No wonder social media platforms can be such emotionally exhausting spaces.

Mood monitoring

In 2017, leaked documents allegedly showed Facebook had conducted research to identify when young users in Australia and New Zealand expressed feelings of insecurity. According to reports, this showed that Facebook can monitor the updates and photos of young people and identify a whole range of emotions, including 'stressed', 'defeated', 'overwhelmed', 'anxious', 'nervous', 'stupid', 'silly', 'useless' and 'a failure'.

When *The Australian* originally published the story, it included a comment from Facebook, which explained that the research was 'intended to help marketers understand how people express themselves'. Why is this a big deal, you might be wondering – isn't it already obvious when people are feeling emotional?

Firstly, it's not clear how this research was put to use – or even if it was used. The simple fact that this kind of data is being collected in the first place could suggest that users can be served certain types of ads when they are feeling certain types of emotions. Hold off on how wrong that sounds for now. It does make business sense for a social media platform such as Facebook to become a more sophisticated ad platform for its customers. Remember the study about impulse shoppers being mostly motivated by boredom? If the goal is to drive views and clicks on ads, what better way to figure out how to do that than by understanding the audience's emotions?

If the thought of this is making you feel uncomfortable, you're not alone. As unsurprising as this kind of platform research might be, it doesn't make it any less exploitative, especially in light of the focus on finding ways to sell to people when they are in their most vulnerable emotional state.

You'd need to delete your social media accounts to be sure you're never going to be manipulated by these kinds of tactics, or even involved in research without you knowing it. But you can manage these influences by stepping away from social media platforms when your emotions are running high. Remind yourself of the emotional regulation suggestions on we explored earlier. None of them involve scrolling and writing updates about how you feel. Instead, they're all focused on the deliberate steps you can take to improve your mood right now.

Checklist

Your devices can affect how you feel. Not everyone has the same experiences. It's up to you to discover how your emotions are influenced by what you see on your screens.

You turn to tech to manage your emotions. This can be positive and improve your mood. But you might have developed ways of coping that aren't working out for you.

Try meditation and mood-tracking apps. These can help you to manage low moods, anxiety and depression. They can also help you to pinpoint emotions, find triggers and learn calming techniques.

Reduce your time online. You don't need to cut down your tech use to zero, but issues like loneliness, social comparison and boredom may improve if you spend less time on your phone. And remember: stop passively scrolling and start engaging.

Create an emotional management toolkit. This will help you quickly find the apps, activities and feel-good stuff you need when you next feel sad, stressed, bored or lonely.

Find more flow. Researchers have linked gaming to a reduction in stress, and it could be because it pushes you into a flow state. But you need to embrace your stress-relieving activities. Approaching them with guilt will lessen their benefits.

Emotions are catchable. You can catch feelings from people online and offline. They may also be manipulated and measured by digital media companies.

Pay attention to your feelings. Often easier said than done, but it will help you to clarify and identify which people, platforms and activities might be having a negative influence on your emotions.

Important: If you're concerned about any of the topics covered in this chapter, I recommend seeking out professional support. Head to a list of resources on page 333.

FOCUS

STAYING PRESENT DESPITE CONSTANT DIGITAL DISTRACTIONS

When I have a new writing assignment, I often feel a bit like Tom Cruise in the first *Mission Impossible* movie, in that scene where he has to abseil into a vault and copy some important data onto a floppy disk (remember those?). My mission, should I choose to accept it, is to write 1,500 words about a smartwatch in three hours. On paper, these two scenarios may seem worlds apart, but they're both extremely high tech and equally fraught with peril.

To fulfil *his* mission, Tom uses a magnetic screwdriver, a microscopic camera embedded in his glasses, a temperature sensor strapped to his wrist, and super-high-strength abseiling equipment. I have a MacBook, a broadband connection, an ergonomic desk chair and a fancy water bottle.

And just as a rogue bead of sweat falling where it shouldn't is all it would take to set off the alarms and ruin Tom's mission, a single new notification could appear on my screen at any given moment and shatter the focus I need to meet my deadline.

The big difference between Tom and me is that he's able to swing in and out of the CIA vault like a special forces Peter Pan without a hitch. I, however, have clicked open a new tab in my browser to check on Twitter before I've barely written a paragraph of my new assignment and my focus has wandered off into a dozen clickbait cul-de-sacs.

Why does it feel increasingly like an impossible mission to keep our attention on one thing at a time? How are we meant to concentrate when the tech we rely on is constantly setting attention traps for us? What can we do to bring balance back to our focus? And where can I get a pair of glasses like Tom's?

BRING IT INTO FOCUS

Right now, you're only seeing, smelling and hearing a tiny sliver of what's happening in the world around you. That's not even counting everything that's going on in your mind, like your memories and your imagination.

Attention is your ability to take notice of something that you find interesting among everything else that's going on.

Philosopher and psychologist William James defined attention as: 'the taking possession by the mind, in clear and vivid form, of one out of what seem several simultaneously possible objects or trains of thought. Focalization, concentration, of consciousness are of its [attention's] essence. It implies withdrawal from some things in order to deal effectively with others.'

I love the poetry in this description. It also helps us to define concentration, which we can think of as the distillation of attention into its purest form. The dictionary definition of concentration is: 'the power of focusing all one's attention' and if we concentrate on something we deal with that one thing above everything else.

And there we have focus too, often used interchangeably with concentration and even attention. It is 'the centre of interest or activity'. Imagine focus as the product – it's what we get if we engage our attention on something and concentrate on it fully.

These terms might all sound similar, but their subtle differences matter. I like to picture how they work together by visualising my ability to focus as an observatory. My attention is the machinery that guides the giant telescope to look up at the cosmos. My concentration is the telescope, allowing me to home in on one specific star, planet or comet. If my attention wanders, I can no longer see it. The greater understanding we have of the various components of focus, the more control we have over improving it and putting it to work when and where we want it to – we need to focus on focus.

We know all too well that much of our connected tech intentionally hijacks our attention. This makes it difficult for us to maintain our focus. Every day we allow the people behind our favourite apps, sites and social media platforms to decide what we do with it instead. We shouldn't avoid the things that call for our attention and never turn our attentive telescopes in the direction of our apps, games, emails and messages ever again. Instead, we can learn how to better control what we focus on and when.

YOUR PHONE ISN'T KILLING YOUR CONCENTRATION

I collect headlines about the tech people use the most. I pay particular attention to the ones I suspect may have been written to scare you into clicking on them. Here are some examples (I've tweaked them slightly, but the verbs are the same):

*'Notifications are **killing** your concentration'*
*'Facebook is **ruining** your brain'*
*'Your phone is **destroying** your focus'*

Notice how violent technology sounds in these. Your phone isn't crawling inside your head and scrambling your brains (promise). And yet here we are. This language sells. People click the links and buy the papers. This doesn't surprise me, because as extreme as this language is, journalists use it to tap into the fear many of us are carrying around: that technology is changing how we think, how we remember and how we concentrate.

Is it possible that the tech you've been using every day – your smartphone, your tablet, your computer – has affected your ability to truly focus on anything? Many of us simply assume they're doing some damage, due to the sheer number of damning articles floating around the internet. Is there currently any way to accurately quantify this?

I've tried my best to answer this question for myself – and it's not easy.

I'm pretty sure I used to be able to remember people's phone numbers with relative ease and even read books a little faster than I do now – before I got a smartphone. The other significant difference here is that I'm simply remembering being younger than I am now. Won't my powers of concentration and recall have changed by now anyway – even if I hadn't spent the intervening years carrying my smartphone around like a pet?

Everyone has now lived through seismic changes in the consumer tech landscape. This makes it harder to argue we haven't all changed to some degree due to having constant, instant access to the internet via smartphones, tablets, laptops and the like. This is our everyday world now, and it's deeply unrealistic to gauge how any of us are using our brains today compared with people's mental activities from 50 years ago.

Think about it: who needs to memorise anything any more when we can get hold of any fact, any map, any calculation within seconds on any screen within arm's reach? Is it, therefore, unrealistic to expect to have an unwavering focus when we have constant notifications to check, likes to look at and new series to binge on Prime Video? None of this tech is going to go 'back in the box', so we're going to need to adapt with it, not against it.

Tech is changing, and it's likely changing us, and so it's no longer relevant or even fruitful to worry about not remembering phone numbers. Instead, we need new ways to find our way in this new and busier-than-ever-before world we're in. The first thing to recognise is that your ability to focus is not a lost cause, far from it. Your smartphone isn't killing your concentration. Facebook isn't attacking your brain. They're just offering you a range of distractions that didn't used to be there. Quick question: how many times have you picked up your phone while you've been reading this page?

Smart devices aren't necessarily making things harder for our focus, but they're not designed to help our focus either, like a friend whom you love catching up with, but who leaves you feeling a bit bewildered because they can't stay on one topic for more than 30 seconds. You wouldn't cut this person out of your life in the same way you're not planning on getting rid of your phone. But there's still a problem to address, which means we need to learn how to guard our energies and our focus.

THE DEAL WITH DISTRACTIONS

Distractions are the enemy of focus, and our days are filled with them. They break our concentration and dilute our attention, swerving us away from what we want to focus on. The words 'distraction' and 'interruption' are often used interchangeably, but some researchers think that despite their similarities, there are subtle but significant differences between the two. They believe a distraction is a type of interference that's irrelevant and should be ignored, whereas an interruption demands attention because it's part of another task or goal.

This is a good distinction to bear in mind, as emails, notifications, instant messages and social media could be classified as interruptions when they interfere with our focus because they're part of ongoing conversations and interactions that we've invited explicitly into our lives. But that doesn't mean they're necessarily any better for us, especially when you consider that it can take 23 minutes to regain focus after you get any kind of notification.

To understand what distracts us, we need to divide these distractions and interruptions into two: inner and outer.

Inner distractions, also referred to as 'endogenous interruptions', are the ways you distract yourself. For example, you start thinking about checking Facebook or writing an email when you're supposed to be doing something else, and then you go ahead and do it. This is often habitual. Remember in the Addiction chapter when we looked at habit cues? Well, a cue that goes something like 'I want some social connection' can lead to one of these inner distractions.

Outer distractions, also called 'exogenous interruptions', happen when something around you catches your attention. This can be people in your office or sounds of traffic passing by. But when it comes to your everyday technology, it's often a notification – a banner that materialises on your screen, a vibration that takes you by surprise, a nagging red dot over your favourite app.

The trouble with outer distractions is they can have *a cascading effect*. This means you might look at your phone for one reason (and that might be a perfectly good reason), then you click a link, open another app, check your emails, and you forgot what you were meant to be doing in the first place. Your phone distracted you from looking at your phone.

These are called within-phone interruptions. One study found they can derail your concentration and take up a lot of time. The first thing you wanted to do can end up taking four times longer than it should have. And, as long as that sounds, I can think of examples of my own within-phone interruptions that never resulted in me getting the first thing done *at all*.

Distractions and interruptions aren't only disruptive because they slow you down. Research has shown that they can make your performance suffer too. Not only is it taking you longer to get the first task done, but you're also not doing it as well as you could either. One study found that distractions of just under three seconds doubled the number of errors people made on a task. That's about the same amount of time it takes to click from one tab to another. Longer distractions of a little more than four seconds tripled the number of those errors. That's about the time it takes to read a short text message. You don't have to be distracted long for your focus to evaporate.

The question of why we can't leave these tech-based distractions and interruptions alone is to do with the tactics we explored Addiction chapter. We feel compelled to check in on our favourite apps, games, emails, messages and everything else that can push a notification our way using tried-and-tested techniques that make notifications feel urgent. What might you be missing out on right now if you don't look? What reward might be waiting for you? By looking, our attention is pulled away from whatever we're doing and towards our screens – where our views, likes and clicks can be profitable.

You're losing time, and you're making errors. But there's something else going on too. Every time you give in to a distraction or interruption from a notification, an email or a text message, you're increasing the likelihood that behaviour will become a habit – also known as a checking behaviour or checking habit.

Think back to the habit loops we looked at on page 42. The cue here would be a notification, and the routine would be that you check it. What that means is that by checking your phone now, you're training yourself to check again and again. You're reinforcing a habit loop. Or, to put it another way, you're making life harder for a future version of you.

Habits refresher

If checking your phone every time you see a banner or feel a buzz has become an unthinking habit, it can be tricky to change, but not impossible.

Open up a notebook or grab an index card (this works best away from a screen) and divide it into two. Write 'inner distractions' on one side and 'outer distractions' on the other. Throughout the day, do your best to make a note of when you notice one or the other. You can choose different symbols to show whether you carried out your phone checking routine or not. It'll look something like the diagram on the next page. The lines are the times I was distracted, and the circles are the times I picked up my phone.

The idea is that this will give you more awareness of how much you're being distracted by your phone – how often you're giving in to distractions – and will help with the next section about notification settings.

If you want to do more to address the root of this habit, go back to the habits explainer on page 42 and work through the steps to identify what new routine you could introduce instead.

Inner distractions

||| OOOO

Outer distractions

||||| ||||| OO

Add a quality filter to your notifications

Notifications are the banners that flash up on your smartphone screen or appear as little red badges over your favourite apps. We've learned to think of notifications as urgent, but they're almost always not.

Research has shown that mobile phone notifications that you don't even look at, but that you know are there, can cause a disruption in performance that's similar to actually picking up and looking at your phone anyway. Notifications make our minds wander and get us thinking about things that aren't to do with what it is we're trying to stay focused on.

You can minimise distractions right now by adjusting your notification settings. Let's break our notifications down into three categories to better understand which you need to cut down, silence or (possibly) stop altogether:

- **People:** These are notifications you get because someone has messaged you, liked your tweet or shared your photo. These are to do with other people.

- **Apps:** These are notifications from apps that pop up at any time, usually as banners on your phone, even when you're not using the app. For example, a workout app might send a notification asking you if you want to do some burpees. (Even though the answer is always no.)
- **Events:** These are messages from apps, but they're about specific events. For example, the Uber app sends you a notification when your drive is nearby.

Now you know what to look for, you can start thinking about how to filter your notifications and protect your ability to focus when you need it. Remember, these are recommendations, not rules, and we're not 'banning' anything. You can apply them and adapt them to best suit your needs and habits.

- **Hear from people – not apps:** Notifications from people, whether that's people on Twitter sending you a DM or your friend giving you a call, are distracting. But I think there's more reason to be distracted by a person rather than by an app that just wants you to check it. Go into the notification settings on your phone and review the settings for each app separately. If a person can contact you through it, like WhatsApp, Messenger, Twitter, etc., keep those for now. If it's an app people can't contact you on, e.g. a fitness app, a shopping app or a map app, then turn notifications off. However, keep notifications from apps that might share important information with you about events, like Uber and Amazon Prime Now.
- **Make a VIP list:** Take that first step further and consider who is *really* important enough to distract you from your focus? For example, I have all notifications from social media apps switched off and the only notifications I allow come from

WhatsApp because I know that's where my close friends and family contact me. I'm also in some groups that I don't want to see every message from, so even though I've allowed WhatsApp notifications, I've muted specific WhatsApp conversations. It doesn't need to be Sophie's Choice, just the people you'll always want to respond to right away, versus the people you can get back to when you take your next scheduled break.

- **Go to airplane mode:** Whatever phone you have, some settings temporarily stop you from getting notifications and calls. I like the 'do not disturb' setting on my iPhone, which silences calls and notifications. You can quickly swipe it on and off – the easier it is to do, the more likely I'll do it. But you can also customise it. You can set a schedule, permit it to switch on when you're driving automatically and, my favourite feature: you can whitelist people, so specific calls always get through. That last one is crucial if you're the type of person who worries about changing notification settings in case there's an emergency.

- **Make a whitelist:** If you use the 'do not disturb' settings on your phone, it's worth making a whitelist to decide whose calls can get through. This will depend on you. If you need to be on call for work, but don't want to hear from friends when you've got a few hours off, whitelist anyone work-related. Or the other way round if you're not required to keep in touch with your boss. It might be that your partner is whitelisted, but no one else is. There are no set rules. It's up to you: work out what will help you concentrate the most, and go with it.

- **Get a smartwatch.** This is the last resort for those of us who have tried turning off notifications but find it makes you check apps, emails and messages even more because you can't stop thinking about what might be there waiting for you. I've been there myself. A way I got around this was by wearing a fitness tracker and allowing notifications to be sent to the much smaller screen on my wrist. This means you'll still get distracted by notifications – and some wearables will enable you to send simple responses – but you won't get sucked into your phone's screen. This will keep you up to date with what you may want to turn your focus to once you're done with your current activity.

There's no universal solution for managing your notifications. You need to try these out for yourself and find out which work best. Maybe it's the magical power of turning off notifications from annoying apps, or the calming energy of 'do not disturb'. Even if you only put airplane mode on for half an hour while you wrestle your inbox, or turn off notifications from that nagging workout app, these are small steps to take back control from your smartphone.

The vampire in your pocket

Notifications are only half of the problem. Have you got your phone near you right now? Don't look directly at it in case it suspects something. It might be affecting your concentration just by existing. I'm not kidding.

One fascinating study called this 'brain drain' and suggested that keeping your phone close by could make you less productive. What I'm saying is your phone, even when it's being quiet and minding its own business, can affect your thinking. Let's be clear here: this isn't to do with any signals it's giving off or that it's cursed. It's about you. It's because you're paying attention to it – even when you think you're not – and can't fully focus on what you're meant to be doing.

What we can take from this is: if you're working, or doing anything else that requires you to focus, you should move your phone away from you to prevent it from sucking all your concentration away. The researchers behind the 'brain drain' study suggest taking time apart from your phone *can* help. But there's a catch. You need to plan for it and make sure there's a way for urgent calls or notifications to get through.

The reason those two points are important to us is that more research has shown that taking someone's phone away from them without warning and forcing separation when they don't want it can make them feel panicked, leading to an increase in heart rate, anxiety and, ironically, worse performance at a given task. We don't want that, which means there's a balancing act here. Don't lock your phone in a drawer or get someone to take it from you. Instead, move it away deliberately and intentionally because you deserve to focus, on your terms.

The simplest way I've found to add some distance between me and my phone is to pick a place to keep it when I'm working that is close enough if I need it but isn't visible or reachable from my desk. I make a point to put it there before I begin work each day.

If you want to test whether this makes a difference throughout your day, think of a place to put it whenever you start a new activity. For example, for breakfast with your partner first thing? It's on a shelf in the hallway. Are you working at your desk? It's hanging out on the bookcase a few feet away. Watching a movie at night? It's over on the kitchen worktop. By moving it away from you consistently, rather than for just one activity, you might be able to create a new habit.

Try this: One way to make this trial separation easier to manage is to use it as a time to recharge your phone battery. Pick a place to charge it that's in the sweet spot of being nearby, but not distracting when you want to focus.

BRAIN TRAINING AND BRAIN CHANGING

It's tempting to hunt for a quick fix to our collective problems with focus – I get it. But we need to be wary. There are many apps and online programs that claim to be able to boost your focus, concentration, memory and overall brain health with games and puzzles. Known as 'brain training', this is a big and lucrative business. If you search online for 'brain training app' you'll see hundreds of recommendations, as well as lists ranking the best ones. Although each app is different, the thinking behind them is similar. Your brain needs to be trained, like a muscle. The more you do it, the better the results. This might sound like a remedy for your easily distracted mind, and something it's worth spending money on. But the simple truth is that your brain isn't like your bicep.

It's unclear whether brain training apps can deliver on their promises. Experts put a number of them to the test, and there's conflicting evidence about whether they work – and what 'work' even means in this context. For example, studies have shown that certain brain training apps do improve your performance. But there's a catch. They improve your performance within the brain training game – not in the real world. More points, advanced levels and trophies when you're playing a game sound fun, but the progress you seem to be making doesn't necessarily translate to your day-to-day life.

You might think that if the experts can't agree on whether these apps help or not, there isn't any harm in trialling a few of them, right? Maybe. But several brain training apps are marketed at older people or those with health issues who have valid concerns about their memory and brain health. This is when brain training can be problematic because some of the companies that make brain training programs also make false promises.

In the US in 2016, the Federal Trade Commission (FTC) filed a complaint against Lumos Labs, the company behind popular brain training app Lumosity. The charges from the FTC alleged that Lumosity deceived its customers with unsubstantiated claims, including that the app could help them perform better at school and protect against cognitive decline. Lumos Labs paid out $2 million to settle the charges and had to notify all of its subscribers.

If there's little proof these apps have a positive effect, I'd recommend focusing on other ways to occupy your downtime. Whether that's taking a break from your phone entirely or using it to play another game you enjoy.

Beware of the brain hackers

Brain training apps aren't alone in making bold claims about your brain. I've lost count of the number of books, online programs and blog posts that allegedly have the secrets to 'rewiring' or 'hacking' the way our brains work. They explain that we all can modify our brains by repeating specific actions. Now, I know this sounds like science fiction. But, in a way, it's true.

Neuroscientists now know that our brains can still change during adulthood. These changes can happen in response to what we do and what we experience. This concept is called neuroplasticity. The problem with it, though, is that neuroplasticity, or simply 'plasticity', is often used to describe changes that researchers have no concrete evidence for. Neurobiologist and author Moheb Costandi explains that the term is a 'buzzword', and it's 'become virtually meaningless', adding: 'If the internet is to be believed, you can rewire your brain to improve just about any aspect of behaviour,' when in reality, it may not be that simple.

It's a very attractive idea that we could all alter and improve our brains if we put the right effort in. It gives us power and control over our flailing focus and dwindling attention spans. But, realistically, there's still a lot that science doesn't know about the brain – let alone how we can change it ourselves. That said, researchers have observed real and significant changes to brain shape and volume when people have trained specific skills over time, including learning a second language and juggling. Tech shortcuts to these changes, like brain training apps, are – without scientifically rigorous evidence of any brain benefits – more Silicon Valley snake oil and it may simply be better (and quicker) to put your phone somewhere out of sight and practise a brain-enriching hobby instead.

There are some activities scientists believe *could* have an impact on our attention, memory and overall brain health more generally. These are the things we all know we should be focusing on anyway: get more sleep, exercise and meditate. Instead of looking for exciting tech-based solutions to our problems, the answers may just lie in the fundamental good habits we already know benefit us. If you were looking for an excuse to go out for a run or download a new meditation app, here it is.

IS MULTITASKING A MYTH?

If you've watched the TV show *Parks and Recreation* I'm sure you can relate to the main character, Leslie Knope, from time to time. For those of you who haven't, she's the deputy director of the parks department in a fictional town in the US called Pawnee. She's driven, she's a perfectionist and she's always trying to do more than one thing at once. I certainly don't have the political ambitions of Knope, but just like her, I'm a multitasker. That's why I always take what her mentor and boss Ron Swanson tells her to heart. In one episode in which she's trying to juggle lots of tasks and getting extremely overwhelmed by them all, he tells her: 'Never half-ass two things. Whole-ass one thing.' It takes 100 per cent of our powers of focus to do a good job of anything. And I think this is a mantra we can all live by, considering many of us try to divide our focus between a dozen different things at once most days.

According to researchers, multitasking requires three things: performing multiple tasks at once, consciously moving from one job to another and performing the tasks over a relatively short period. We all do more than one thing at once all the time. We walk and we talk. We eat snacks and watch YouTube. We write emails and listen to music. But not all tasks are created equal, and so not everything is suitable for multitasking.

Imagine you're sitting opposite a friend. You're having a conversation, so you're listening to them, then talking back to them. Then you hear a conversation between two other people on the table next to you. No matter how much more interesting that other conversation might seem, you wouldn't be able to listen to and take part in both simultaneously – at least not well or without confusing everyone else. Multitasking is a tricky subject. It's certainly not the holy grail of productivity some think it might be. We have research to prove it doesn't work for most of us. But that's not the whole story. We also have research to suggest it suits some people, but only some of the time.

The problem with technology and multitasking is that it is far too easy to do, and we don't realise how it might be affecting our focus. When I realised how many screens I had open in front of me while writing this chapter, I had a sudden feeling of horror. I was watching Netflix on my TV, while scrolling through Twitter on my phone, while my laptop was open in front of me and I was trying to come up with a writing plan and, to top it all off, my iPad was at my side because I was about to FaceTime my brother to say hello. I was splitting my attention in at least four different directions but concentrating fully on none of them. I'd managed to write three sentences in nearly as many hours.

This kind of scenario might have become the norm for many of us throughout 2020 as we did our best to juggle work, fun, keeping up with family and friends and all of those Netflix shows we'd meant to watch. I gradually became more attuned to which activities could be done in tandem with others and which needed my full attention. I found I could pick a maximum of two things to do at once as long as one felt easy or mindless: working out on my exercise bike while watching YouTube on my iPad or putting a call with my mum on speakerphone as I cooked dinner. But if I combined two tasks that both needed my full attention, I may as well have been doing nothing at all.

One study found that people who multitask are, despite what we might tell ourselves, not fully concentrating on any of the tasks they're carrying out and are instead distracted continually by each of the different things that they're doing, making people who multitask far less productive than we might think. This study also suggests that people who multitask could be sacrificing performance on the first thing they started doing to let in all of those other sources of information. What this boils down to is: by doing more than one thing you're getting nothing done. Especially that first thing you *really* needed to do.

A lot of the research suggests the same thing: multitasking rarely makes us more productive – it often does precisely the opposite. It's not all bad news, though. There is evidence to suggest that all of the switching back and forth between tasks could be making us better at noticing multi-sensory stimuli. One study found those who multitask regularly can better prepare for unexpected information. The participants took part in a colour change and audio tone task and the multitaskers were better at responding to incoming audio sounds; which you'd expect if you're continually checking every email, beep and little red dot.

We also know that the nature of the tasks matter. One study of older adults discovered that those who pedalled on a stationary bike at the same time performed better on a series of cognitive tasks and even cycled faster. The positive effects decreased as the tasks got more challenging, but the researchers were still surprised by their findings. They suspected this could be because cycling is easy to do and automatic. It might also be because exercise increases arousal in regions of the brain. 'What arousal does is give you more attention to focus on a task,' Lori Altmann, one of the lead researchers and an Associate Professor at the College of Public Health and Health Professions at the University of Florida, told EurekAlert!: 'When the tasks were really easy, we saw the effect of that attention as people cycled very fast. As the cognitive tasks got harder, they started impinging on the amount of attention available to perform both tasks, so participants didn't cycle quite so fast.'

This might explain why some of my most successful multitasking sessions have involved combining cycling on my exercise bike at home (an easy-to-do exercise) with other tasks, like watching TV shows, replying to emails and even dictating parts of this book to a voice notes app on my phone (these require more focus).

If you're reading this and thinking you *can* multitask, you might be what's known as a supertasker. Researchers estimate that only a few of us – about 2.5 per cent – can actually do more than one thing well at once. So I don't know whether you are one or not, but the odds are against you that your multitasking is anything above mediocre. On that note, we also know that people who think they can multitask well are often the ones who aren't good at it at all.

It's not hard to understand why we multitask. There are always lots of things to check and do at any one time, and our devices are always demanding our attention – and that's just in our personal lives. In many workplaces, it's considered the hallmark of productivity to handle lots of things at once. Many jobs require people to switch between meetings, emails and calls quickly. That's not counting the jobs that rely on multitasking, like those who work in the military or in a high-pressure medical setting.

For all of the criticism that's levelled at it, what I find fascinating about multitasking is that we might all do it naturally. In their book *The Distracted Mind: Ancient Brains in a High-Tech World*, neuroscientist Adam Gazzaley and psychologist Larry Rosen write that multitasking happens because 'at our core we are information-seeking creatures.' In the same way we learned about the dopamine response in the Addiction chapter, we look for new rewards whenever we can – multitasking is no exception.

Interestingly, the same productivity problems we face with multitasking might also apply if you stop doing one task and move quickly on to another – called task switching. One 2009 study suggested this problem is down to something called 'attention residue'. When you stop one task and move on to another, there might be residual thoughts and focus from the first one left over, which impairs your performance on the next one.

Hold up, how would we get anything done if we can't move from one thing to another? Well, the researchers suggested some key findings might help us. The first is that the initial task needs to be fully completed – switching when it was unfinished had an impact on performance. Secondly, more time pressure can help. It's unclear why that is, but I know if I have a specific deadline to work to, I'm more likely to hit it. Either way, I think the answer to our multitasking and task-switching problems are to learn to focus on one thing at a time: to become monotaskers.

> ### Save things for later
>
> One of the main reasons I multitask during the day is because I come across something genuinely engaging and relevant to my job that I want to read and go ahead and read it – no longer concentrating on what I was initially doing. An excellent way to deal with this is to find a saving or bookmarking system. I like Pocket, an app which allows you to save articles, as well as Evernote to keep everything else – think of it as a virtual notebook.

Why there's no shame in becoming a monotasker

The main message coming out of all the research into multitasking is that you *might* be getting things done if you're doing relatively simple tasks in a relaxed and leisurely environment. If, however, you have an important task to get done, you really should concentrate on just that and nothing else. You need to become a monotasker.

To get myself focused and ready to monotask effectively, I pick three things that I want to get done today and choose one to get on and complete straight away. Here are some of the considerations you might want to make, to set yourself up for some serious monotasking:

- **Your space.** Wherever you can find it, you need to have a space to work in, whether it's your desk at an office or a kitchen table at home. Make sure there are no books or papers in the way. If there are, spend a few minutes sorting them into neat piles. You also need to throw away rubbish. Take used bowls and cups to the kitchen. Wipe the surface.

If you're working out and about, grab a napkin and clean the table. Sit so you're not facing the entrance where people are moving about. Put your bag somewhere that feels safe; that way, you're not thinking about that when you should be working. Make sure your phone is in a pocket out of sight.

- **Your body.** It's tempting to tense up and ignore everything your body needs right now to get this one task done. But if you're uncomfortable, hot, slumped over your laptop, or anything else, you'll get distracted, start multitasking or just stop working altogether.

Take a couple of deep breaths. Make sure there's a bottle or glass of water at your side and keep drinking it. Do everything in your power to ensure the temperature feels good. (I'm one of those people who would happily work in a fridge if I could find one big enough.) Do your best to sit up straight and uncross your legs. Adjust your chair and table if you can so it's a little more comfortable.

- **Your technology.** Follow at least two of the notification suggestions from page 99. Get used to having only one tab open at once. Yes, only one. Close that email tab. If you're working on a laptop, turn off notifications there too – especially the kind that fly in from the edge of the screen.

Try one of the focus apps on page 333 or visit the directory in the back of the book. Make sure your device is fully charged, or you know where your power lead or battery pack is in case you need it in a hurry.

- **Your priority.** All of this is pointless if you don't know what you're meant to be getting on with. Write down the three things you must get done today. Highlight, underline or put a big circle around the one thing you need to do right now.

When I need to focus, I write all the tasks I need to get done on separate index cards and set them in a pile, putting the most pressing task at the top. If you get distracted, the card is there to keep bringing your focus back to that one priority. If I'm feeling stressed, this method works better for me rather than writing a list, which gives me an excuse to try and do the top three things all at once. You could also write it on a Post-it and stick it in the corner of your laptop so that whenever your (literal) focus drifts, you come back to it. If you need to leave your phone out, take a photo of your list and set it as your wallpaper, so that whenever you pick it up, you're reminded of the task in hand.

Approach monotasking as a focus experiment. You don't need to do it all the time, but take what you like from my steps above and put them into practice – even if you just choose one thing for each step, that's going to help.

THE PAST CONTROLS THE PRESENT (AND VICE VERSA)

Focus isn't only significant because it helps us to get things done – it might also give our memory a boost. Before we look at how that works, let's define the basic types of memory and briefly look at how the technology we use every day impacts our ability to remember – for better and for worse.

Working memory and short-term memory

These are terms to describe the way we temporarily hold on to information. Our short-term memory holds on to bits of information, like numbers, words and names, for a brief time. There's a lot of debate about exactly how much information our short-term memory can store. Researchers believe it roughly holds four to seven chunks of information at any one time. This could be six letters, around five short words or seven digits – but that differs from person to person.

Working memory holds on to a similarly small amount of information to short-term memory. The key difference is, it's the job of your working memory to use that small amount of information to plan and to carry out behaviours, like reading, learning and working. Neuroscientists Earl Miller and Timothy Buschman describe working memory as 'a mental sketchpad, providing a surface on which we can place transitory information to hold it "in mind"'.

Researchers think your working memory is directly related to how well you can multitask. If you have a good working memory, you're more likely to be able to switch between multiple tasks, better deal with interruptions and, therefore, focus better.

Long-term memory

New information moves through different stages and can end up in our long-term memory. This is a big store of knowledge with many different elements to it. One part of it is implicit memory – where you store the things you know, but might not be aware you know them. This is knowledge you probably acquired unconsciously and now use without thinking, not deliberately.

Procedural memory is a type of implicit memory, think writing or riding a bike. You know how to do those things, but you don't sit and think, 'How do I write my name?' in the same way you might think, 'What's the capital of Venezuela?' This leads us to another aspect of long-term memory. Explicit memory (also known as declarative memory) is the opposite; it allows us to recollect events and facts. These are the things you know.

This can be divided into more parts: semantic and episodic. Semantic memory refers to knowledge of the world. This system stores information about the meaning of words, concepts and facts. This is where you'd find dates, names and all of that useless trivia you've picked up at pub quizzes over the years. In other words, these are all the things you turn to Google for.

Episodic memory is a type of long-term memory for personally experienced events that have occurred at particular times and in specific places. Sometimes called autobiographical memory because it's *your* collection of past experiences. This is where memories from a holiday are stored or your graduation. I like how psychologist and author Dr Julia Shaw describes episodic memory in her book, *The Memory Illusion*. She writes: 'It is our personal memory scrapbook; our mind's diary; our internal Facebook timeline.'

Our devices have become external storage space for our episodic memory. We might have once remembered with diaries and photo albums, but now there are reminders every day of what you were doing two, five and ten years ago, whether you like it or not.

There's more to memory, many models and distinct processes, but here we've touched upon some of the essential kinds in regards to how we focus: now, let's explore the link between the two.

The link between attention and memory

The relationship between what you pay attention to and what you remember is not yet completely understood. But what we do know is they need each other to function.

Memory has a limited capacity, which means what we turn our attention to can determine what information we will and won't hold on to. Surprisingly, it also works the other way around – memories of past experiences can guide what we pay attention to in the present moment.

Here's an example. Let's say you need to find your way to a place you've never been to before, but you don't have your phone with you, so you can't use Google Maps. Instead, you're following directions that someone told you a minute or so before. These directions are (for the time being) in your working memory. One of the directions was to look for a yellow garage then turn right. You need to pay attention to what you see and look out for a yellow garage. The contents of your attention and your working memory overlap.

Attention and long-term memory are also linked. In the example above, you have long-term memories that inform you what a garage is, which helped you to work out the directions, using what's stored in your long-term and working memory to guide your attention.

When you think about it, it's common sense to assume that attention improves memory. If you don't pay attention to something in the moment, you'll struggle to recall the details of it later on. It may be you have no memory of it at all, or it's tucked away in your implicit memory. You're more likely to be able to recall that information easily if you're paying attention at the time when you first experienced it. That way, you are creating memories that are more readily available in your explicit and episodic memory. Interestingly, for all the convenience that GPS-enabled smartphones give us, the physical detail of a yellow garage is more likely to stick in our minds than the abstract blue line of a route on Google Maps.

CAN CONCENTRATION HELP US TO CREATE BETTER MEMORIES?

There's no way of knowing for sure, but rough estimates suggest that we might have collectively taken more than 1.4 trillion photos in 2020. More than 100 million (or thereabouts) are uploaded to Instagram per day, and many more are stored on all of our phones right now because they're not grid-worthy.

We're taking and sharing a staggering number of photos, but do you remember much about what was going on when you took them?

Let's conduct our own experiment. Go to the photos on your phone. Scroll back about five times and take a look at what you see there. Pick any photo that you took (this won't work if it's a Baby Yoda meme or an inspirational quote you're going to share later on Instagram). Are you able to remember what you were doing when you took that photo? Do you remember what you could hear and smell? What were you thinking and feeling?

When I try to do this, I struggle to answer with any certainty. This gives me cause to consider whether I'd have forgotten these moments altogether if I hadn't taken a photo, and what I was even focusing on at the time if I still can't recall the moment in any detail. Since photography went digital and no one has to worry about how many exposures are left on the film in their camera, we're all taking thousands of photos throughout the year, so it's worth taking a little time to understand what's happening in these moments as we're capturing them, and what happens to our ability to focus in the moment when we're continually capturing it for later on.

Cognitive psychologist Dr Linda A. Henkel conducted two studies that I think are important to look at when it comes to photos and memory. She aimed to find out how taking photos with a camera might shape what people then remember about their experience afterwards. (Her studies looked specifically at digital cameras, but I think we could apply some of the same thinking to our phones.)

The first study took participants on a guided tour of an art museum. They were asked to look at 30 objects, including pottery, paintings, sculptures and jewels. They were told to photograph half of the items and observe the other half. Later, when they were asked to describe the objects, they couldn't remember the ones they photographed as well as those they didn't.

What a thought-provoking finding, right? Bear that in mind for the next experiment. In this one, there were 27 objects. Participants were asked to photograph nine of them. Then they were asked to photograph another nine of them by zooming in on a specific part or detail. The final nine were observed but not photographed. When recalling the objects later, those the participants zoomed in on and those that were observed were remembered with similar accuracy. But, yet again, the full, regular photos weren't remembered as well. Wait, there's more. Zooming in on one bit of the object then had a knock-on effect. It seemed to make the whole object more memorable – not only the bit that was zoomed in on.

Let's remember this is only one study. But what I like to take away from this is that when we act passively, by which I mean when we just take photos for the sake of it or so we can bookmark the moment for later, we don't pay attention to what we're seeing, hearing and experiencing. We're concentrating on photo-taking and little else. So it's no surprise we don't remember the moment well. However, when we make a point of zooming in, the heightened focus required to look at only one small part of the object might enhance our memories of the moment.

Another study suggested that taking photos could actually boost your memory of what happened and what you saw. But here's the notable part: participants only took pictures of scenes around them that they were interested in. Researchers believe this is important and shows us that people have a better memory for photos that are self-relevant. Simply put, if we care about what we're photographing, we're more likely to commit what we saw and did to memory. And if you feel like you're creating disposable memories, don't be surprised if you can't recall them well later. Instead, make a deliberate choice to record the moment you find yourself in – and focus on everything that's going on in it.

This isn't only about being more deliberate, looking around you and taking in what you can see, smell, hear and how you feel, but staying present. As in, not thinking about what caption you'll write underneath the photo or who might or might not like it later. I know that when I start agonising about what my followers will think of a photo I plan to put online, I either don't want to take a picture any more because I've sucked the fun out of it or the resulting photo ends up looking a bit contrived. There's research to back this up. One study found that participants who took a photo with the intention to share it with others enjoyed the experience less than those who were taking pictures for themselves. The researchers suggest this is because taking photos that you're going to share comes with the added icky feeling that you might be evaluated or judged by others.

The research acknowledges that sharing the photo at a later point might not feel this way at all. Instead, it could trigger emotions of pride or joy and drive connection. But it focuses on how this intention to share affects the enjoyment of the experience in the moment. And it's often not a good one.

There's more evidence to suggest that our recollection of events is skewed when we have social sharing in mind. Another study found that when people take photos to share, many remember what happened from a third-person perspective not from how it actually felt to be there. This suggests that taking photos solely for social media might make people only concentrate on how what they're doing would be evaluated by an observer.

This is a significant point. We're focusing when we take a photo, but often on the future. We care more about what our photos might look like on our Instagram grid and how people might perceive them than what it's like to take them. It might help to consider taking pictures as an enjoyable activity in and of itself. Put them in albums and *then* decide if they'll go on social media or not later.

You might think this isn't a big deal. But consider how much time you spend thinking about photos, taking them, posing for them, lining them up perfectly, editing them and writing captions to go alongside them. I can't speak for you, but I really don't want all of that time to be rushed, forgettable and a bit miserable.

Finding focus

One of the best ways I've found to stay focused on what's happening right now is to ground myself in my senses. Do that by focusing on what you can see, hear and smell around you. Is there also something you can touch too? Another thing I like to do when I know I need to escape from my spiralling thoughts is to focus on how my body feels. This can be quick. Plant both of your feet on the ground and notice how strong, supported and grounded you feel. Then pay attention to each body part: legs, torso, arms, head.

In a number of her guided meditation sessions for the Calm meditation app, psychologist, author and meditation teacher Tara Brach invites us all to notice the 'aliveness' in parts of our bodies. This has always stuck with me, so when I'm trying to bring myself back to the present moment, I'll find some of this magical aliveness. This could be as simple as paying attention to how my hands feel and then flexing my fingers. By focusing on physical sensations and senses, we're telling ourselves to pay attention to what's happening **right now**, not what's going on in our heads or what we think might happen tonight, tomorrow or in the distant future.

THE POWER OF RECALL

Take a minute now to think of all the times you use the technology around you to do the work your memory (whether that's long-term, short-term or working memory) could do. I'll get you started. You use it to remember past events through photos and updates. You use it to remember facts, essential information and birthdays. You use it to remember maps, directions and the way to go. You use it to remember future events with calendars, notes and reminders. You use it to remember things as you think, like numbers in a calculator and notes on a page. I'm sure there are plenty more. But you get the picture. We use our technology to remember many things for us.

This is sometimes called cognitive offloading. It's the process of thinking using our bodies and other things in the external world. Why do we do it? Because it's easier. We can overcome our own limitations and, in doing so, improve our memory, perception, counting and much more.

We know the technology we use every day, like smartphones, tablets and the internet, is novel and different from the kinds of media we had before. But what's surprising here is that cognitive offloading isn't new. It's been around for a very long time. For example, people write down notes on a notepad so they don't need to keep them in their working memory. They might keep a diary so that they can remember past events. Put photos in a real-life photo album. Turn to an encyclopedia for knowledge. Use an abacus to count or even their fingers. These are all examples of using physical actions to ease the load on our learning, memory and problem-solving abilities. Screen-based technologies are just the first time all these actions have been in one place.

Psychologist Betsy Sparrow and her team conducted several studies that show cognitive offloading in action in our day-to-day dealings with tech. In one study, researchers asked participants to read 40 trivia statements. Things like: 'An ostrich's eye is bigger than its brain.' They were then asked to type each statement into a computer. One half of the participants were told the computer would save what they'd typed. The other half believed the statements would be erased. Everyone was then asked to write down as many of the statements as they could remember.

Interestingly, those who believed the computer would erase what they typed remembered more of the statements. Those who were told the statements had been saved didn't remember as many. The researchers suggested this is because the participants believed the computer would remember for them – so they didn't need to.

Another study gave participants more trivia statements along with details about where each one was saved into a folder on the computer they were working on. They were then asked to write down as many statements as they could remember, as well as the folder names into which they were each saved. The results showed that participants recalled the places where the statements were saved better than they recalled the statements themselves. The 'where' was prioritised more than the 'what'.

I find these results fascinating. Have we adapted how we remember because technology can remember for us? The study suggests this might be true.

You might think this is lazy or detrimental to our own ability to focus on what we're doing. But to me, it seems that we've come to treat the internet as a resource we'll always have access to. Or a computer folder as a safe space to store information. We remember the things we need to instead, like making a mental note of where we can find information later, and discarding everything else.

After analysing results like this, researchers have suggested that we treat technology, especially the internet, as if it's a close friend, colleague or member of our community. Let me explain. Whenever humans are in a group, whether that's a team at work or a long-term relationship, they develop what's called a transactive memory.

This is a way to hold on to knowledge that's bigger and more complex than your own memory could handle on its own. This means individual members of a group will remember certain things. For example, one person might know where to get the best food; another might know how to prepare it. The only thing people need to know is who knows what. The benefits of this group memory are easy to see. This way the group can hold on to a wealth of knowledge that's bigger and more complex than one person could ever handle on their own.

The internet might be the newest member of our memory group. This could let us off the hook when it comes to our focus and committing everything we see, hear, feel and do to our own memory – but it's not without its drawbacks.

HOW THE INTERNET IS (AND ISN'T) LIKE A GIANT EGG

We might be using the internet, our computers and our phones like an external memory or even a friend. But are there any dangers to doing this? The short answer is: we're not sure yet.

The biggest problem is the internet – sorry to state the obvious – is not a person. It doesn't have a regular memory. It can do much, much more. That's why some researchers and psychologists refer to the internet as a supernormal stimulus.

A supernormal stimulus is something that 'hijacks' our thinking. The best way to explain it is to look at the animal kingdom. Some birds give preferential treatment to larger eggs. This makes sense. Larger eggs are, often, more viable than smaller ones. The problem is even if an impossibly large, artificial egg is placed next to one of its own, smaller eggs, the bird neglects its own egg in favour of the big fake one. Even when it gets bigger and bigger. There are more examples, like male Australian jewel beetles who prefer big females to mate with. This means they get confused by beer bottles, which are shiny and brown like the females are, and mate with the bottles despite the fact they're way bigger than a female could ever be – often getting eaten by ants in the process.

I'm not saying the internet is the same as a big fake egg or a shiny bottle, but we can all agree there are some similarities. Like the size of the eggs, a computer's ability to store memories and process information is exaggerated. It's available all the time, has a vast breadth and depth of knowledge and can provide answers immediately.

Some researchers think this could lead to long-term changes to the way we remember. Because it's so big, so effective and so supernormal, it might reduce the amount of information we store. With such vast amounts at their fingertips, why remember anything at all? But more than that, it could get harder to pinpoint problems because we might not have a great sense of what we do and don't know. One study found that when we're relying on the internet, we might overestimate what came from our mind and what the internet found for us. Participants thought they knew things they didn't know, things they actually found online. This wasn't intentional either. They convinced themselves they knew all along.

CAN WE TRUST OUR TECHNOLOGY?

I like to think of the fact that the internet, our computers and all of our other smart devices are, collectively, in our new memory group as a positive thing. Right now the benefits of using our devices to offload various functions, like counting, remembering past events, making a note of future ones and storing valuable information, seem to outweigh the risks of relying on the supernormal status of our connected tech. What I'm saying is, we don't have to carry everything in our heads any more – and that's okay.

But we do need to be wary. I can't say hand on heart that this will always be the case. We don't know enough about our long-term relationship with modern technology yet, because in the grand scheme of things we haven't been using it long enough. Some risks come with storing information that we need to consider, such as information getting hacked or deleted, passwords being stolen and human error.

On the one hand, you can trust technology to remember things for you more than ever before. On the other, you can also trust the unexpected to occur.

There's a balance to be found here in which we're smart about what we 'outsource' to our technology. For example, we might decide important information is safe on our devices and in the cloud. But, as we explored with the research about taking photos, we might realise relying on tech to store memories of important moments is causing us to miss out on real-life experiences.

The key is to make more deliberate choices and not blindly defer to our tech.

Safeguard your essential stuff

Everyone should learn how to back up important information. This means making copies of work, essential details, photos and memories and storing them in different online (and even offline) locations – then remembering to repeat this process regularly. Here are a few of the most important steps you can take to safeguard your important stuff:

Back up your phone. Search online for the different options available to back up your particular handset. The best option is to use a cloud-based service, like iCloud or Google Drive.

Back up your laptop or computer. You can buy a hard drive, which is a device that connects to your computer. Or you can also save important information, work and anything else you want to be sure you won't lose to a cloud-based service.

Change your backup settings for your most used apps. Some apps, like WhatsApp, have their own backup settings. This is so if you lose your phone or get a new one you'll still have your chat history. Enable these settings for the apps you care about the most if they offer them.

Save important documents and work in more than one place. If you're working on an important document or project, make regular backups to more than one location. When I was writing this book, I was working on a writing program called Scrivener. I also saved backups to my computer and had backups automatically sent to Dropbox too. I didn't want to take any chances.

Keep important phone numbers in a few places. Important contacts, bank details, even passwords (maybe) should be written down or stored somewhere safe. Take a look at the Privacy chapter for more about safeguarding your important information.

Store your photos in the cloud. To save space on your phone, and make sure you don't lose all your photos, regularly upload them to a cloud-based service. Google Photos is a good option that's reliable and easy to use.

Carry a powerbank with you. Make sure your devices don't let you down by simply running out of juice. Buy a small but mighty powerbank that'll give your phone at least one full charge in case you're caught out while you're on the move.

Checklist

Change your notification settings to manage distractions. Use 'do not disturb' and only keep notifications on if they're from people. Bonus points if these are only VIPs.

Distance yourself from your phone when you're working. It doesn't have to be locked away, switched off or even silenced. But find a new place for it when you need to concentrate.

Learn how to monotask. Multitasking might work in certain situations, but it's not worth juggling multiple screens and jobs when you have a significant task to complete that needs your full attention.

Your ability to focus is affected by your memory – and vice versa. The more you focus on what's going on in the here and now, the stronger your memories will be. Use your photo-taking habit to test this.

You use your technology like an external memory. The technology you use every day is new and different. The way you use it to help you remember is not.

Safeguard important information. We can trust our technology. But we can also trust that things go wrong sometimes. Learn what information you need to back up and why for peace of mind.

CONNECTION

WHY OUR TECH RELATIONSHIP STATUS IS 'IT'S COMPLICATED'

A movie came out a few years back about a man who falls deeply and sincerely in love with his smartphone. It was called *Her* and it starred Joaquin Phoenix as Theodore, a lonely middle-aged man whose heart belongs to Samantha, the AI virtual assistant on his phone – like a super-advanced version of Siri or Alexa – voiced by Scarlett Johansson. Theodore takes the bodiless Samantha out on dates using a Bluetooth earpiece to talk with her and pointing his smartphone's camera out from his shirt pocket so she can 'see' what he sees.

I recommend this movie to people *all the time* because it offers a refreshingly even-handed exploration of intimacy in a world fast filling up with super-smart technology. Even though Theodore's pursuit of a purely digital partner isolates him from real people, he experiences happiness and a sense of connection that is already missing from his day-to-day interactions.

While the movie's message is, broadly, that synthetic love is no replacement for the real thing, it also acknowledges that connections through tech can actually still be fulfilling in a bunch of ways.

The connections we make through our screens help bring us closer to people – never more so than during the forced absences we experienced due to the Covid-19 response – as much as they can *add* distance without us even noticing.

When we ask questions about tech and relationships, like, 'Which is better – talking with people online or offline?', I think we too often hope for definitive answers when the truth is just too fidgety to pin down.

I think of our device screens as opportunity portals – the connections are there and it's up to us where we let them take us. We use our devices and the apps on them as ways to start and strengthen friendships, find communities to join, and nourish family relationships when distance and schedules get in the way. We can also use them to find lasting and genuine love, through a whole host of digital matchmaking ways.

No app developer or platform provider can guarantee us a healthy connection. You can have thousands of online 'friends' and still feel lonely. Social comparison can breed envy, screens can become barriers to physical intimacy, and digital romances can be swiped away in an instant.

In this chapter, we take a look at how we can better manage devices that allow us to reach across the world in moments *and* keep our closest friends at arm's length. Don't worry, none of the advice is 'embargo instant messaging', 'denounce dating apps' or 'veto video calls'. What would be the fun in that?

WE JUST WANT TO GET ALONG

Psychologists and researchers believe we all have a strong, built-in need to connect with others and belong to a partnership, family or community.

To understand the importance of belonging, I think it helps to take a look at where it sits in relation to all the other needs we have. You've probably heard of psychologist Abraham Maslow's hierarchy of needs before. As a quick refresher, this is a five-tier model (often imagined as a pyramid) of things all humans need and, therefore, what motivates them. Each level has to be satisfied to move on up to the next one.

At the bottom, you'll find basic physiological needs, like food, water and rest. The next level up is safety needs, to feel secure and like you're not in danger. The next level (the third level) is the need to belong and love, and this is where friendship, romance and intimacy factors in. Above that, there are esteem needs, which covers feeling accomplished, and the final one (the top of the pyramid) is self-actualisation, fulfilling your potential and being creative.

Belonging might not be as important as food and water, but it certainly forms the foundations of what makes us human and shows us what we *need* as humans to function at our best. Without it, we don't have a solid sense of our identity and who we are, the protection of a community, the support and caregiving benefits of close relationships with family, the intimacy and pleasure of a sexual relationship, and the feeling of belonging that comes with romantic relationships that can lead to a long-term partnership and, possibly, building a family together.

It's no surprise then that a lack of connection to others has been linked to loneliness, ill health and depression – if you don't have community, relationships or family around, you slide down the pyramid. The opposite is also true. Strong connections and long-term social ties can lead to considerably more health and happiness. Reams of pages have been written by many different researchers to qualify this. One review of several studies about the link between social connection and health found that having secure relationships might mean you live longer. Researchers suggested the influence a lack of social connection has on your risk of death is about the same as other well-established risks we take way more seriously, like alcohol consumption and smoking. Feeling connected to others might, literally, keep you alive.

But what qualifies as connection nowadays, with our phones helping (and hindering) us along the way? Social psychologist Roy F. Baumeister and Mark R. Leary, a Professor of Psychology and Neuroscience at Duke University, put forward the belongingness hypothesis. This is the idea that, yes, we need to feel like we belong. But reaping the rewards of belonging requires you hit some specific criteria. In their opinion, the most important factors are that interactions should be lasting, positive and significant. This means you don't only need social contact, but the strength of your connections to other people counts, as does how long you've known them, how you feel about the relationship and the part they play in your life. Understanding this is essential when it comes to getting to grips with how we can use our devices to connect with others. They can give us an abundance of opportunities to fulfil our needs to belong, but quality over quantity rules here: something we're still learning how to measure on our phones.

Built for belonging

Because belonging is so important to us, it's no surprise that the technology we find most irresistible has been created to encourage connection and community.

It's one of the primary reasons why we feel (even if, sometimes, only temporarily) satisfied by email, messaging and social media platforms. Much of the technology we use every day is built on the promise of connection. Of bringing people together to talk, share and grow closer. Technology built to bridge and strengthen our connections can sometimes make me feel uneasy. That's because, as we've looked at again and again throughout the pages of this book, we can draw great benefits from our connected technology – but it doesn't come for free.

The spaces you and I use to connect with people are the same spaces that are expertly engineered to take up hours and hours of our time, monetise our attention and encourage us to hand over more and more information in the name of being social.

Most of the major social networking platforms are not digital safe spaces built solely to fill your life with love. They're intentionally designed this way because that's what we all want. But the broader aim is, put simply, to collect information about you and what you like and work with advertisers to sell products to you. This changes the quality of the connection: there's a condition attached, and what's more, a lot of the time it is a condition we can't even see.

We are often nudged into connecting more than we might want to or even need to, which can lead to exhaustion after putting unnecessary pressure on ourselves – because as we'll learn soon, we're not built for continual conversations with hundreds of other people. This is why all of the mechanics we looked at in the Addiction chapter exist, including likes, comments, shares and messages. They encourage us to do more, say more and connect more. In the same vein, messaging apps, like WhatsApp and Messenger, add pressure to reply with read receipts and status features that tell us who's available to talk at any given moment. We need to be aware of these things.

We need to understand the benefits of online connection and make the technology work for us. And it never worked as hard as it did during the Covid-19 pandemic.

THE POWER OF DIGITAL BONDS

When Covid-19 restrictions were put in place, we all clung to our phones for comfort, familiarity and reassurance. Our devices became powerful bonds to the people we love and care about.

It's this connection that I think our devices should be celebrated for the most. Technology isn't the reason we're driven to connect with others. But over the past few decades it has equipped us with the means to connect with whomever we want, wherever we are. Previously, there was no way you could become part of a community that wasn't, literally, on your doorstep. Now, location is no longer an obstacle. You can talk to someone on the other side of the world via WhatsApp in seconds, meet them in Animal Crossing or see them face to face on Zoom. I don't need to tell you how great this is. And, for that reason, it's easy to imagine how this level of connection could not only be beneficial for all of us but genuinely life-changing for those who, for whatever reason, don't have access to offline communities. That could be due to disability, chronic health conditions or illness, in which case online communities can provide a tremendous amount of support. Or marginalised groups who might feel discriminated against in offline communities – or fearful of becoming a part of them.

There are countless other reasons why online connection can be vitally important and, in some cases, even a means for survival. But, for now, I think we can all agree that messaging apps, forums, online games, social media platforms, video apps, and any other way you can think to connect online, can all be hugely positive for us. This is why it bugs me when online communities are sometimes dismissed as trivial by sensational news stories or when generational differences mean relatives reminisce about how romance or friendship was 'better' in their day.

It's also why I roll my eyes when I read someone has dramatically announced they're leaving social media, messaging apps and even the internet alone for good, encouraging the rest of us to do the same. Yes, it is a privilege to have access to this technology in the first place. But let's not forget it's also a privilege to be able to tell people who are dependent on these connections, to whatever degree, to log off and that their lives would be better without them.

LEVEL UP THE WAY YOU CONNECT WITH YOUR TECH

Having said all that, I think it's worth taking a look at what we can do to better understand how we connect with people online so we know what kinds of conditions and behaviours promote connection and which could be a path to loneliness. This includes learning that we have friendship limits, identifying passive behaviours and realising the importance of balance when it comes to prioritising between online and offline connection.

The importance of online/offline balance

When it comes to unpicking the differences between online and offline connection, I like the way it's described in one research paper as 'a new playing field for the same game'. We don't need to view face-to-face relationships and virtual relationships as distinct, but linked and both as essential as each other, especially because many people have plenty of overlap between the two – the people we know offline we often follow or are friends with online, too, and vice versa.

Researchers suggest that the social connections we form online are processed in our brains in a similar way to the way they work offline. This supports the idea that they can be carried from the internet to help shape and inform real-life connection. Put simply, connection online isn't always constrained to online.

One series of studies found that when people meet virtually, they might like each other better than having met face to face. But then, interestingly and thankfully, the connection they developed online can survive a subsequent real-life meet-up.

The researchers believe there are a few ways to explain this and the most important is also maybe the most obvious: many of us are better able to express our real selves online without what they call 'gating features', like appearance (to a certain extent), shyness or social anxiety, getting in the way.

Speaking of anxiety and shyness, the researchers also believe that online relationships and friendships can be particularly beneficial for anyone who sometimes finds offline connection more challenging. But that doesn't mean they *only* connect online. Or, as the researchers put it: 'People, it would seem, want very much to make a reality out of the important aspects of their virtual lives.' This study was from way back in 2002, so I was unsure about whether we could still draw conclusions from it today – we know tech moves fast, really fast. But it resonated with me because when I chart my relationship and friendship history over the past ten years, many started out in the virtual realm before becoming an IRL reality – including my relationship with my present-day partner. I think this is to do with the fact I spend a lot of time online for my job *and* I'm an introvert who does, at least initially, feel more comfortable communicating without those pesky offline 'gating features'.

However, this isn't just the millennial condition. I know plenty of people just as 'online' as me who would always opt for a face-to-face meeting over a virtual one. With that in mind, I'm not proposing any universal recommendations here. I don't believe we should be debating which rules supreme. As the belongingness hypothesis suggests, maybe this is much less about online vs offline and, instead, what we need to focus on is the quality of our connections.

Research about loneliness online suggests whether we feel lonely or fulfilled or not depends on how we use our technology. For instance, it's a useful way to enhance existing relationships and make new connections – this can reduce loneliness. But when people rely on it to 'escape' from the pressure of being social offline, that's when feelings of loneliness can increase. This proves that what we need when it comes to the demands of both offline and online relationships is balance.

You can't be friends with everyone

How many friends do you have? I don't mean Facebook friends, but people you could have a conversation with right now who you would stop and chat to in the street if you saw them approaching. The opportunity to talk to millions of people online might make it seem like our devices can get us closer to more people than we could in real life. But some psychologists and researchers believe that the number of people you can truly click with is fixed – regardless of how many thousands you might be following on Twitter or Instagram right now. That doesn't mean you can't feel interested or invested in someone's life. But the level of time, energy and connection probably won't be spread evenly across everyone. There's going to be a disparity between the close circle of friends you have on your close friends list on Instagram and the people you follow on Twitter because you like that they share funny animal videos.

Anthropologist and psychologist Robin Dunbar first wrote about the maximum number of people we can connect with in the 1990s – a number that was dubbed Dunbar's Number.

Later, in his 2010 book, *How Many Friends Does One Person Need?*, he explains: 'The number of people we know personally, whom we can trust, whom we feel some emotional affinity for, is no more than 150, Dunbar's Number. It has been 150 for as long as we've been a species. And it is 150 because our minds lack the capacity to make it any larger.'

This isn't to do with how many people you have access to or which social media platforms you're on – it's to do with your brain, which has limited space for connections.

But how does this play out online? Has technology enabled us to enlarge this magic number? One study put this to the test by analysing the conversations that 1.7 million users had on Twitter over six months. The researchers discovered most users can maintain 100 to 200 stable relationships on Twitter.

Another study, carried out by Dunbar himself, aimed to test the same theory on Facebook. I bet he wasn't all that surprised to find it showed that the number of Facebook friends we can feel truly connected to is similar to the number of friends we can successfully juggle in offline networks.

Dunbar's Number holds up, which suggests that we might have the same finite capacity for friendship online and offline.

If you're shaking your head at me right now, then let's take a look at who exists outside of that 150. Dunbar himself has since followed up with a theory that suggests we can visualise circles of connection around us with different numbers within them – some which go above 150. What he calls 'circles of intimacy'.

Imagine a dartboard and you're at the centre, sitting on the bulls-eye. Your closest circle likely has no more than five people in it. This is where good friends you'd turn to for advice and comfort reside. The next larger circle has about 15 people in it. Wider still, there's a bigger circle of about 50 people. And there might be a final one with 150. A pattern that increases by a factor of roughly three each time with different levels of interaction frequency and different levels of closeness in every one.

It's been suggested that some people could have even larger circles of 500 and 1,500 people. These would be classed as acquaintances, so you wouldn't consider them friends or family, but you could put faces to names and, possibly, have a conversation with them.

Even if you aren't connected to more than 150 people, that doesn't mean you might not feel something for the people who are on the periphery of your inner circles. This is where something called ambient intimacy might apply. This term can be used to describe that feeling of closeness you can get when you've followed someone for a while on Twitter. It could be a stranger or a celebrity. But it's also a way to describe the level of connection you might have with people from your past, maybe former colleagues or people you knew in school – friendships that might have faded otherwise. So although we might have this little limit in our brains that dictates how many people we can call friends, we can still derive some sense of intimacy and connection from people online – it's good to know our limits. Obviously, everyone is different. The accuracy of Dunbar's Number has been proved in a variety of different settings, but it's not set in stone. However, the important lesson here is: we can't feel deeply connected to an infinite amount of people.

That means, although our devices give us access to a great deal of different people, we don't need to connect with them all for our well-being. This makes me think back to the idea that our technology, the internet and our social media platforms, could represent a kind of superhuman stimulus (see page 123).

We could never feel connected to hundreds of thousands of people; it's just not possible. But thanks to technology, many of us are pulled towards the idea that we *could* be and that doesn't work well for us because we're just not capable of closeness and intimacy that extends way beyond our limits.

I think knowing about these limits relieves some of the pressure that we put ourselves under to have massive numbers of friends and connections. It also makes sense why some people advocate for following only a small amount of people online and limiting how many virtual friends they have. Although we don't intend to or want to feel a deep connection to every person we follow, this mindset might help with some of the overwhelm that often accompanies time spent on our screens.

Being active is the key to enjoying time online

In the Mental Health chapter, we looked at the differences between lurking and engaging when you spend time on social media platforms. This is the difference between passively looking at other people's posts, photos and videos, and actively commenting on them, sending a message or uploading your own.

This is such an important issue (and one that's central to the topic of connection) that I wanted to bring it up again here. I know first-hand how easy it is to fall into the trap of thinking you're engaging with what you see online. Sometimes I'll think I'm connecting with someone, but I've only been watching a few of their Instagram Stories. Other times I'll think I've given a friend encouragement, but I 'liked' their achievement. As you'll know, when someone does this to you, a small 'like' on a post from a close friend is no match for a call or a proper text. No wonder social media can sometimes feel a little empty.

Admittedly, my online activity gets more passive when I'm feeling low. I'm interested enough (or interested in procrastinating enough) to want to check social media platforms. But once

I'm there, I don't feel like chatting or connecting. This is fine sometimes. The last thing I want to pile on you all right now is the expectation that you need to start a deep and meaningful conversation each time you open up an app. But it's important to be aware that the more time you spend passively scrolling, the lonelier you might feel (and make others feel, too).

Many of us will instinctively know that being passive makes us feel icky. But there's research to suggest that it can act as a barrier to connection and negatively impact our well-being.

A 2016 study of 1,910 Facebook users found people get benefits from communicating online, but there's a catch. This communication needs to be from people they care about and it needs to be tailored to them. For example, the study found that any personalised communication (composed text) from people considered close to them improved their well-being. But the text that was easy to produce or one-click styles of communication, like likes or auto-replies, from both close friends and not-so-close friends, wasn't found to improve well-being.

This is kind of obvious. An 'HBD!' is never going to cut it compared to a 'Happy birthday! I loved your article about your trip to France. I can't wait to read more!' But I think we can get lazy online and assume a generic reply is better than no reply at all, when in fact waiting until you have the time and energy to craft a thoughtful birthday wish, even if it is a little late, will always be more appreciated.

A generic response online should perhaps be seen as the equivalent of going to a party but standing in the corner and refusing to speak to anyone. It means other people are less likely to connect back with us: connection is reciprocal, after all, and the result is we feel lonely. One reason that these kinds of generic replies can lead to loneliness appears to be that passive use of social media can breed social comparison and envy.

One US study even suggests that passive social media use (which in this case meant reading and watching things online and not commenting or posting content) is associated with an increase in depression.

The researchers do raise the point though that people might use social media platforms more passively because they're already depressed, which could be similar to the experience I described above about feeling low and finding it challenging to play an active role online. As I began to learn more and more about the problems that could arise from being more passive, and the benefits that come from being active, like creating social capital, and also stimulating feelings of belonging and connectedness, I was able to make some changes I think have been beneficial.

The most simple but significant one is to switch my default reaction, which is liking, for something more active, which has been commenting. I've found that social media platforms have become much more enjoyable spaces since I made this shift to be present in the activity.

But I also know this doesn't always come naturally to me. So instead of logging on when I'm feeling down, I use other social media platforms or games that don't require me to be as switched on and ready for a chat. For me, that's Pinterest. I never feel too tired to add stuff to my boards, and the images often soothe me.

Tip: Being active online has also been shown to reduce the chances you'll experience social comparison; for more on that, visit page 67.

You need to keep your FOMO under control

Whenever I talk to someone about social media and FOMO (Fear of Missing Out), they think I'm joking. But FOMO is real, pervasive and can be shutting you off from genuine connection in a bid to connect with all of the people all of the time. We looked at FOMO briefly back in the Addiction chapter, but it's well worth revisiting as it drives much of our tech usage.

FOMO is defined as an apprehension that other people might be doing better, fun and more exciting things than you are. And it shows itself through a desire to be looking at and thinking about what other people are doing constantly.

One of the most significant ways we can learn to have a healthier balance with social media platforms, as well as make sure we are crafting genuine connections, is to get a handle on our FOMO.

That's because there's a good chance it's responsible for how much we overuse social media. To be clear, FOMO doesn't necessarily mean 'they're at a party, I want to be at that party too!' The more insidious type is the niggling feeling many of us get when we need to know what's happening at any given time – among everyone we know, on all platforms. It's not necessarily that we want to be at all social events all the time (although I'm sure some people do). Instead, it's a constant curiosity that never feels fully satisfied.

And that's because it never *is* satisfied. This is one of the reasons likes, comments, shares and notifications exist. Tech companies know we hate missing out so do their best to make sure we keep checking things to always feel up to date. But this is an illusion. Unless you have ten screens open all at once and you're gobbling in text and photos and videos, like Neo in *The Matrix*, you can't possibly know what's going on all the time in the lives of everyone you follow.

Here's how we can reframe it: we *will* miss out. It's just how life is. This realisation might not help people who are suffering with long-term loneliness and social isolation. Still, it will hopefully serve as a wake-up call for those of us who think of ourselves as lonely and not in the loop far too often, when in fact we're doing the best we can.

This renewed focus might also enable you to pay more attention to just a handful of closer friendships instead of wondering what everyone in your social feeds is doing all the time. I've heard this school of thinking described as the Joy of Missing Out (JOMO), which sounds extremely cringeworthy to me, but maybe it's the kind of silly acronym we'll remember when we need it the most.

HERE'S WHY DATING CAN FEEL EXHAUSTING

Anyone who's been looking for love at any point between around 2012 and today will know that it's official: dating apps have become the main way for single people to meet.

One 2019 study from the US found that heterosexual couples are more likely to meet a romantic partner online than through friends nowadays. The study, which is comprised of surveys from 2017, found that about 65 per cent of same-sex couples meet online, and about 39 per cent of heterosexual couples do, figures which I imagine will have increased dramatically over the past few years since then.

However, what anyone who's been through the process of selecting the right images, crafting a perfect bio and swiping until their thumbs hurt will also know is the whole thing can feel tiring and, after a while, disheartening.

Online dating has been around for a while, and nowadays there are lots of options to cater for different types of people and all kinds of interests. But Tinder is, at least at the time of writing, still the most popular dating app. Even though you might be tired of it, it's easy to see why it's so popular. You can set up a profile within minutes and then easily hunt for digital romance as you sit in front of the TV watching Disney+ or while you're eating a sandwich at your desk on your lunch break. The lure and possibility of connection is right there at your fingertips at all times.

The thing is, this ease is exactly what can make it exhausting – especially if you've been swiping for years and you're looking for a relationship rather than something casual. It isn't a game, but it often feels like one. The swipe left for no and right for yes gesture has become ingrained in our thinking, second nature for our thumbs and has since been added to many other apps too, like Bumble. But, over time, this encourages the super-passive mode of connecting I described earlier.

To make the process feel more enjoyable, active and, hopefully, successful, those of us looking for a partner need to hit the brakes and take more time considering our options. But that conflicts with how many dating apps are designed. For example, Tinder gives you a way of approving or disapproving of someone else's appearance in an instant – with the added anticipation of finding out if they approved of yours. If they do, you have the option to keep playing the game, I mean swiping, or send them a message.

It's this fast-paced and seemingly endless experience with the promise of rewards that keeps people using it and using it for hours and hours at a time – in a similar way to how we become hooked on social media platforms that offer up 'bottomless' experiences. But, after a while, the fun ends and you become tired.

This is because the rejection mindset can kick in. This is when it feels like you've got access to a limitless number of partners. Sounds promising, right? Wrong. This virtually endless choice makes people more pessimistic and rejecting of potential dates and the whole dating process.

One research paper described three studies in which there was a 27 per cent decrease in the chance that the person swiping would accept someone from the first to the last partner option. With every new person you see, the likelihood you'll want to match with them drops off dramatically. The researchers explained this was due to an overall decline in not only satisfaction with the pictures but dating success generally. They compare it to the law of diminishing returns. In short, the time and energy some people put into online dating might not be worth the rewards.

What's interesting here is the more choice of people you have to date, the quicker the rejection mindset kicks in. As participants in one of the studies were shown more and more options, the rate that they'd want to date any one of them decreased. So perhaps an app with more selection criteria than Tinder would be a more sure-fire way to find a partner?

But there might be a sweet spot that could help us out. In one study, the rejection rate was stable until 30 choices were shown, then it decreased rapidly. The researchers suggest this might be because the rejection mindset kicks in when participants no longer expect real interactions. It seems 30 might be the tipping point where we think, 'Nah, this is too much. This is one big swiping game and nothing more.'

The researchers believe there are two key elements to the rejection mindset: feeling more and more dissatisfied with the pictures participants were seeing coupled with an increasing pessimism about the likelihood of finding a partner. Other studies have added more suggestions. It might be that we don't want to regret our choices. After all, with many potential partners available, how do we know we should pick that person over that person? This doubt then makes us feel less enthusiastic about any choices we do later make.

The researchers ask whether this rejection mindset might be part of a broader shift. Are we as indecisive about other things, like buying a house or which pizza topping to choose? Speaking from my own experience, that might be true. But dating comes with much more baggage.

REFRESHING YOUR ONLINE DATING MINDSET

If you're experiencing the telltale signs of a rejection mindset and you're feeling fed up with dating apps, here are some suggestions to reboot your enthusiasm.

Put a limit on your swiping

The main advice from all of the research about the rejection mindset is to restrict how long you search for, which should help you limit how many people you see – this might prevent your swiping fatigue from kicking in. As tempting as it is to keep swiping, scrolling and searching until you find your perfect partner, make do with five or ten minutes each time you open up a dating app – set a timer if you need to. Or you could only swipe 30 times – the tipping point from the research that appears to pinpoint when you start to feel the most fed up.

Take breaks

Whether it's for a few days or months at a time, take a break from dating apps whenever you want to. There's no rule that if you're single and looking for love you need to be actively using Tinder all of the time – or ever. It might be the best way to meet new people because it's easy, but that doesn't mean you're obligated to be always on the lookout.

Try a non-swiping app

Many apps have implemented the same swiping features Tinder became well known for. But others aren't all about swiping, giving you a little more time to stop and decide if you want to talk to someone or not instead of judging them solely on a filtered selfie you've seen for a few seconds. We know the rejection mindset can be due to the vast amounts of choice, but an app like Hinge gives you more time and less choice, which might sound like a bad thing but is exactly what someone with a rejection mindset and Tinder fatigue might need.

Remember the positives

Yes, online dating can suck sometimes. But we're lucky to have the opportunity to find love through our screens at all – I know a lot of people felt that way throughout the initial Covid-19 lockdown when pubs, bars and other ways of meeting people were suddenly off limits. Being introduced to someone new through friends or a chance encounter out and about might sound more organic, but dating is always awkward. At least we now have more freedom to look for someone while we're also catching up on Netflix.

Accept the ups and downs

One day there might be a dating app that guarantees rewarding experiences each time we log on. But that doesn't exist yet. It pays to accept this isn't easy; that dating apps come with uncertainty, disappointments and a whole lot of thumb ache. Acknowledging that everyone else is going through the same grind is also important. No, it's not ideal. But it's the best we've got, and it can bring all kinds of good things into our lives: a chance to meet new people, learn more about what you want and have fun.

SWITCH ON TO YOUR ATTACHMENT STYLE

When people enter a relationship or start dating someone, they can sometimes begin acting a little differently. You might have noticed this in a friend, a partner or even yourself. Maybe before they considered themselves a chilled-out person but now they feel worried if they don't get a text back straight away. Perhaps they're into someone they've met recently but find themselves scrolling through that person's Instagram friends list in a miserable detective game of 'guess who their ex could be'. These behaviours might not be good for us, but your attachment style can often explain them and give you tools to address them.

This is relevant to how we use our devices in a relationship because attachment style can dictate how we communicate and what we need from others. The idea of attachment style requires us to take a look at some relationship theory. Don't worry, this is much more interesting and, potentially, transformative than it sounds.

The idea of attachment theory comes from a psychologist called John Bowlby. In the 1960s, he was working with children and became interested in how they formed relationships and became attached to their parents. He called this the attachment system, something which he found was made up of emotions and behaviours that ensured the children were safe and protected by their loved ones. This makes sense. As children, in order to survive, we need people to look after us and love us – that's the job of the attachment system.

Fast-forward a few decades later, and psychologists Cindy Hazan and Phillip Shaver explored how the same types of attachment might also apply to adult relationships.

The book *Attached* by psychiatrist and neuroscientist Amir Levine and psychologist Rachel Heller provides examples and a framework for couples to find out more about their attachment style. I'll be referring to a lot of their thinking over the next few pages. Although it might not apply to everyone, it comes up again and again in research about relationships and how we use technology. So even if it doesn't feel relevant to your experience, it might be helpful for better understanding other people in your life.

There are three attachment styles: secure, anxious and avoidant. There are tests in the book (and plenty you can take online too) that will help you determine which style best describes you, but here's a quick summary:

'Basically, secure people feel comfortable with intimacy and are usually warm and loving; anxious people crave intimacy, are often preoccupied with their relationships and tend to worry about their partner's ability to love them back; avoidant people equate intimacy with a loss of independence and constantly try to minimise closeness.'

The thing is, you might not know what your attachment style is if your relationship with someone else hasn't felt threatened. If it does, that's when your attachment system is activated. It won't calm down until you find out your partner is there for you and your relationship is safe.

Anxious, avoidant and secure. Each style has a different way of viewing and dealing with conflict, sex, communication and expectations. So it's worthwhile figuring out which style might apply to you – and your partner if you have one – because it's a powerful way to understand (and possibly even predict and change) behaviour in a relationship. Not everyone might fit neatly into these boxes, some people might be a mixture or move between styles as they get older or enter into new relationships.

We can see evidence of our different attachment styles in how we use our tech. For example, people who have an anxious attachment style are more likely to call, text and email a lot, as well as waste time and energy waiting for a phone call. Those with an avoidant attachment style could be frustrated by texts and calls, so might avoid them.

What's more, someone with an anxious attachment style is more likely to monitor a partner's activities on social media platforms. This can lead to a lot of excessive monitoring, as well as a chance anything ambiguous they find will result in jealousy or rumination.

I know this might sound a little overwhelming. Still, it pays to be switched on to these attachment styles. The behaviour you might feel shameful about, or have been called out for by a partner in the past, whether that's ignoring calls or worrying about what they're doing online, could be all to do with your attachment system. This then allows you to talk to your partner about what you might need – both as a couple and as individuals, to feel more secure. And there are plenty of steps you can both take to feel better.

In *Attachment*, there's a story about a woman called Georgia who had an anxious attachment style in her relationship with Henry. He was frequently busy during the day at work so she'd call or text and hear nothing back from him. That's because he had an avoidant attachment style and would get frustrated by her contacting him when he was trying to work. When they discussed their conflicting needs, they realised Henry could send a prewritten text whenever he was thinking of Georgia. This was enough to make her feel calm and cared for because her attachment system was no longer activated.

Tip: if you have an anxious attachment style, it might also be helpful to notice your behaviour, whether that's constant texting or checking social media platforms, and treat it like a habit. Your cue would be that you feel unsafe. Your reward needs to stay the same so that you feel comforted. But is there a trigger that could work better for you and your partner? Head back to Addiction chapter and look at habit loops with these fresh insights.

Important: Some worry is normal. But attachment styles aren't excuses to breach someone else's trust or privacy. If your partner is regularly accusing you of things you haven't done, asking for your passwords or checking up on what you're doing with the help of devices without your knowledge or consent, you need to discuss what is and isn't acceptable. Everyone has a right to privacy within a relationship – whether that's online or offline. If you can't talk to your partner about it or you're worried a current or an ex-partner might be looking at your messages, tracking your location or you suspect they've tampered with your tech in other ways, check out the resources at the back of the book.

WHY YOU NEED TO START PUTTING YOUR PHONE AWAY MORE

We've covered the ways our devices can help us to better connect and communicate. But what about the effect our screens have, quite literally, on the way we relate to others in real life?

You might know this as phubbing (phone snubbing), and I bet you've experienced it many times before. It's when you're with someone, and they get their phone out and start checking it. Sometimes this feels rude. But most of the time you probably don't even notice it's happening any more because it's become commonplace for many of us.

There's heaps of advice online about how you can stop phubbing other people and ask them to stop doing it back. But my question is: because our phones are everywhere now, do we need to change anything? Is phubbing just a part of life these days? Maybe. What's important here is that research shows phones can affect how we feel about someone we're with purely by existing (we learned a similar thing about the effects a silent, minding-its-own-business phone has on our focus on page 102.

Researchers who conducted a 2012 study assigned 74 participants into one of two groups. The first group had to split up into pairs and sit with nothing but a notebook in front of them. The second group did the same, but there was a phone resting on a book just out of their direct view. The researchers then asked all of the pairs to spend ten minutes talking about something interesting that had happened to them over the past month. They then measured a bunch of factors all about how well they felt they had connected with their partner, like their relationship quality and their emotional sensitivity.

Results showed the mere presence of a phone undermined how close the participants felt to each other, as well as the level of connection they reported experiencing and how they judged the quality of the conversation.

Interestingly, the participants didn't realise this was happening at the time – that the phone was responsible for sucking all the connection out of the room. The researchers proposed a couple of theories about why this might be. One suggested that our phones prime us to think about wider social networks, including different events and people. Therefore, this draws our attention away from the person in front of us.

In a similar study, 300 participants were asked to share a meal at a restaurant with friends and family. Some of the people were told to keep their phones on the table; others had to put them away. When phones were out on the table, people reported feeling more distracted. This, in turn, reduced how much they said they enjoyed the time they spent with their loved ones.

The fact our phones have the power to weaken closeness and conversation quality and boost distraction when they're not doing anything is surprising. But it does mean we already know what to do to prevent our devices from hijacking our experiences: if we can, let's put our phones away more often.

You might think putting your phone on the table in front of you occasionally when you see a friend for a coffee isn't cause for concern. But the more pressing implication here is that you could influence the closeness you feel to the most important people in your life – including your children – and how close they feel to you.

Researchers conducted two different studies to discover how connected parents feel to their kids when the adults spend time on their phones. The first took place in a science museum in which some parents were told to use their phone more than they usually would and others were told to use their phone less than normal.

The second was a more thorough 'week in the life' diary-style study, which aimed to chart how phone use would affect how connected the parents felt to their kids over the course of six days.

Both studies showed that the participants felt distracted when using their phones, which then meant they reported feeling less connected to their children in a number of situations because their attention was being drawn somewhere else – to their screens.

So, let's be clear here: it's not that phones have a connection-crushing superpower. But it's the same thing we learned when we took a closer look at distractions. Which is that our devices are forcing us to multitask – but this time between what we do with our screens and what we do with people around us.

As you might expect, there are fewer of these adverse effects when there's no opportunity for connection. For example, if parents are with their children but there isn't a chance to interact with them – the research gives the example of a parent watching their child at sports practice while they're sitting alone. In that situation looking at their phone probably wouldn't have the same effect. So we needn't worry *all* the time.

I know what you're thinking. This seems to fly in the face of a lot of literature and research about not letting phones distract us. But there's nuance, which we need to become attuned to. If being on your phone doesn't distract you from an opportunity to connect, that's okay. My concern with that though is: will we miss out on an opportunity to connect because we've been scrolling through TikTok non-stop for an hour?

Interestingly, there are exceptions. In the same study, researchers found that the negative effects of phone use were reversed when parents used their phones to access apps or information that was relevant to what their children saw at the science museum. Using the phone as a tool to find out more about their environment ended up boosting feelings of connection and enhanced everyone's experience.

This shows the value of being mindful that if we use our devices around others it can and should be to enhance our experiences – not distract from them. You could do all kinds of things, like take a photo. Or find out more information about what's going on around you using an augmented reality (AR) app, which adds a fun virtual layer to the real world using your phone's screen. This is positive for setting guidelines about what is and isn't acceptable when you and your family want to connect. It provides a useful, simple question to ask yourself when you get your phone out around others: is this going to make what's happening even better, or put up a barrier? The opportunity to use our screens to reinforce our relationships is also one of the reasons I don't recommend banning phones – especially not for kids and teens.

We've learned about phubbing. But did you know there's also something called Pphubbing? This is partner phone snubbing. (I'm not suggesting you use these made-up words by the way – I'm not sure how you even say this one? – but it's important you know them so you can better understand articles or research about them.)

Pphubbing is the same as phubbing – and causes many of the same problems – but there are some considerations specific to being in a romantic relationship that also tap into attachment theory. The most important thing we need to learn here is that some of us might find that we believe our need for attachment is at risk if we sense that our partner isn't present in a conversation and is looking at their phone instead.

As you might expect, people with an anxious attachment style are likely to feel the adverse effects of a partner looking at their phone when they're together more strongly than others.

This could be because they're jealous of whom their partner might be talking to online. But more than anything it's likely down to a strong need for closeness. It's not hard to see why some people might think time spent on devices could jeopardise closeness. This can lead to relationship conflict as well as even higher levels of attachment anxiety.

Pphubbing isn't something to shrug off and just try to get over if it's bothering you. That's because this isn't about only mild frustration.

If you feel constantly ignored and distanced from your partner, it can have a wider impact on your general life satisfaction over time too and can even lead to depression.

You need to get a handle on this problem soon using some of the tips below – whether you're the one Pphubbing or feeling Pphubbed.

RECHARGE YOUR RELATIONSHIPS

I'm not a big believer in strict digital etiquette guidelines. But I think we can all agree that if we want to connect with someone, whether that's a partner, family, friends, colleagues or anyone else, we need to put our phones down more often. But here's the thing: how that looks for every one of us, and each of our individual relationships, is likely to differ. Banning phones from meals, only getting them out to talk through ideas, checking them if there's an email, checking them freely whenever – what works for one friendship or relationship might not be the best choice for another. Understanding this is better than trying to follow universal laws, which might be deeply unrealistic for you and the people in your life.

Our relationships with our partners, kids, family and friends are here to stay – and so are our devices. That means we need to talk about what we do and don't like. What we can all agree to and how each person feels about screen time. That way, you can come up with agreements together – not impose bans, which can cause both adults and kids frustration and even distress.

I know some couples have a 'phones on silent in our pockets' policy when they're out having dinner and some parents have no phone zones at the dining table, which is a good start as it's flexible and realistic. This last bit is essential. You need to strive for a good outcome, but also stay grounded when you're deciding when you and your partner or your family will and won't use your devices.

One study that aimed to explore the tension between parents, teens and their devices explained that romanticised ideals of what family time should look like aren't always real to life. There's a perception that family time is when parents and children need to put all tech away and be constantly engaged with each other, talking and smiling, without screens – but that's not always the case or the most conducive to a genuinely happy and relaxed family life. Holding on to this ideal means you're likely to be disappointed.

What's more, as we learned earlier, when tech is used to enhance experiences, it can be an extremely positive force. I'm not saying all family time needs to be centred on sharing screens, but being too strict will mean there's no opportunity for that to happen: no chance for your children to show you the videos they've made, the games they've been playing or the cool things they've learned how to do that they want to share with you.

To combat this, researchers from the University of Michigan call for 'a more nuanced interpretation of family time'. I'm not saying let people in your life stamp all over your boundaries, but there's a balance to be found here. It might be worth adjusting your expectations, which could relieve the pressure for everyone.

The parents and teens in the same study echoed this. Surprisingly, they didn't want more attention from each other. But they did want expectations about what screen time and family time looks like and for those expectations to be shared across the whole family. In one study, everyone in the family considered using devices acceptable when they were together as long as everyone's attention was also split with a device or another activity. It's not hard to see why this is important to everyone in the family. I know parents who tell their kids they can't use their phones and then end up setting a bad example by using theirs. It makes more sense that the expectations, family time and screen time are all shared.

We can also apply this thinking to our romantic relationships. I don't think my boyfriend should be swiping through Instagram Stories when we're out for a meal, but I'm not going to suggest he stops playing video games in the evening. I know how important they are for him to unwind. And anyway, when would I get a chance to scroll through Pinterest or play around with new fonts on my website?

Expecting anyone to be screen-free all the time isn't realistic. So ask yourself and your loved ones: what can you all agree on?

DOES YOUR SMARTPHONE HAVE A SOUL?

An exploration of connection and technology wouldn't be complete if we didn't also acknowledge our relationship with our technology. In other words, why is it that you frequently feel closer to your phone than you do to other people?

Throughout this book, we've already identified the evidence to suggest that your smartphone is way more than a shiny gadget. It's a friend, a therapist, a matchmaker, a coach and hundreds of other things depending on how you use it.

Therefore, it's no big surprise that many of us have strong connections to our phones that go well beyond how we might ever even conceive of feeling about another object or even another device – imagine cradling a smart speaker in your hands 24/7?

There's evidence among the research too which points to the conclusion that – if it wasn't already obvious – it's clear our phones mean a great deal to us by the way we behave with (and without) them.

For example, the fact that we personalise our phones can give us an insight into how we feel about them. Customising the appearance of your home screen, putting on a case, changing settings so it works how you want it to work. These changes are small but significant. Research has suggested that personalisation is evidence that we've become emotionally attached to our phones, as well as a consequence of being attached.

We also know that some people can become upset and emotional when their phone is taken away – or they worry it might be. This is sometimes referred to as nomophobia (no mobile phone phobia).

According to researchers, symptoms can include anxiety, breathing problems and agitation. However, it's difficult to pinpoint whether this is a condition in and of itself or if it's a part of existing anxiety disorders.

The way we relate to our phones can also be an indication of our attachment style. For example, one 2016 study found that most people have a strong attachment to their phones, but anxiously attached people crave more contact through their phone and, therefore, might use it more excessively than those with a different attachment style.

The bond we have with our phones is particularly intriguing if we stop to recognise just how mass-produced they are. There are, literally, millions of other people who have the exact same phone as you. What is it about yours that feels special to you?

The more I dissect my own feelings about my phone, the more I realise my attachment isn't to my phone at all. I can easily get a new one and it'll still feel like the same phone. It's not the object that I'm attached to, but what my phone enables me to do. I see my phone as a gateway to love, connection, excitement, distraction and everything else.

Whichever phone you put in my hand, in the place of the one that's there right now, you'll create the same gateway. This is strengthened by the fact that we can now move all of our content and settings from one device to the next with ease. I like to think of it like this: the soul of my phone (all my stuff and what it allows me to do) gets put into new bodies (a shiny new handset) if I choose to upgrade it.

Therefore, it's not the phone I'm connected to – not really – it's the portal it opens to other people and places. It's tricky to define in the context of a relationship because it's different. But that doesn't mean we can't afford to pay attention to the quality of the connection to our phones, regardless of how strange that might sound, as we would with any other kind of relationship. Because if we continually feel more connected to our phones than the people around us, it's time to start drawing some boundaries.

Checklist

We all want to belong. Our devices present us with more opportunity to connect with others and seek out love, friendship and community.

Our brains can only handle a finite number of friends. One hundred and fifty. That's Dunbar's Number and it means we can't keep up with everyone we follow and friend online – no matter how long we might spend trying.

Balance offline and online friendships as much as possible. Both types of connection are as crucial as the other. Prioritise both and don't be afraid to take online friendships offline.

Start conversations online. The more passive we are online, the higher the chances that we'll experience social comparison, loneliness and even depression. Make an effort to be more active and comment on and share things you like. If you don't feel like it, stay off social media platforms and do something else with your time instead.

Learn to be okay with missing out. We (quite literally) can't keep up with everything, so accept that you will miss out – remember JOMO.

Take a break from dating apps. Have a Tinder time out or limit the time you spend swiping. This could reduce the chance that the rejection mindset will kick in – which we now know is a shortcut to dating-induced burnout.

Learn your relationship attachment style. This can help you to understand how you (and your partner) behave in relationships – and what you both need to feel loved and secure.

Put your phone away more often. Research shows its presence can impact how connected we feel to other people. But don't be afraid to use it if both parties will benefit or if you communicate clearly with your partner, friend or family member first.

WORK

HOW TO SWITCH STRESS OFF AND SWITCH BALANCE ON

On 24 March 2020, when the UK government announced a national lockdown, many people had to rapidly transition from working at a desk in an office to working at their settee in their living room.

With nearly half of the UK's total working population moving from a regular office to a 'kitchen table office' as of June 2020, I count myself extremely lucky that, as a freelance tech journalist, my home has been my workplace for almost my entire career. What surprised me, though, was the impact of having my boyfriend suddenly working from home alongside me and the logistical tap dancing we had to do to make both our jobs work from within our tiny flat.

We only have space for one desk, which led to us having to build a makeshift 'standing desk' out of a pile of books on the kitchen worktop and alternating our time between the two. We had to coordinate when we'd each be on video calls to make sure we didn't drown each other out, and reorganise the one part of the room visible during back-to-back Zoom calls to mitigate the uninvited eyeballs peering into our home and give the appearance of living reasonably grown-up lives.

Having greater flexibility to work from home is something many office workers have been requesting for years, and the circumstances of 2020 helped to prove what many bosses had long been denying – that WFH is in fact productive and viable, and not just a 21st-century reinvention of pulling a sickie. As I write this, companies across multiple industry sectors are formalising their flexible working policies, giving employees greater choice over where they work – while a number have got rid of their rented office spaces entirely.

Technology was, of course, critical to making all of this work and demonstrating that virtual offices can be a viable, long-term reality. Being able to connect with colleagues through collaboration tools and messaging apps on laptops, tablets and even our phones is nothing new. However, people using and doing all of these things in vastly greater numbers than ever before has created a sea change in the work-life balance debate.

The statistics show that a staggering number of apps, digital services and video chat platforms were downloaded in March 2020. My favourite stat comes from app tracking company Apptopia, which tracked a leap from 56,000 daily downloads of Zoom in January to 2.13 million downloads of Zoom globally on just one day in March – the day the UK lockdown was announced.

As we know, smart technology can deliver genuinely life-changing benefits to our lives, in and out of work. It can also bring along a brand new host of challenges and difficulties. People working from home during the pandemic became acutely aware of the impact of a constant email stream, discovered the very real phenomenon of Zoom burnout, and learnt that being confined to our homes quickly created an expectation that we would be constantly and immediately available to our employers.

Now, tech doesn't exist in a vacuum. By which I mean that we can't blame our laptops for how much time we spend staring at them. It's the combination of technology with the always-on expectations of clients and line managers that creates a perfect environment for elevated stress, exhaustion and burnout – whether we're in the office or our favourite armchair.

STRESSED OUT, BURNED OUT AND ALWAYS ON

We all know how stress feels. (If you don't, seriously, *what* is your secret?) Maybe you get irritable, your worries take on a life of their own, or you're increasingly concerned there's a lot to do and precisely no time to do it in.

It's normal to feel this kind of pressure sometimes, especially in relation to your job. Many of us experience situations that cause stress every day, called stressors. Like when a difficult assignment that makes you feel queasy lands on your desk or when a blunt email from your boss that you're frantically picking apart line by line lands in your inbox.

The telltale physical signs of stress are that your heart beats faster, your breath gets quicker and you tense up. For most people, these symptoms come along with anxious thoughts – like worrying that you're not going to be able to complete a piece of work on time.

Experiencing stress now and again isn't particularly pleasant, but it is normal. However, persistent stress over time can have a significant impact on your mental and physical well-being. This could lead to health issues, like depression or a weakened immune system, if left unchecked.

Prolonged stress can also lead to burnout, which the World Health Organization (WHO), explains is a syndrome that's the result of 'chronic workplace stress that has not been successfully managed'. The WHO's definition of burnout specifies it's used to describe stress associated with work. But these days it's become a broad shorthand to label the mixture of stress, exhaustion and worry brought on by all kinds of different aspects of our lives – especially the way we use tech (like Zoom burnout, Tinder burnout and email burnout).

Trying to pinpoint the specific causes of burnout isn't easy – especially after 2020, a year filled with worry, upheaval and fear. But psychologists Christina Maslach and Michael Leiter have compiled one of the most comprehensive lists, which includes having too much on your plate and not enough time to do it all, experiencing micromanagement, not getting enough acknowledgement, not getting enough pay, feeling isolated, being discriminated against, experiencing ethical conflicts and being given meaningless tasks at work consistently. If you're feeling stressed just reading that list, you're not alone. A 2018 study of more than 7,500 employees found 23 per cent of people reported feeling the symptoms of burnout at work 'very often', and 44 per cent reported feeling burned out 'sometimes'.

The specific problems we can experience as a result of burnout are not only about work but our attitudes to work and rest – namely we work too hard and we rest too little. According to research, burnout has several different symptoms, including cynicism, exhaustion and being bored of the same old routine. I'm not sure I know many of my friends or peers who don't experience at least one of these on a regular basis – no wonder millennials are frequently referred to as 'the burnout generation'.

There's little doubt that stress and burnout are significantly influenced by our technology. Like most of the issues in this book, these aren't new problems *caused* by our devices, but they can make them worse. It's not hard to see why when we pick apart what technology brings us: instant, constant access to all kinds of things and all kinds of people whenever we like and wherever we are. It's the always-on nature of technology, coupled with the always-on expectations of work, that have a large part to play in work-induced stress.

Whether it's a working day or the weekend, many of us are constantly checking in with social media platforms, emails and touching our phones every few minutes. Suppose for some reason we're *not* continually available. In that case, we're always worried about what we might miss – whether that's FOMO tied to friendships or fear of missing an email (is that FOME?) that could turn out to be vitally important to a project you're halfway through.

This gets particularly tricky when we use the same social media accounts or email addresses for both our work and our personal lives. Still, even if you do have a firm split between your work email and your personal Twitter, the urge to check to see what's new is the same – a need for connection, validation and reward. It's no surprise that in some professions the line between tech for work and tech for play has blurred so much we can no longer identify it.

The significant shift to working from home for most of 2020 might have made some of these problems worse. We don't have the data on it yet, but think about it. Not only are our work and personal lives already muddied thanks to technology, but our physical spaces are too. Video calls during the pandemic lockdown restrictions were a great example of this. They granted everyone you work with access to your home, as well as a very real look at the lives we all lead outside of work, including pets, kids, bookshelves and questionable decor choices.

Everyone had to communicate in the same way whether they were an intern working at a big company, a celebrity calling in to a chat show to do press for a new movie, a CEO talking with senior management or a politician addressing the nation. But there are problems when work life and home life become too enmeshed, which can result in, you guessed it, significant amounts of stress.

Several studies have looked at what's called work-home interference. This is when there's a conflict between your work and your home domains, whether that's time demands or a spillover of stress and strain; like a conference call with colleagues in another time zone that you have to take in the evening; or you're looking after your children when you're also trying to hit a deadline; or a project that eats into your weekends so you can't enjoy time with your family and one week merges into two with no rest in between. Importantly, but unsurprisingly, the effects of this kind of work-home interference have been found to lead to poor health, low sleep quality, exhaustion and burnout.

There's no easy solution to stress or burnout. Taking a break from work or booking a holiday certainly sound like good ideas on paper, but simply stepping back isn't simple at all when you consider the huge amounts of work-based pressure, societal pressure and self-inflicted pressure many of us find ourselves under. What people who are significantly impacted by stress and teetering on the verge of burnout need instead is perhaps a mindset shift.

I love the way writer Anne Helen Petersen puts this in her widely shared BuzzFeed essay about modern-day burnout and her realisations about addressing it: 'This isn't a task to complete or a line on a to-do list, or even a New Year's resolution. It's a way of thinking about life, and what joy and meaning we can derive not just from optimizing it, but living it.'

This chapter will acknowledge the problems with always-on working, the pressure we pile on ourselves to be productive and why we all need to step away from our screens more often. It will look at the ways we can use technology to tick things off our job lists, tackle our emails and work better, as well as flipping that question on its head to ask ourselves: but do we need to?

MEET YOUR INSTANT GRATIFICATION MONKEY

We all have mixed feelings about procrastination. Some of us joke about how great we are at it. Others do everything they can to rid themselves of it. A few talk about it as if it's an evil curse they're destined never to shake, so why try?

Put simply, procrastination is 'intentionally deferring or delaying work that must be completed'. It's similar to the distractions and interruptions we explored on page 96. If your phone vibrates and you get a notification, this might also delay you from getting work done. But procrastination is a little different in that it's *intentional*. What that means is a lot of the same advice from the Focus chapter applies, but it deserves special attention here in the Work chapter. That's because people who procrastinate (hi!) have a tough time getting things done and a lot of the technology they need to get those things done can enable it. Remember, the minds behind your favourite social media platforms do not want you to feel productive and focused throughout the whole working day because they'd lose out on a lot of your attention. Instead, they want you to check if you have new messages, friend requests and likes. They want you to feel like you're missing out if you're not always looking for what might have happened in the past four minutes since you last checked.

To better understand procrastination, and why we'd choose to delay work rather than do it, let's look at what the creator of the blog Wait But Why, Tim Urban, calls the 'procrastinator's system'. In a 2016 TED Talk about procrastination, he explains that in everyone's brain there is a rational decision-maker. But in his brain, a procrastinator's brain, which is easily distracted and leaves deadlines until the last minute, there's something else: an instant gratification monkey. (No, this isn't scientific, but bear with me as the characters are useful for explaining why many of us do the things we do.)

He says the instant gratification monkey only cares about two things: easy and fun. This means when you need to do things that are challenging or unpleasant, your monkey draws you to all kinds of other activities instead, which drowns out the rational decision-maker.

In my experience, this might mean starting another piece of work and leaving the one that needs to get done for future-me to finish. Or scrolling through Instagram in the name of research. Or falling down a research hole only to return after I've learned the detailed history of the Mayans.

If you're new to working from home, you might have realised just how many ways to procrastinate are hiding in cupboards and behind doors. Many of us clean, organise and tidy as a form of procrastination, which somehow feels more acceptable than social media scrolling – but I'm afraid it's still procrastination in disguise.

Not only does doing whatever the monkey wants to do mean you don't get your work done, but you quite often feel bad about it too. Urban says that giving in to the monkey means you're working in what he calls the dark playground. He says: 'The fun you have in the dark playground isn't actually fun because it's completely unearned and the air is filled with guilt, dread, anxiety, self-hatred – all those 'good' procrastinator feelings.'

There's a third character in this procrastination play: the panic monster (imagined as a big, red scribbly character on Urban's blog). This wakes up when a deadline gets too close, or your career hangs in the balance: crunch time. The monkey is terrified of the panic monster, so it runs away to avoid it. Finally, with the instant gratification monkey gone, the rational decision-maker can take charge and work. Often with only a terrifyingly small window of time to get it finished.

It's great to visualise your own procrastination patterns in this way. Not only is it helpful in understanding why procrastinators live in a state of either procrastination or panic, but it gives procrastinators a way to talk themselves out of procrastination. 'Okay, I don't really want to be on Instagram now, this is just my monkey running the show. I'm going to hand the wheel back to the rational decision-maker', is something I've definitely said to myself more than once. (And drawn too, but that was probably another form of procrastination.)

I think even the non-procrastinators will agree that the dance between the monkey, decision-maker and monster sounds tiring and not at all good for us and our work. But the question is: how do we stop procrastinating?

I wish I had an easy answer to save you from procrastination for good, but there just isn't one – at least not one that'll work for all of us. When I was researching the depths of procrastination, I found there are all kinds of reasons why we do it. The good news is it's not that you're lazy or you lack self-control – it's more complicated than that. Maybe you're scared of failing. Perhaps it's a habit loop you're yet to break, or maybe you don't feel confident in yourself right now, so you always choose some kind of instant relief over a challenge.

I think the most important thing here is that the goal should not be to stop procrastinating forever or try to rid yourself of it, like you're exorcising a demon. As far as I can tell, there's no magic time management tip or simple app to cure it – it's far too tied up in the ideas we have about our work, our emotions and our abilities for that. But there are a few different approaches we can take to reduce its effects on our working lives. If you are struggling with procrastination, have a go at all of these and be open to different approaches at different times.

Figure out what it looks like for you: Procrastination doesn't always look like wasting time and doing fun things. Many of us procrastinate with activities that aren't always fun, just different. Think putting a wash on or alphabetising your skincare (things I absolutely did not do before writing this chapter). The first step in better managing your procrastination is noticing how it manifests when you're trying to work. To start, just try labelling it. You don't necessarily have to stop doing what you're doing; instead, notice you've stepped away from work (physically or metaphorically) and just say, 'I'm procrastinating.'

Make it difficult: Technology doesn't cause procrastination, but it makes it a hell of a lot easier. Change which apps are on your phone's home screen to make sure it's as minimal as possible and either delete the most irresistible apps temporarily (especially the bottomless ones) or put them in hard-to-reach folders. While you're at it, add content blocker extensions to your phone and your browsers too (see page 333). If you really, really, *really* want to procrastinate, you'll find a way around these obstacles. But sometimes all it takes is a few seconds to pause and realise you should be focusing on work before the panic monster arrives and not the other app, site or game you were about to open.

Build your own panic monster: This one comes from Tim Urban. It's aimed at people who don't have a big deadline or some reason to get work done. This might sound good, right? But think about it. If there's no deadline, there's no panic monster. If there's no panic monster, the instant gratification monkey has free rein forever. Set a deadline if you need to get something done and put it in your calendar. Tell a colleague if you need to as a way to hold yourself accountable.

Notice your emotions: A lot of the research on procrastination refers to it as an emotional regulation strategy (head to page 54 for more on emotional regulation). This means if you notice you're procrastinating it pays to think about your emotions and ask yourself if there's a bigger reason why you're putting off this work. Are you worried you won't get it right? Or maybe you're not sure you want to do well because then you'll get a promotion and have way more responsibilities to deal with? Get used to noticing you're procrastinating and asking: 'Why?' If you're anything like me you won't have all the answers, but just pausing to question your actions might bring you a bit more awareness.

The important bit here isn't to rid yourself of any negative feelings you might find – or feel bad about feeling bad. Instead, let the emotions be – accept them (because anxiety, insecurity and fear of failure are all very normal, after all). Label them if it feels right, like 'I'm overwhelmed' or 'I'm worried I'll screw this up' and come up with another way to address them rather than banishing them. Go to page 72 for emotional regulation tips or visit the meditation resources on page 333.

Go easy on yourself: People who procrastinate don't usually treat themselves well. That's because procrastination tends to have two default settings: allowing yourself to indulge in good things that make you feel full of shame almost straight away or feeling riddled with panic and berating yourself for not getting your work done earlier. It's no surprise that researchers have found the enormous amounts of stress that go hand in hand with procrastination can be linked to how little self-compassion procrastinators show themselves.

Rather than expect to become kind and compassionate overnight, focus instead on the future. Consider what you can do next rather than berating yourself for what you did before. A solid piece of advice you've likely heard before but always shifts my mindset is: talk to yourself like you would someone you love. You wouldn't tell your best friend how rubbish they are for not getting something done. You'd be kind, soothing and get to work on a plan to hit that deadline together.

Important: Another way to get a handle on procrastination is to minimise distractions. Remind yourself how to do that by revisiting the Focus chapter. Your procrastination might have also become habitual, so review how to create new habit loops on page 42.

MAKE YOUR SCHEDULE WORK FOR YOU

I love job lists. I have a handwritten one that I start each day and scribble all over or write my most important tasks of the day on index cards, as well as a running list of actions for the next fortnight that I keep in Evernote. This is a note-taking app that has lots of different templates. I use a checklist that's perfect for that extremely satisfying 'ticking things off I've got done' feeling. There are plenty of other scheduling apps that I've enjoyed using in the resources at the back of the book.

Of course, you could download all of the best job list apps to all of your devices and still not get anywhere. It might be because they're not for you – maybe you can hold everything you need to do in your head, or you don't need more than a simple notebook. The key is noticing whether the system you're using is working for you, and tweaking it if it isn't. But you won't know unless you try – and it could be that you're falling into some familiar traps that make scheduling difficult – or at least not as effective as it could be, regardless of the apps you use. Let's take a look at three common traps I've fallen into before – as well as ways we can avoid them in the future.

Trap one: you're addicted to getting stuff done

This is called completion bias. Many of us love to get things done then cross tasks off our lists. This sounds positive, but it means we're often drawn to the quick and simple things on our schedules rather than the deep work that takes time, energy and focus. That way we can get the satisfying 'ticking things off' feeling earlier – who wouldn't want that?

Research has shown that starting the day with simple tasks can be positive, giving us a hit of dopamine, which has a positive effect on attention and work. But if you're not careful, you might spend all day doing the small, easy-win jobs. That means the big ones never get done and the pressure, stress and procrastination could mount up. Red alert: panic monster incoming.

One answer to this is an approach called eating the frog, which we looked at briefly in the Addiction chapter. This is the idea that you should get the most challenging, most unpleasant task on your job list out of the way first – you need to eat the metaphorical frog. This is a good idea if you're prone to putting off rubbish tasks for days at a time.

- **Schedule in both types of tasks.** Deliberately pick small, warm-up tasks to ease yourself into your day – but strictly keep it at two or three. Then select the same number of essential priorities – these must get done by the end of the day, no excuses. To stop the more straightforward tasks from spiralling, make sure you know precisely what these bigger tasks are and how to complete them. This way, even if you do fall for completion bias at some point throughout the day, you'll have at least ticked off the top jobs by the end of it too.

Trap two: you underestimate how long things will take

Do you often think something is going to take 20 minutes tops and then four hours later you're *still* working on it? This doesn't mean you're bad at managing your time. It's another bias, called the optimism bias or planning fallacy.

There are a lot of studies about planning fallacy and what it looks like across a range of industries, but the universal lesson is that people often don't consider their past experiences enough when they're estimating the time it'll take to finish something. They're overly optimistic about how quickly they'll whizz through it – which is rarely the case.

Not only will seeing this fallacy in yourself help you to create better job lists and more effective scheduling, it can also be helpful if you share calendars at work or have time management software installed too. That's because you might think things take you ages (your boss might think things are taking you ages as well), but you're not underperforming, you're underestimating.

- **Track your time then plan accordingly.** Dedicate a week or two to tracking your time with an app. There are some suggestions on page 333. This will show you how long tasks are really taking you. Sure, this won't be exhaustive. You won't cover every task in a fortnight. But it's an excellent place to begin to get a more accurate picture of how you work and what a typical day looks like. You might be surprised by how long admin, emails and seemingly small jobs are eating up your time. From there, you can create job lists and schedules with these more accurate times in mind. If your job allows it, add small buffers between tasks to give you some insurance in case you do run over.

Trap three: the work you have to do always fills the time you have to do it

Are you ever surprised when you thought you had days and days to get something done, but somehow you filled all that time with, well, *nothing*?

This is called Parkinson's Law, thanks to historian and author Cyril Northcote Parkinson. In an essay in *The Economist* in 1955, he wrote: 'It is a commonplace observation that work expands so as to fill the time available for its completion.'

Using the time you have available to get something done is useful if you're on a tight deadline. But not so much if you've got a distant deadline and time to fill. Chances are you'll find ways to fill it, either by procrastinating or making lots of changes and revisions to what you're working on.

Does that mean we should set shorter deadlines for ourselves? Unfortunately, it's not that simple. One study found that time pressure can make performance worse. That's because there's less time and energy for thought and exploration. You might get something done quicker, but the quality will suffer. Then again, giving people too much time isn't always a good idea because there might only be slight improvements in the work.

- **Set (mini) deadlines.** Working to a deadline is essential to getting things done; otherwise, you'll find one way or another to fill the time. I think the answer is more awareness about how you work and what you need, then get as realistic as you can about when to set deadlines. It's also a good idea to break big projects down into smaller deadlines that only you know about, regardless of the longer project deadline that someone else might have set for you. That way, you're guaranteed to get things done. This approach could also activate a lot of tiny panic monsters, which, admittedly, sounds terrifying, but could be beneficial if you've been procrastinating too.

BRING BALANCE TO YOUR INBOX

I find it fascinating that emails can be vital lifelines, job lists, nuggets of connection, lists of complaints, offerings of support, and yet also the bane of our working lives. It's no wonder many of us find it challenging to manage them and why we avoid them, loathe them or compulsively check them – often while wincing.

What's almost as annoying as our constantly too full inboxes is the advice to tackle them. This might seem hypocritical. But my point is that many productivity experts have been talking about how we can get a handle on our emails for years. It can be overwhelming to choose which advice to follow. Because of that, we end up doing what anyone who's overwhelmed does: burying our heads in the sand. Or, more precisely, in the pile of mounting emails all marked urgent.

When I asked people I know why they dislike emails so much, they gave me lots of reasons: never knowing the right etiquette, how differently some people use it, the fact that colleagues email into the night and at weekends, that they're never-ending. But the most persistent problem (at least among people I know) is how much time they take up. We need to send them, read them, reply to them, sort them and unsubscribe from them. I've heard people joke that tackling their inbox could be a full-time job, but that's probably quite accurate.

Tackling inboxes doesn't really even take into account the amount of time we spend checking our inboxes. I know leaving a tab to my inbox open while I'm working is a distraction, so I close it. But my instant gratification monkey has been known to swing by and open another tab to check in on what's happening as a way to avoid something else. That means, throughout the day, I'm often opening and closing new tabs to check my inbox. Why do I, and you and almost everyone else with a pulse and an internet connection, feel compelled to check them, obsess over them, refresh them? For the same reason, we can't stop watching Instagram Stories or scrolling through Twitter or anything else because they've been designed that way.

Remember the variable reward schedule we looked at on page 30? We can see it in action in our inboxes too. We don't know if we're going to get something great (yay!) or something rubbish (nay!). But either way, we want that hit of dopamine. Like scrolling to refresh, refreshing your inbox over and over shares many similarities with slot machines and games. The rewards are rarely worth it, but the anticipation that builds when you're waiting for them, that's still often irresistible.

Whether you love them or loathe them, emails are here to stay. Every so often there's a new app or service that wants to 'kill' or 'reinvent' email as we know it. Some workplaces are using Slack more and more, but few have done away with email entirely, which means we need to make peace with our inboxes – at least for the time being. Now we've got a clearer idea of what emails are doing to our brain, here are some strategies for managing them.

Decide when you check your inbox

One interesting study from 2016 continually logged 40 participants over 12 working days to see what impact emails had on their stress and productivity levels. People who self-interrupted (as in, they didn't wait for a notification or had them switched off) and checked their emails at specific times rated their productivity higher than those who relied on notifications and checked them continually throughout the day whenever a new one arrived. The researchers suggest this might be because those who decide to check rather than waiting for a notification feel like they have more agency over their work because they choose when to interrupt themselves – rather than letting a notification decide how they will spend their working day.

So, a good place to start would be to turn email notifications off and intentionally plan email time into your day. How often you schedule your email checking will depend on your job. Once or twice a day is ideal, but if you need to be checking it more often go for once an hour at the most – it doesn't matter as long as you schedule it in. You could write this down or literally block out time in your calendar. This last option is a good idea if you work somewhere with shared calendars. That way you'll ensure the time stays free and someone doesn't schedule a meeting when you're meant to be sorting, replying and deleting. Not only will scheduling in email-checking time rather than doing it whenever you feel like it mean you get more done, it could help to reduce the desire to check your inbox for rewards continually – but that could take time, so be patient. Try it for at least a fortnight, and see how it works for you.

Schedule emails to set boundaries and delay replies

There are several different services that you can use to schedule when you send an email. This means you receive an email and reply to it, but the reply won't send until you want it to – you can choose from an hour in advance to any other time with the help of a little pop-up calendar. This is a good idea for setting boundaries: people will learn not to expect instantaneous replies. It will also stop your inbox from clogging up – if you don't reply until later, they won't reply until later still. Yes, that sounds like you're delaying the inevitable because you are. Buying time is useful if you're inundated with hundreds of emails a day. I use Boomerang, and I also really enjoy the sense of control it gives me over what, at times, can feel like a chaotic carnival in my inbox.

Scheduling emails is also a good idea if your working hours are different from others in your team, whether that's because you work varying shifts or your colleagues are spread out across many time zones. That way you can control when they get your email, and you won't feel pressured to reply outside of your working hours and neither will they.

Send fewer annoying emails to receive fewer annoying emails

We all want to think it's our emails that are clogging up our inboxes. They're the problem. It couldn't possibly be us, right? Often the way we approach emails can make situations more frustrating than they need to be. Keep emails as clear and concise as you can. You don't need to be rude. But it does mean you should get to the point. If someone has asked for a call, reply with availability and how best to contact you. What could have been another few back and forth emails full of things like 'sure' and 'okay, what's the best way for us to talk?' can be decided in a single email. Keep it focused and to the point.

Figure out if folders are for you

Some productivity experts swear by sorting all of their emails into carefully labelled folders. I have folders nested in folders, and things are (for the most part) neat and organised. But here's the thing: if you forget which folders you have or have way too many, sorting your emails is going to take up as much time as responding to them. It has to be straightforward from the start or don't bother with folders at all.

You could begin by taking author Nir Eyal's advice from his book *Indistractable*. He says we should only touch an email twice. Once to read it and decide when it needs to be dealt with and once again to deal with it. There are two options at the first stage: 'Today' or 'This Week'. Anything that doesn't fit into these can be deleted or archived. You could decide on a colour to flag each of these or sort them into two folders. Then schedule time each day to address everything in the 'Today' folder or colour as a priority. Schedule a little time each day to tackle the 'This Week' folder, so it doesn't build up but is slowly chipped away at over the next five or seven days.

Consider other people

This might feel out of place among a lot of productivity advice, which often focuses on you and no one else. But if someone needs a response, it won't take you long, *and* it'd help them to receive a reply, consider replying.

I was working on a big branded content project in 2019 with lots of different deadlines. The project manager had emailed me to ask if I could move one of the deadlines a little earlier. I happened to be sorting emails at the time, so I saw it as soon as I received it, but didn't reply immediately and decided instead to sort it at the end of the day. She followed up because this was an important piece of work for us both, and clearly it was something she needed to know. All it would have taken was something like: 'Hi, I probably need a week on this one. Thanks.' Or something else as short and sweet, and I didn't do it, and that meant she needed to email again.

I'm really *really* not telling you to reply to every email instantly and pander to every request. But if it's a working relationship and there's a tight deadline or a lot of moving parts to a project, and acknowledging you've at least read the email wouldn't take long, do it. There's no official rule here. But I often think that in the pursuit of being more productive, optimal versions of ourselves, we forget the worry a lack of a reply can pile on to the responsibilities of other people that would have taken seconds for us to sort.

Important: You could lose days implementing all of this advice, so here's a gem of a time-saving tip: don't. Take one suggestion or two to free up more time. If they work out, keep making changes. But with a lot of time, energy and emotion tied up in our inboxes, the last thing we need is another endless checklist to work through. Just keep trying things until you hit on some helpful solutions for you.

More than anything, I think what we need is an attitude shift. Taking charge of your emails does not have to be a monumental ordeal or a constant nag (promise). It's a place that can be trained, cultivated and used to work for you and not against you: this will look different for everyone, so stay in your lane and find your own solution.

UPGRADE YOUR WORKING FROM HOME ROUTINE

For many people, working from home used to be a rare occurrence. I know plenty of managers who considered it an excuse for doing nothing all day. However, working from home has become the norm for large numbers of us. Many companies have realised that (surprise, surprise) most people do work well at home and don't need anyone watching over their shoulder to make sure they do a good job.

That said, the transition wasn't easy for everyone, especially last year when it coincided with the anxiety of an unprecedented global event. Plenty of people I know said they felt happier and more efficient working from home. At the same time, others found juggling childcare, small spaces and work a huge challenge – not to mention the constant worry about the pandemic and temptation to check the news every few minutes. Like working in a regular office, for most people there are pros and cons to working from your kitchen table: the key is spotting them, working out what they mean for your individual working style and tweaking, so it suits you best.

The key to working from home is accepting that it can look different for everyone. Not only because we work in different jobs and live in different spaces, but because we all have more choice about what our working day can look like, what it can include and exactly how we work outside the constraints of an office.

For example, some people feel their best if they wake up at the same time as they'd usually head into the office, get dressed, go for a walk and then return to settle into working at a desk. Others like to mix up their schedules and work in comfy clothes on the sofa for an hour and then choose to transfer to a desk or the dining room table for a few hours later. There's no one way to work from home – despite what some people might say.

With that in mind, I'm not going to repeat the same working from home advice you've heard before. You know the kind: get dressed, get some fresh air, talk to people. There are countless great articles online about how to get the basics right. Instead, here are a few suggestions you can use to upgrade your home working set-up, as well as the way you communicate with your colleagues. I've spent the best part of the last ten years working from home, so I've learned a lot about what works and what saps your time, energy and motivation.

Improve your Wi-Fi signal as much as you can

A good Wi-Fi connection is essential if you're working from home. But poor internet connection can be a big problem, especially in rural areas. If you've been working from home with unreliable Wi-Fi, consider this your prompt to do something about it. There's nothing more frustrating than getting started on work or joining a video call for the connection to drop out seconds later. You've got a couple of options, including changing the position of your router, updating your router if it's old, buying a Wi-Fi extender (a good choice in larger homes) or plugging in a powerline adapter, which is super-easy to set up and can improve the strength and speed of your connection. It might also be time to switch to a different type of broadband or even a different provider. Don't be afraid to chat with your broadband provider about faster speeds; they might be more helpful than you think.

Build your day

Without the structure and norms of an office, you need to schedule your day. This doesn't mean account for every minute, but at least get clear about what you need to do and how you'll break up the next eight hours. Use a job list app or your calendar to do that and timers if you need to keep yourself on track. Knowing what you've got ahead also gives you structure. When you've got no one watching you at home, it can be tempting to allow your instant gratification monkey to take the wheel and start scrolling, cleaning or playing a game on your phone. With a basic schedule, you might find it easier to stay on track. For some, having a weekly schedule might work, but for you, it might be something which changes every day. Try out both and see which you prefer.

Divide work and life

Social media scheduling tool Buffer published a report in 2019 about remote working. The company spoke to 2,500 remote workers and, even before Covid-19 flipped everything upside down, people said the biggest struggle they faced when working from home was unplugging after work. Working from home can feel strange if you don't have plans in an evening. It means you clock off and then that's it, you're done. But without a commute home or the ritual of leaving an office, it might not feel like you are. All you've really done is walked a few feet from your 'kitchen table office' to the settee (which sometimes also doubles as an office). Do something to mark the end of the day. Set an alarm. Go for a walk. Make a tea. Work out. It doesn't have to be something big or time-consuming. But deliberately draw a line under your day. This will help you to leave work stress and troubles behind more effectively.

Get clear on communication

We all know it's important to talk with other people and colleagues – either via a call, video call or using messaging apps – when you work from home, so we don't feel isolated. But it pays to put the same consideration into how you communicate with your boss, team, colleagues and clients. For me, this is one of the biggest obstacles I see when people go from office working to home working. Get clear on how you will communicate. How you do this depends on your role. Put processes in place, know what's expected of you and, if you can, set boundaries. For example, is everyone talking on Slack or can you default to email? Does your boss need to hear from you once a day via an email update or can you wait for your catch-up call every Wednesday? Do you need to make sure you have one meeting-free day a week for big projects and to get through your inbox? Get clear about what's expected of you so you can get clear on what you need to work well.

Push back on video calls

2020 was the year a specific type of work stress became widespread: Zoom burnout (or Zoom fatigue), which is that exhausted feeling you get after being on endless video calls. There are many reasons why video calls can make you feel tired and fed up, including (but certainly not limited to) tech glitches and the lack of body language. But Zoom burnout was also a product of the pandemic, during a time when we were all starved of social interaction. Video calls brought people closer to us, but also made them seem somehow further away. To avoid video call fatigue in future, you could turn off your camera when you need to or hide your face so other people see it, but you don't. I'd also recommend asking whether a video call is really worth it – can the same thing be done in a regular call or even an email?

Take breaks

As well as knowing what you need to do throughout the day, decide when you're going to stop working. Think about how much time in an office you spend chatting to people, making coffees, faffing about with your stationery, Googling how to readjust your armrests, getting to meetings. Working from home doesn't mean sitting at a desk for eight to ten hours with one tiny lunch break spent eating a sandwich and spilling crumbs all over your keyboard and then frantically searching online for 'how to get crumbs out of a keyboard'. In most roles, you can afford to take regular breaks – and these are important. You need breaks from work, breaks from tech and breaks from the same screen. This can mean stopping work to check Twitter. But you'll get the most significant benefit if you do something that'll nourish you in another way: play a game, stretch, go for a quick walk. Not only is this good for productivity, it also gives your eyes and back a rest from whatever position you've been in, which is a whole topic in and of itself we'll look at next.

IT'S TIME TO STOP HUNCHING OVER YOUR SCREENS

One of the biggest problems with working from home is that our homes are not designed for all-day working. That's why people struggle to feel comfortable working from their 'bed office'. Working from your settee, your bed, that nice armchair with the squishy headrest, might feel right for you, but it could lead to back, neck and shoulder pain.

There's a huge amount of advice online about how you should and shouldn't be sitting all day, and there are many ways you can upgrade your home working set-up. For example, I'm a big believer in the value of a good office chair, and a monitor hooked up to my laptop, so my eyes don't feel as strained. But let's prioritise and look at the most pressing problem: hunching over your screens.

We all know how this feels. You might even be doing it right now. Your head is tilted down, and your shoulders and upper back are rounded. This can cause neck pain, shoulder pain and stiffness in your upper back. Many of us naturally hunch over when we have a screen in front of us. If you have a laptop on a low table or your lap, you're hunching. But at least a laptop screen can be leaned on something. Holding a phone at chest level, keeping it propped up with your hand, hunching your back and angling your neck down means your posture is compromised even more.

The best solution to your hunched-up habit is to elevate the screen you're looking at to eye level. That means, however you're sitting, you're not putting quite as much strain on your back and your shoulders. You could sit at a table and place your laptop on top of a pile of books to quickly try this out or a small, desk-sized laptop stand. Position this an arm's length away from your face. You'll then need a separate keyboard and mouse that sit on the top of the table or surface. Ideally, your elbows should be at your side at 90 degrees.

If you have the room and the money, I'd also recommend investing in a good chair. There are some fantastic office chairs available these days. Look for one that has adjustable parts and, if possible, has lumbar support to keep your lower back happy. But the most important consideration is it feels comfy, and it allows you to sit back a little rather than lean forward and keep both feet planted firmly on the ground.

'Should I get a standing desk?' is something I've been asked a few times throughout 2020. First up, there isn't any conclusive evidence that standing desks are much better for us than regular sitting desks. But the reason I recommend them is to add variation to your working from home day. This is important if you don't have access to a desk or chair and spend time working from not-so-ideal spaces.

You don't have to buy one, though. Start with a makeshift standing desk by stacking books on a table or kitchen worktop so that your laptop screen is at eye level when you're standing in front of it. Try this for a few hours for a week or two and see if you like it. If you do, there are plenty of small, foldable stands you can buy. Some of these are made from cardboard, which is ideal if you need to pack away your 'standing desk' at night.

HOW TO SLEEP MORE AND SCROLL LESS

Less sleep for us can, as you probably know all too well, have a big impact on our mental and physical health. I'm writing about it in this chapter because it can also influence how you work, how productive you are and how stressed you get from day to day too. This is particularly true now more of us work from home, and daytime naps are a genuine possibility.

The CEO of Netflix, Reed Hastings, was once asked who the biggest competitors to Netflix are. His answer: sleep. Here's what he said:

'You know, think about it. When you watch a show from Netflix and you get addicted to it, you stay up late at night. We're competing with sleep, on the margin. And so it's a very large pool of time.'

When I first read this response, I laughed. I remembered how many times I hadn't managed to switch off Netflix before it continued playing another episode. And the bittersweet feeling of accepting my fate and sacrificing another 50 minutes to the binge-watching gods.

But if we look deeper, it's worrying. Technology companies knowingly monetise your attention and carve into our precious sleep time. No matter how enjoyable, entertaining and soothing that might sometimes be, it also means less time and less sleep for us, leading to more stressful days at work.

It's no secret that time in front of screens affects our sleep. There are countless studies about how disruptive our technology can be to our sleep with the consensus being that electronic devices and social media use increase the chances we'll have a bad night's sleep – especially among teens –although, interestingly, some studies suggest time online only affects our sleep by a few minutes each day. This means if you don't have a problem with sleep, keep doing what you're doing, and lucky you.

If you want to make some changes, let's take a look at some of the reasons why tech use might influence sleep quality and duration – and what we can do about it.

Get the light right

Your circadian rhythm is your internal 24-hour clock. It determines when you want to sleep and when you want to wake up, as well as other things, like when you should eat, how you feel, your temperature and even your mood.

Light plays a major role in how this internal clock works because it prompts your body to produce melatonin. Melatonin is a hormone that signals it's time to sleep. The problem is, when you've exposed yourself to lots of artificial light (the kind you can get from screens) melatonin isn't released.

Studies have shown it's short wavelengths of light that disrupt the circadian system, which is the blue light your devices emit. In contrast, warmer light aids sleep because it helps melatonin do its thing. Too much blue light and you're effectively telling your body to wake up. It's the equivalent of hopping on a plane and flying through a couple of time zones in the space of time it takes you to watch some Instagram Stories or an episode of your favourite TV show.

Luckily, many devices now have built-in features that allow you to amp up the warmth of the light in your screens at certain times of the day. As I'm typing these words right now, my laptop screen is slowly being infused with yellow tones. Tweak the settings in each of your devices and set a schedule for when you want the warmer light to kick in, as well as how intense you'd like it to be when it does.

But there's more to do. One study found that these settings alone won't make a big difference – brightness is essential too. This means you need to turn down the brightness of your screens at night and get as much brightness as you can during the day. That's when blue light *is* good for us. Plenty of bright light, especially natural bright light, can improve sleep timing, daytime sleepiness and executive functioning.

Don't stop at your screens. One of the pieces of tech I recommend the most for day and night is a smart light bulb. These bulbs can connect up to your phone, which means you can choose from millions of colours, change their brightness and set schedules. After learning about the power of warm light in the evening, I now change the colour of the smart bulbs at my desk to ease me into sleep as well.

There's a lot to remember here, but simply put, we want bright light during the day and warm, soothing light at night.

Limit what you look at

Looking at something frustrating, anger-inducing or work-related before bed can be the difference between a restful and restless night. Try limiting how much tech you look at before bed – charging your phone on the other side of the room can help.

If you must look at a screen, make sure you're not doing anything that can trigger unhelpful feelings. For me, this means email is out, as is Twitter, Instagram and anything that can be classed as doom-scrolling.

What is allowed? That's down to your preferences and what riles you up or calms you down. I sometimes allow myself Pinterest and meditation apps on my phone, but my Kindle for reading is always the safest bet. Everything else would be too much of a gamble.

Set a sleep alarm

Tech eats into sleep time. It doesn't matter if your screen is pumping out a restful, warm light and you're looking at soothing images. If you don't nod off because you're too busy looking at screens, your sleep will suffer.

I'm sure we've all been aimlessly scrolling or working on something or checking Twitter and Instagram in an endless loop, but know it's about time we got some sleep yet still can't seem to stop. (Remember, that's how your favourite apps are meant to work.)

A straightforward way of addressing this problem is to set a sleep alarm. You set one in the morning so set another at night too. This is when you have to switch off (in every sense of the word) and start getting ready for bed. You can't ignore your morning alarm if you want to keep your job, so the one you set at night has to become immovable too.

You could swipe-proof your night-time sleep alarm by changing the settings on your phone to ban apps after a particular time. That way, you're more likely to focus on sleep, not apps.

The tech that can help you sleep

Our screens might prevent us from sleeping well sometimes, but there are also apps, devices and tech tools that can help us to get a better night's sleep.

There are lots of meditation apps with sleep settings. Calm even has a section that features celebrities lulling you to sleep with bedtime stories. I love listening to white noise while I sleep.

You can find plenty of white noise tracks online – use an app like Noisli, which gives you ultimate control over the types of sounds you hear or even buy yourself a white noise machine. Check out page 334 for more sleep resources.

FROM OPTIMISATION TO OBSESSION?

People often ask me whether using tech to track your sleep with a fitness tracker you wear on your wrist or a small device that tucks under your mattress is worth it. The answer is: it might be.

As a general rule, sleep tracking could be a useful way to find out more about how you sleep. For example, you could discover your nights aren't as sleepless as you thought they were, but you wake up at 3:00am consistently. You can then start making changes or asking yourself: is there something changing in my environment that's causing that? Like the heating switching on? Or a smart gadget switching off?

If you have serious sleep problems, collecting information about when you sleep and how you drift through the different stages of sleep (or not) can arm you with insights to take to see a GP or specialist. What's more, as sleep tracking tech advances, we can expect the information our devices collect to become more and more useful.

However, sleep tracking isn't for everyone. I've spent a lot of time reviewing tech designed to track sleep over the years, and I've had several different experiences. Sometimes I'd track my sleep for weeks at a time with no problems, but other times I'd forget to do it. On occasions the tech would be so uncomfortable I'd have already taken it off before I nodded off. And a few times I've become preoccupied with the information my sleep tracker serves up each morning; to the point where I began making all kinds of changes to my days, my routines, my lights and my bedroom in a desperate bid to improve it.

That last point can be a problem, and I'm not alone in experiencing it. There's even a name for it: orthosomnia. Researchers decided to call it this because they felt the preoccupation with trying to perfect your sleep and then track it was similar to the preoccupation with healthy eating, which is called orthorexia, and *somnia* is derived from Latin and is used to refer to sleep.

Researchers describe this as 'a perfectionistic quest for the ideal sleep in order to optimise daytime function'. In their study, these same researchers looked at three different cases of people receiving therapy for poor sleep. They found that each of them experienced unintended side effects of sleep tracking, and most of the time this was a preoccupation with sleeping and ways to improve it, including excessive amounts of time in bed.

The reason I'm telling you so much about sleep tracking is that I think it opens up a broader discussion about our preoccupation with becoming 'better', especially with regards to optimising ourselves to work better, longer and smarter – often to the detriment of our well-being.

I believe many of us have our own 'perfectionistic quest' that we often embark on, whether that's being hyper-focused on improving our sleep, obsessing about email hygiene or insisting on a time-consuming side hustle when our day jobs are already gruelling enough.

Modern work culture, unfortunately, is partly to blame here. Companies want to maximise working hours and staff just as much as we want to maximise our sleep, our energy levels, our ability to work, focus and do 39,508 things at once.

Our tech enables many of these perfectionistic quests by allowing us to check up on work emails, stay connected continually and, importantly, quantify our lives with emails, likes, sleep scores and calendar invites. But I think we need to get a handle on this because it seems to me like it's a shortcut to burnout.

Unpicking why some of us are so laser-focused on these number-based goals, both in our personal and professional lives, can be difficult. But for now, I'd like you to ask yourself: what if how everything is right now was enough? Even if that means a messy inbox and a mediocre night's sleep ahead. What would life be like if every little piece of ourselves didn't have to be measured, optimised and, sometimes, monetised? If every second didn't have to be filled with an activity, a goal, a reason for being? Would we be happier? More creative? More free?

The big one for me, which I make a point of writing down and asking myself regularly, is: how would this moment feel right now if you focused not on maximising what you could get done, the calories you could burn, the things you'd learn, but on getting joy and meaning from it instead?

There is no right answer. But stopping to ask these questions is a bold move in a world pushing us to be better versions of ourselves and takes you (even temporarily) out of what I like to call the optimisation game.

The three rules of sleep tracking

If you can afford to take a gamble on a sleep tracking device you don't know will work (many aren't cheap), then here are my tips for developing a healthy attitude towards it:

1. Give yourself permission to take it off and miss tracking every so often.
2. Accept that your sleep graphs and sleep scores could be low, and there might not be anything you can do about it.

3. Stop tracking if you feel yourself becoming preoccupied with the graphs, numbers and sleep scores you get each morning.

HOW TO (CAREFULLY) TAKE A STEP BACK

Whether you feel stressed out, burned out or like you'll scream if you get just one more damn email, there are steps you can take to distance yourself from your tech temporarily. This won't be a miracle cure. A few hours avoiding emails won't make you a shiny new person (if only), and some of us have more autonomy over how we work than others. But I hope some of these suggestions will give you a much-needed breather.

Create an auto-responder

These aren't just for when you're going on holiday. If your biggest problem is the number of emails you get each day, this might be an excellent way to manage expectations about when (or if) you'll reply. You could say anything you like: you get a massive amount of emails, so it might take a while to respond; there's someone at your company or who works for you who might be better placed to deal with most queries; you don't always respond to press releases (that's one for fellow journalists).

Make sure people know how to contact you

You're trying to cut down on communications; I get that. But let's say someone needs you for a work emergency or you're in a job that doesn't allow you to take a tech break. Make sure people know the best way to contact you. Suggest one form of contact with everyone. You might not have a choice over what that is if you work at a company with specific policies. But speaking to your boss and colleagues on email, Slack, WhatsApp and Zoom is bound to be exhausting. Streamline as much as you can.

Tell your followers

If you don't live and breathe social media, this might seem a bit self-important. But if you make a living online, it makes sense to keep everyone in the loop. You can let your followers know you're taking time off and when you might be back. Think of it as an auto-responder, but for people who keep up with you via your Instagram, not your inbox.

Get clear on what you need (and don't need)

Many of us know we need to do less, but we're not sure what less looks like. Get clear on what your most significant tech stressors are. Maybe you're finally at the end of your tether with video calls, so on days when you have a lot of them you need to be super-careful of taking lots of breaks around them. Maybe it's emails that are driving you up the wall. Perhaps you can't keep up with a running challenge you've entered on your fitness app. To do this, simply make a note anytime you're feeling stress and see if you can identify those triggers. If we don't find out, we end up thinking everything is the problem, and that becomes unmanageable. Either delete these things for good or temporarily to give yourself space. Most of us won't be lucky enough to press pause on everything, so get specific about what it is that causes the biggest drain to your time and your energy instead.

Redefine urgent

We've been conditioned to think that every notification is urgent. An email from your boss and a retweet can both feel just as important to check. They show up as red notifications, make a sound and nag us if we don't attend to them. But there's a scale of urgency, and I think a lot of us forget that when we're busy. Remind yourself some things are more urgent than others. Then treat them with the urgency they deserve. Maybe this is how you divide up email folders: urgent and non-urgent. Maybe only urgent apps are allowed on your home screen. Or you could revisit the notifications settings on page 99 and make sure only the genuinely urgent ones get through to you.

Important: If you want to take prolonged time away from your devices and it won't get you fired, go for it. If you're worried it will get you fired, but you're feeling overwhelmed, talk to your manager or someone from the HR team at your company. I'm not sure it works for all of us, but there's further reading on page 334 if you think you might never want to see another screen again – or at least not for the next fortnight.

BEWARE OF PRODUCTIVITY PROMISES

Sometimes it doesn't feel right to recommend new apps, devices or services. I know you probably weren't expecting to read that from a technology journalist who has written a book with a lot of recommendations in its pages. But that's because I believe many of the changes we should make to the way we use our devices are tied up in our thinking and behaviour, not in getting more things, whether that's more apps, more devices or more tips about how to sort emails or manage your time.

But the people who make these things know what you want. You want to be more productive at work. You want things to feel more manageable. You want to tick everything off your job list. You want to look like you've got everything together. And their job is to sell you things they tell you will help you to achieve those goals.

Advertising and marketing are built on promises like these. New running shoes aren't just new running shoes. They're a promise of peak performance. You can be the best with them strapped to your feet. Apps, services, devices, new software – these are all the same, which means there's sometimes a disconnect between what we believe a new product will bring us (the promise) and what it does bring us (the reality).

A new productivity app is something we believe will make us more productive. A new laptop will improve our work (and the Apple logo on the front will make us feel more professional). A new smartwatch packed with features might finally stop you from procrastinating and make you feel and look like the kind of super-organised person you always dreamed of being. These things *could* all be true. But it's not always easy to unpick what we're led to believe about something new and what it can genuinely add to our lives.

This isn't unique to technology. But I think, as we touched upon above, over the past few years there's been more pressure to be more productive, to measure what you're doing, to improve your scores, sales, work and life. To be the best we can be with little consideration about what the destination of 'best' even looks like.

We know we can improve our stress and burnout symptoms by cutting back, not adding more. But when new tech, new services, new apps and plenty of new promises are readily available and appealing, it can be tricky to put on the brakes and exercise some critical thinking.

There's no right or wrong answer here as to whether you should or shouldn't buy, subscribe to, listen to or sign up for something new. There is nothing wrong with buying new things sometimes. (I don't think we should all be minimalists and I know many of us wouldn't want to be anyway.) But I think we can all agree that we want to feel like we have control over what we're buying and that each choice is deliberate.

An enduring question I think we need to practise asking ourselves, again and again, is: just because we have access to something, does it mean we need it? The answer, more often than not, is no.

Checklist

Learn the signs of stress and burnout. This is important. If you know what to look for, you can better care for yourself when you spot the symptoms. Or make changes to the way you work now to prevent them.

Look out for your instant gratification monkey. Procrastination is normal. But it can have an impact on your work and well-being over time. Put steps in place to prevent your instant gratification monkey from taking over and ask yourself why you might be avoiding a project or task.

Be mindful of completion bias. Are you doing things because they need to get done or so you can tick them off your list? You might be putting all of your time and energy into tasks that aren't worth it. This leaves nothing left over for tasks that are.

Take charge of your emails. This doesn't have to involve multiple steps or new apps. A few changes to the way you organise, send and even think about your emails can ensure your inbox works for you – not against you.

Pay attention to your posture. Many people have now had a taste of working from home. But if you want to keep it up without aches and pains, you need to position your tech and your body in the right way.

Get the right light at different times of the day. Sleep is vital for your mental and physical health. It also has a significant impact on your work, productivity and stress management. Add warm light to your night-time routine and bright light to your days.

Question whether you need to track and improve upon everything you do. It's easy to get swept up in optimising your work, your routine and yourself. This can make you feel like you're never enough. Ask yourself: what if things were okay right now, just how they are?

Step away from your tech when things get overwhelming. You don't have to detox or lock away your phone. But taking a break from the things that are causing you stress can be extremely beneficial if you do it slowly and considerately.

PRIVACY & SECURITY

THE SIMPLE STEPS TO TAKE FOR PEACE OF MIND ONLINE

One sunny afternoon a few years ago, I received an unusually frantic call from my mum. She was calling from the Leeds Library, where she'd been researching family history on the microfiche readers. Half an hour into her research, she realised her handbag, which she'd placed within touching distance on the floor, was gone. Her phone was in it, so the library staff let her use their phone first to call the police and then to call me.

Many of us have first-hand experience of that sinking feeling that comes with the realisation your phone, your wallet, your laptop isn't where it was five seconds ago. For me, it feels as if my stomach has hit the floor, my head's turned into a cloud of cotton wool and my hands to warm liquid. Then the 'what happens next' worry kicks in, followed by the guilt of 'how did I let this happen?'

What's interesting to me is how often we only take preventative action *after* we've had something stolen. After someone stole my wallet from my always-slightly-open handbag in my uni days, I bought a smaller one that fits into my pocket. My neighbours across the road put up security cameras *after* they'd had a break-in. My mum now has a small bag she wears on a long strap all the time and attached Bluetooth trackers to every valuable bit of tech she owns. We put so much more thought into our personal security *after* things go wrong, to avoid having to go through the same distress all over again. This makes sense, but it means many of us act when it's already too late. When there are so many more sensitive details about our lives and finances now online, how many of us are waiting for something to go seriously wrong before taking steps to protect our digital privacy and security?

I get it: updating old passwords, ticking and unticking privacy settings, trawling review sites to find out which is the best VPN (or even what a VPN is) – they're just more things we need to add to the endless to-do list you haven't got around to yet. But remember that 'liquid hands, cotton-wool head' feeling when your phone goes missing? Hopefully, you'll never discover your bank balance or phone or email account has vanished. But why aren't more of us actively making sure that we're as safe as we can be right now?

As it turns out, 'privacy fatigue' is a very real thing. Like other tech-induced fatigues (see also: Zoom fatigue and email fatigue), privacy fatigue is a mixture of exhaustion and cynicism brought on by endless privacy breaches and hacks in the news that means taking steps to do anything seems pointless, confusing privacy controls that change often and no clear sense of how our personal information is being used. If you're nodding along right now, you're not alone.

But we do need to take action. I don't want you to leave it until your email account gets hacked because you used a lame password and it feels like an endless maze of calls to (if you're lucky) get it back, or a quiz you signed up to take on Facebook is discovered to be leaking your personal information for you to do something about it – no matter how hard that fatigue hits.

I'm sorry if it seems like I'm trying to scare you. I'm really not. But this *is* scary. While there is a very slim chance any of these things will happen, it's no guarantee that they won't. We're not just talking about a problem with a password that you can easily reset anyway. Every topic in this book is impacted by privacy and security. You'll lose your online identity if yours is stolen or your memories are erased. Your mental health might be affected if someone figured out your passwords and got hold of your personal information. Connection with others could feel less satisfying if you thought it was through an app that's also selling on your data.

The seed of these problems might be one rogue, reused password. But when they grow, they can influence nearly every part of your life.

PRIVACY PRIMER

To make sense of what we need to do and why, let's take a look at some definitions. Because although privacy and security are similar, they're not the same, and understanding the difference is key to understanding those lengthy privacy and security emails we all get when we sign up to a new service or social media platform.

The International Association of Privacy Professionals (IAPP), a non-profit organisation for people working in the privacy industry, defines privacy as 'the right to be let alone, or freedom from interference or intrusion.'

When we talk about privacy in the context of technology, we're referring to information privacy, which the IAPP explains is 'the right to have some control over how your personal information is collected and used'. Personal information can mean anything from bank details or health records through to social media posts, photos, things you type into search engines, what you say to your Alexa voice assistant and much, *much* more. There are, therefore, all kinds of ways your privacy could be compromised. For example, a new app you signed up for might sell information about you to a marketing company. Or a smart speaker company might hire people to listen to recordings of what you say in your home to improve how the next version works. These are things that you'd expect to be kept private, right?

Security (in the digital sense) is whatever you or I or the companies that host our personal information do to protect it from breaches and hacks. An example of a security compromise could be if cybercriminals gain access to a banking app's database and can see who has signed up for the app, what their bank details are and lots of information about their finances.

To explore these differences, and how we might spot a privacy or security compromise in the future, here's an example:

You've downloaded an app to store photos, let's call it 'FavPics'. You've filled in your name, location, interests and added your photos to it. But, uh-oh, a month later you spot a headline about FavPics in the news and find out it sent all its users' details (including yours) to a marketing company without your say-so. This marketing company might have used information about you to advertise to you, to send you emails or to sell on again to another company that deals in this kind of data, without you expressly giving your consent. This is an example of your **privacy** being compromised by a company you trusted to behave ethically.

Let's consider another scenario. This one is likely more familiar if you watch a lot of movies and TV shows that involve hacking. This time, FavPics did *not* give away your personal information, but it was not careful with its security. Which means it got broken into by hackers. The hackers were able to steal the photos that you and every other user uploaded. That means the **security** of the information you've shared with the app provider has been compromised.

There's more to this one, though. If the app provider's security is compromised, someone could also compromise your privacy at the same time. Hackers might be able to access private account details, like your password, phone number or home address and sell this information for profit or publish it online to embarrass the app provider.

There's no way to be sure if or when compromises like these might happen. That means if you want to be 100 per cent safe, you need to give up on technology entirely. But, like telling teens the best form of contraception is abstinence, I know that's not helpful.

What's more, even if you *did* give up on tech entirely, there's probably information about you in so many different digital spaces after years of living your life online that you'd have to be extremely thorough about deleting your virtual self. Even then, there's no guarantee it'd be genuinely gone anyway.

So, in the absence of keeping things how they are and running the risk of a privacy or security nightmare, or, scrubbing our virtual identities from every single app or service we've signed up to over the past few decades, where does that leave us?

I think there are two key things we need to do:

1. Learn about the steps we can take to ensure our information and accounts are as secure as possible.
2. Become more aware of how easily we hand over information about ourselves and how tech companies might use that information so we can make better decisions about whether to share or not to share.

This chapter acknowledges that, yes, we are collectively tired of privacy talk and likely haven't been doing enough to protect our personal information so far. But no, we're not too late to make a difference and cannot afford to ignore these issues either.

I'll be selective about stories, stats and step-by-step instructions that could lead to overwhelm or go out of date within days and focus instead on a few of the key concerns many of us have about how to keep our private information private.

THE POWER OF THE PASSWORD

Your passwords protect all of your online accounts and are, therefore, keys to your life.

Cracking your password, which might mean guessing it based on personal details, using one that was used elsewhere or trying loads and *loads* of combinations, is one of the top ways someone could get their hands on your personal information.

If there's only one thing you take away from this chapter, let it be this: stop using the same password for different accounts and apps. (Yes, even for boring accounts and apps.) This is another bad habit that a lot of people find it hard to break – yours truly included.

If your password is compromised in one place, by which I mean a hacker knows what your password is and what your username is or has posted a list of them online and yours are included, anyone can use these to log in to your other accounts. This is called credential stuffing. Hackers will try and 'stuff' your username and password into other services. Think of this as a domino effect – it only takes one for lots of others to fall.

Significant breaches that give hackers access to loads of credentials happen more regularly than you might expect. This means if you use the same password across more than one account, you need to change them. Luckily, some services, including Google and several password managers (more on those soon), will alert you if a password you use in one place might have been compromised elsewhere.

There's also a simple way to check. Go to haveibeenpwned.com. This is a site run by security researcher Troy Hunt, where he keeps track of breaches for free. Enter your email address, and you can find out if it's been compromised in a hack, along with your password. At the time of writing, more than 572 million passwords exposed in past data breaches are on the site.

This means you need to do two things from now on: think of unique passwords for each service you use and figure out a way to remember them. Unless you have a truly incredible memory, you won't be able to remember all of your unique passwords. Here are the ways you can use tech to help you:

Get a password manager

One of the best ways to dream up the best passwords and remember them is to use a password manager. Think of it like a secure vault where you can store your passwords and other important information. Password managers can generate random passwords (with a mixture of letters, numbers and symbols) that would be almost impossible to guess. All you need to do is remember your master password. This is how you log in to the password manager.

For many people, password managers are a reliable option. But they're not perfect. For example, if you forget your master password, you could be in real trouble. There are what's called recovery options, which you can fall back on if this happens. But it's just not possible to reset your master password every time you forget it in the same way you might do with other accounts. For that reason, some people have lost all of their passwords because they forgot their master password. Don't let this put you off password managers altogether, but do protect that master password like your life depends on it.

What's more, you obviously don't want anyone to get into your password manager because then they'll get *everything*. Luckily, most password managers are super-secure. But there have been reports of vulnerabilities in the past. This means they haven't been hacked, but researchers have found some of them could be. You'll need to weigh up the pros and cons and read the reviews before you hand over all your important information to one place. I've included some password manager suggestions in the resources section on page 335 to get you started.

Write them down

Never write down your passwords. That used to be the first rule of smart online security. But nowadays it *might* be a good option to scribble them down. After all, you can't hack paper, right? The Electronic Frontier Foundation (EFF), a digital rights and privacy group, recommends keeping passwords you write down somewhere safe, like in a wallet. But lose the wallet and, again, you've lost everything. As the EFF points out though, at least that means you'll know when your passwords get stolen – keep things online and you're often clueless until you make an effort to check. Don't go with this option if you think a flatmate or partner might be looking for ways into your accounts.

Set up two-factor authentication

There's always a chance someone will hack your password manager or find your secret password notes. Whichever method you use, there's a way to make sure your passwords are more secure: two-factor authentication (sometimes shortened to 2FA). You might already have two-factor authentication activated on some of your accounts, but as a quick refresher, this is combining something you know (your password) with something you have (your phone).

Whenever you withdraw money from a cash machine, you're using a type of two-factor authentication. You combine something you know (your PIN number) with something you have (your bank card).

With two-factor authentication you'll need to enter a random string of numbers after you've entered your password. Some apps generate these numerical codes, like Google Authenticator or Microsoft Authenticator, or you can have them sent to you via SMS, although SMS is considered a little less reliable because you need to have signal and security researchers believe they're easier to hack if someone *really* wanted that code.

There's more you can do to secure your accounts. For example, you can get a physical two-factor authentication key that you slot into your USB port to use instead of your phone. But, for the time being, these are the basics: stop using the same password, pick a way to remember them and add two-factor authentication whenever you can.

Important: Beware that false sense of security.
Adding more security steps might make you lazy. In one study, researchers found that people who use two-factor authentication – in this case, something you know (a password) and something you have (a fingerprint) – chose weaker passwords than those who didn't.

This is called risk compensation theory. People sometimes change their behaviour in response to perceived risk. In this case, they might behave *less* securely when they're interacting with accounts because they think they're better secured and that means there's less risk. The result is they might be undoing that added security by playing fast and loose with their personal information. Don't compromise on the strength of your password just because you're using two-factor authentication: you still need to be just as careful.

WHAT WE'RE UP AGAINST

One of the reasons privacy and security issues can seem overwhelming is because many people don't have a clear idea of what – or who – might be a threat. If I listed every possible risk, they might fill the rest of this book. So instead, here are some of the key definitions it's important we get clear on.

Hacking

This is an umbrella term for any activity that exploits security weaknesses in web-connected tech, such as your smartphone, your computer or even the Wi-Fi network you're on. A successful hack can affect individual people, entire companies and even whole governments.

Here are some helpful need-to-knows:

- Hackers are highly proficient and talented. Sometimes systems are exploited just to show other hackers how skilled they are.

- Often, hacking is carried out for financial gain, through methods like fraud and stealing bank details.
- 'Black hat' hacking is basically any kind of hacking activity with criminal intent.
- 'White hat' hacking is when companies hire hackers to hack their systems, find vulnerabilities and fix them.
- There are also 'hacktivists', like Anonymous, who are politically or socially motivated hackers.

Phishing

Phishing is when something appears to be a trustworthy source, let's say your email log-in page, and it prompts you to sign in as you usually would. But it's not the real thing – scammers have made it to look like it is. The result is your sensitive information, including your password, is now in the hands of whoever set the page up.

There's another type of phishing: spear phishing. Whereas phishing emails are sent to hundreds, or even thousands, of people, spear phishing is targeted at one specific person. This is how celebrity photos have been leaked and how hackers have gained access to large networks and tech companies.

Phishing doesn't just happen online. You can also get a phishing phone call, which is sometimes imaginatively referred to as 'vishing'. And there's also 'smishing' which is the same thing but via SMS text messaging. Essentially, it's anything that makes you voluntarily hand over information because you think it's legit whereas really it's a criminal gotcha.

Phishing is sometimes considered a type of hack. But the difference is hacking means getting hold of information from you or a company or a government involuntarily. With phishing, you hand it over. Hackers sometimes use phishing scams as one element of breaking into an account or network.

Scammers use both hacking and phishing for identity theft. This is when someone uses stolen information to open up a credit card, take out a loan or do anything else in your name.

Data brokers

Data brokers are companies that collect information that's either publicly available about you, like property records and voting details, or private information bought from other sites, apps or social media platforms, including your buying history or web browsing history. Most data brokers don't have contact or any direct relationship with the people they collect information about. This means it happens without you knowing.

They then package up this information and sell it to other companies, like marketing companies, investors or anyone else interested in buying it. Luckily, since the General Data Protection Regulation (GDPR) came into effect in 2018, data brokers have had to be more careful with how they collect and store data to avoid breaking the new rules and being fined. In fact, several data collecting companies have had complaints filed against them, but many are still operating as usual.

Technology companies

The companies you know and (for the most part) trust don't hack into your accounts or fake log-in pages to steal your personal information – you've handed over a *lot* to them already, often without realising it.

This is because the privacy agreements you accept when you sign up to a new app, service or social media platform are often hard to understand. So it's no surprise many of us ignore them and scroll to 'I accept'. There are now more rules in place to make these more straightforward, but not all companies have made the right changes.

This means your personal information might be used in ways you didn't know about or didn't feel like you consented to. This is what we're going to explore in more depth next.

Signs of a scam

Phishing isn't always easy to spot. Scammers use tactics to get you to part with sensitive information, which they then use to steal money from your account or gain access to even more sensitive information.

Many people think they're immune. This is something that just affects our grandparents, right? Not so much. Scam calls and emails sound and look professional. They're also becoming even more sophisticated and harder to identify.

Here are some of the key points to look out for, whether it's a phishing scam via email or someone has called you and is pretending to be from your bank.

Identity

Is this person who they say they are? Watch out for random email addresses and phone numbers that don't match with the company. Scams are advanced nowadays, which means email addresses and phone numbers can sometimes look like the real thing. The best step to take if anyone contacts you is to find the official number online or on a bank statement or letter and then call them up yourself to check. If it's urgent and real, you'll get through to the right person who'll be able to help. Or you'll realise it's a scam and a lucky near miss.

Urgency

When you're worried, you act fast and don't think clearly. Scammers know this. Watch out for calls, emails and texts that tell you it's in your best interest to act right away. You haven't paid your HMRC bill, someone has hacked your account and you've got loads of charges that need paying before bailiffs show up. These tense stories get our attention the most – and scare the hell out of us. Many coronavirus-related scams in 2020 played on the fear of job loss and catching the virus.

Security

There are several things to look out for in a scam call, text or email. For example, a bank will never text you with a link to get you to log into your account. Similarly, your phone company won't email you and ask you to click on a link to pay your bill. These are tactics to play into your sense of urgency. It's highly unlikely a company will contact you via email or call or text and ask for your personal details. What's more, they'll never ask for your password or PIN number.

If you think you might have received a scam text, email or call: Hang up if it's a call. Delete the message if it's a text. Don't open links, mark it as 'spam' and send it straight to the bin if it's an email.

If you think something was a phishing scam but you're not sure, follow the identity step above and call the official number of the bank or company that claimed to be contacting you. This way, you can find out if it's genuine. If it's not, you can let the company know about the scam.

If you think you might have been the victim of a scam: If you've clicked a link, chatted to someone who you think is a scammer or handed over any details, you need to call the company the phishers were pretending to be from and explain what's happened. The quicker you do this, the better the chances any damage that's been done can be reversed. You might also consider contacting Action Fraud, the national reporting centre for fraud and cybercrime. Head to the resources at the back of the book for more information.

ARE BIG TECH COMPANIES SNOOPING ON ME?

The short answer is: yes. But not always for the reasons you might think. It's safe to assume any device that connects to the internet is giving some company somewhere some information about you.

Let's take what Google knows about you as an example. Suppose you use a lot of Google services. In that case, the company likely knows your name, your payment details, who you email and what you say in those emails, the videos and photos you have stored, the documents you work on, the YouTube videos you upload, the YouTube videos you watch and which you comment on, what you search for, what you buy, your browsing history, your location and much, *much* more.

This is the business model many of the tech brands we consider household names are built on. Simply put, they give you something: maps, email, a smart assistant, a social media platform, a search engine. You give them something in return: information about you.

This doesn't mean these companies hired someone to sit and read all of your emails or check up on your location 24/7 (or it's at least very, very unlikely). Instead, it means this information can be utilised and, most importantly for that company, mone-tised in a variety of different ways.

What happens to your information varies from company to company, and we'd need to wade into the privacy policies of each one to find out *exactly* what they're doing with it. Trust me, that would make for one hell of a boring read. Instead, here are a few key ways your information *might* be used, and therefore what to look out for in those extended privacy policies you need to agree to.

To personalise ads

Many companies make money from advertisers. These advertisers will get the best results (that's clicks, shares and purchases) if you're shown ads for things you care about. Things you look at online, search for, write about and even email your friends about could all be used to show you ads you're more likely to like, which in turn means the company can sell more ads as they seem more convincing.

To measure the performance of ads

Advertisers want to know how well their ads are doing. That could mean straightforward information, like whether or not you click on an advertisement for a T-shirt.

But it can also mean more personal forms of information gathering, like being able to track your location or see a list of everywhere you've been.

According to a report in the *Guardian*, Google has allegedly been known to allow its advertisers to track how effective their online ads are at driving customers to their bricks and mortar shops, as well as allowing advertisers to target their ads at people in specific locations.

We don't know exactly what Google does with this information and what advertisers see. But, as a simple example, here's how this *could* work: a company might have shown you an ad for coffee online. You might have then visited that coffee chain, which a map app could track if your location settings are switched on. With this information, the advertiser could learn the specific ad that encouraged you to take that particular action.

To personalise products and recommendations

Information about what you like, what you click on and the topics you're interested in is used to serve up recommendations about products, services and suggestions you're likely to want.

For example, this information could be used to figure out products you might like and you'd then see a recommendation on Amazon for them. Or maybe your smart assistant can learn more about your routine to make better suggestions about when to switch off the lights.

To improve products and services

Learning more about you allows tech companies to use the things you upload, search for or share to improve automated software, like voice assistants or facial recognition technology. This means your selfies, commands and videos are making the tech that runs our lives smarter.

This sounds like a good thing, and it can be. But there have been several issues with the way we 'teach' voice assistants to become smarter. For example, a Bloomberg report explains that teams of real people listen to the things users say to Alexa. This is so they can transcribe their commands and conversations and feed back to the smart assistant. Yes, this makes the voice assistant more intelligent, but at the cost of someone listening in to what you say to Alexa in your home.

To inform research

On page 77 we looked at an example of data being manipulated and collected for research purposes. Publicly available data is also collected – often without your knowledge or consent.

For security reasons

Your emails are regularly scanned by malware and virus software that companies use to detect any threats.

To be clear, these are the ways companies might use your information *right now*. But, as with everything privacy-related, there's a chance more is going on behind the scenes we don't know about – at least not yet anyway. Until that day comes, let's focus on the main thing here: companies know *a lot* about you.

THE CONFUSING TRUTH ABOUT PRIVACY POLICIES

We absolutely can, and should, put more time and energy into finding out what an app, service or social media platform plans to do with our information – whether that's personal details or things we create, like photos – before we sign up.

You can imagine how this is more of a priority for some people than others. For example, a freelance photographer has more at stake when it comes to whether a photo app owns the content they upload to it than I do uploading pictures of leaves that I've liked. But there are some things we all might care about, like whether a face-transforming selfie app might use photos of you in other places, or to advertise the app or to feed to a facial recognition algorithm to make it smarter.

The first step to figuring out how tech companies will use your information is to read the privacy policy. This is an agreement between you and the tech company that lays out all of the ways your information might be collected, stored or used. When you first sign up to a new app or social media platform, you'll be asked to read it and need to acknowledge you agree to it to start using it.

If you're anything like me – and the majority of other people – you will scroll through this as quickly as possible and hit the button which usually says 'I agree', or something similar.

But we need to take the time to read it and find out what might happen to our personal information if we consent. I'd recommend searching the next privacy policy you need to agree and looking for some keywords, like 'share', 'affiliates' and 'third parties' to figure out whether the tech company you're signing up to might pass on information about you to other companies.

As well as 'recommendations' and 'advertise' to see how your information might be used by the company to figure out what you'd like to see more often and how your information might be used to sell things to you. You should also look for 'store', 'encryption' and 'delete'. This might help you to figure out if what you share will be kept somewhere – and whether you can remove it if it is. If you're reading the privacy policy on an app on your phone, get on to a laptop or computer so you can search for these words more easily. Most policies will be available through the company's website.

I've made this sound relatively straightforward – and, sometimes, it might be – but more often than not privacy policies are lengthy, confusing and full of legalese. If you start reading one and can't make sense of it, you're not alone.

The *New York Times* summed this up nicely in a 2018 report calling privacy policies an 'incomprehensible disaster'. The same report discovered some policies exceed a college (university here in the UK) reading level. That's because they're not really there to inform you, but to protect the company in case anyone takes legal action against them if they find out their information is being used in a way they didn't expect.

Luckily, several privacy policies that belong to major tech companies have changed in recent years thanks to pressure from researchers and privacy advocates calling for more transparent, shorter agreements, as well as new GDPR rules, which now require privacy policies to adhere to specific requirements.

According to data security and analytics firm Varonis, the reading grade level, amount of words and time it takes to read those words has been reduced on many (but not all) privacy policies since the introduction of GDPR. This is a good step in the right direction.

But don't think that means these are easy reads. It'll still take you nearly half an hour to get through each of the privacy policies for Facebook, Wikipedia, Twitter, Instagram and eBay. That works out at two and a half hours for all five. Seriously, who has time for that?

Luckily, there are some sites and services to help you. One is Terms of Service Didn't Read (tosdr.org), a project launched in 2012 that rates privacy policies and flags up the most important bits. You can check the website or add the Terms of Service Didn't Read extension to your browser. That way, when you visit a website that the extension has rated, you can click on an icon in the browser that tells you what that rating is.

I'd also recommend checking out Polisis (pribot.org/polisis). This AI-powered site creates visualisations of popular policies. You'll have to check it out for yourself to see exactly how it works. But what I like about it is it's useful for those of us who prefer looking at colours and charts to process information rather than long lists of pros and cons.

Despite policies becoming clearer, learning what keywords to look for within them and finding services that can lend a hand, many are often still difficult to wade through. I tried reading some of the privacy policies for the most popular apps I use while I was writing this chapter and I kept getting bogged down in the language. With that in mind, I think the answer for most of us is to do the best we can, read the policy, take time to research, look to third-party sources and, finally, accept that we might not spot every potential problem because the odds are stacked against us. I'm reminded of this quote from the *New York Times* report:

'Until we reshape privacy policies to meet our needs – or we find a suitable replacement – it's probably best to act with one rule in mind. To be clear and concise: Someone's always watching.'

Remember: Ironically, one of the terms in a company's privacy policy might be that the policy can change. That means it's worth revisiting policies every so often, especially if you start using a service differently. For example, let's say you start putting your design portfolio on an image-sharing site. You'll want to check whether the site can, in theory, use your designs elsewhere.

CHANGING YOUR SETTINGS

Privacy concerns and GDPR laws haven't just changed privacy policies. Some companies have also ensured settings are more straightforward and easier to control once you've signed up. This is great news for us because it means there are more opportunities to have a say over the information you do and don't share, as well as options to opt out of sharing other things entirely.

Let's take a look at how we can change the settings in our favourite apps, social media platforms and services right now. You don't have to change all of these – some will affect how your tech works. Instead, they're choices you can make to allow you to take back a bit more control. Some people reading this might be more worried about smart voice assistants listening in to their private conversations and less about if their work emails are scanned – and vice versa. Pick and choose which privacy boundaries to set for yourself.

Although settings differ, the basics of securing your personal information online are mostly the same across different services. I recommend searching online for step-by-step instructions to implement the settings below on your app or device. The most important thing to remember is: assume the default privacy settings don't have your best interests in mind – you'll need to change them.

Mute your microphone

Most devices with a microphone have settings that allow you to mute it from within the app. Others, like the Google Home Mini and Amazon Echo devices, have a handy physical mute button. If you use a smart assistant, I recommend muting the mic regularly, especially when you want to talk about (or do) anything you wouldn't want someone else to hear. That means muting (or even unplugging if that gives you peace of mind) these devices during confidential work calls, in deep heart-to-heart conversations with your partner and, it goes without saying, in the bedroom.

Delete things you've said

Most smart assistants, whether you talk to them through a sound-bar or your phone, will allow you to delete the saved history of everything you've ever said to them. Deleting this history may affect the relevancy and accuracy of what your smart assistant recommends for you in the future, but that's the trade-off if you're worried about your recorded utterances ever being heard by anyone else.

Opt out of enhancing performance

Dig into privacy settings. In many apps you'll find ways to opt out of improving your experience and helping to inform new features. If you're using a smart assistant, this should stop your recordings from being used to better train Alexa (or Siri or Google Assistant), as well as reducing the chance a human might listen to them. You might not be able to opt out of all data collection, but you can reduce it.

Opt out of recommendations

I can make peace with Gmail scanning my emails to make suggestions about which events to send to my calendar, but if you're not comfortable with that, you can change these settings. Turning off suggested replies and calendar integration in emails is an option if you want to keep your emails more private. Opting out of smart assistant recommendations would be advisable too, and, in some cases, you can even turn off personalised ad recommendations. This means you'll still see ads, but they won't be shown to you based on what the company knows about you.

Pay attention to permissions

As well as agreements, look out for permissions. When you download a new app, it'll ask for your consent to access information about you. Pay attention to what it's asking for and question it. For example, why does this shopping app need access to my contacts and my microphone? If it looks fishy, don't bother. As well as new apps, go back through your old ones. Most phones now allow you to toggle permissions on and off for each app from within your settings, like location, access to your photos and Bluetooth.

Turn off location tracking

Whatever phone you have, there's a way to turn off all location services in an instant. This will mean several apps won't work correctly. As a longer-term fix, venture into the settings and toggle location settings on or off for each app. You can also specify whether you want to grant location tracking permission all the time or only when you're using an app – in most cases, I'd go with the latter. There's a cool new setting in iOS14, Apple's latest operating system at the time of writing, which allows me to grant access to my general location, rather than my specific coordinates. This means you can get the benefits of location tracking and use cinema apps, weather apps and anything else that needs to know roughly, but not exactly, where you are.

Remember: If you use work emails or a work laptop, it's always worth bearing in mind that your IT department probably has access to what you do online. Sure they shouldn't be monitoring what you say or do all the time – and if they do it should come with plenty of warning. But it's always best to assume they might. Use technology you own or your personal email account for anything sensitive – especially if you're applying for new jobs.

When cookies don't taste good

When you visit a website, you've probably seen a pop-up that says: 'This site uses cookies to improve your experience. Please accept cookies.' Or something to that effect.

Cookies are a way for websites to remember who you are. They exist as files that contain small bits of data that are unique to you. When you visit a site, this file is downloaded on to your computer or smartphone. Next time you visit, the website knows it's you again.

And, because this is how they work, they improve your experience online. It means if you click away from a site, your shopping basket will still be full with all of the things you just added to it. Or you won't have to log in again if you accidentally closed a tab. Or the site remembers some of your preferences, like the types of news you want to read or the types of products you like, which means it can suggest similar ones.

These things all benefit us and make shopping and moving around the internet easier. Most of the time, if you're visiting trustworthy sites, there's no reason to worry.

But there are other cookies, and these are called third-party cookies, which allow advertisers, analytics companies or other big tech companies to track your browsing history across the internet. This is usually because you've visited a website with an ad on it, which generated a cookie – even if you never clicked on the ad. That means you can then be tracked based on other sites that contain that ad. This can create a big picture of what you do online and the sites you visit. It's also the reason you might look at a coat on one website and then you find the same coat follows you around the internet for days after you first looked at it. This is called retargeting and it means you now have a solid explanation for why you're being haunted by a parka.

Since the General Data Protection Regulation (GDPR) came into effect in 2018, websites must be transparent about the cookies they use. The Information Commissioner's Office (ICO), the UK's independent body for information rights, explains that people must be told there are cookies on a website. They must also be told what the cookies do, and also ask for a user's consent.

Luckily, some browsers can block cookies entirely. Others can remove the ones you have stored. Search for how the browser you use works, and dig into the settings.

The thing here is, many cookies work to personalise ads. This is, at the same time, a relief and a little worrying when you consider what it all adds up to. Once companies have information about you, you can't get it back. It might be naive to think this is all just to make online shopping more bearable when it's also to sell things to you.

I recommend disabling cookies where possible to see how your online experience is affected. At least then you can choose to re-enable them if you're an online shopper and don't feel like it makes sense to turn them off. This way, you can pick and choose which sites you allow them on rather than selecting 'yes' and agreeing to everything without thinking about it by default.

THE PROBLEM WITH OTHER PEOPLE

One privacy concern many of us overlook is it isn't a solitary pursuit. Networked privacy is the idea that privacy is a collective effort and requires cooperation from people you connect with on social media platforms. A friend might tag you in photos without you knowing, record a video in your home, share your location and check you in on Facebook, tell you *after* a very personal conversation in person that there's a smart assistant listening in, or download an app that uses all of her data and yours too if it's not secure enough.

I'm not saying you should unfriend everyone who might put you and your information at risk. But do consider whom you share information with, especially if your accounts are private. Think twice before you accept every friend request or follow everyone back and tell people you know what you've learned about the importance of permissions and privacy too.

I like the super-simple but memorable way author and Associate Professor Carissa Véliz puts this in her excellent book, *Privacy is Power*: 'Privacy is collective and political – it's not just about you.'

She stresses that this works both ways too: 'privacy etiquette is important'. She urges us all to ask for consent before posting a photo of someone else online.

Véliz also recommends an idea I think we could all do with trying: privacy zones. These are spaces offline where people are urged not to take photos or videos. This might help people to unwind more at a party or debate with added confidence at a conference without the worry about what will or won't end up online in a few hours.

WHEN YOUR LIKES ARE USED AGAINST YOU

You can take precautions to protect your privacy – and even warn your friends. But it's not always possible to stop your personal information from getting into the wrong hands. One prime example is when data analytics and political consultancy Cambridge Analytica got hold of the profile information of tens of millions of Facebook users. This story is a few years old now, but I think it's worth revisiting as a lesson in how your personal information – which you might think is mundane – might be used to influence you.

Cambridge Analytica worked with a Cambridge University academic who created a personality test app that required Facebook access. It collected personal information from 300,000 Facebook users who took the test. They consented to their data being collected to take the test and were told the results from the test were for academic use. But not only was *their* data collected, which they'd consented to, but so was the data from all of their Facebook friends too, something which they couldn't agree to – that wasn't even allowed on Facebook.

As if that wasn't creepy enough, the reason this incident proved to be even more controversial was that Cambridge Analytica used this gigantic amount of information from Facebook to create psychological profiles of many millions of users – 87 million users is the best guess. These profiles were then used to develop personalised political Facebook ads designed intentionally to sway the opinions of people who were identified as on the fence about political issues and to do that by playing on their worries and their fears.

This is the strategy the company is alleged to have used to inform the work it did on Donald Trump's 2016 presidential campaign. There's also been a lot of ongoing speculation that it might have been used to inform the work Cambridge Analytica did for the Leave.EU political group in the Brexit campaign too.

There's a lot to unpack here. Firstly, the question that comes up whenever I talk to anyone about Cambridge Analytica is: did Facebook know what was happening? The official line from Facebook's CEO Mark Zuckerberg in his 2018 testimony for a hearing about the Cambridge Analytica controversy to the United States Senate Committee on the Judiciary and the United States Senate Committee on Commerce, Science and Transportation went like this:

'My top priority has always been our social mission of connecting people, building community and bringing the world closer together. Advertisers and developers will never take priority over that as long as I'm running Facebook.'

Cambridge Analytica's data collection went against Facebook's policies at the time, which only allowed app developers to get information from friends of friends to improve user experience and that's all. But although Facebook claims it wasn't complicit, it's been heavily criticised since by users, governments and privacy campaigners all over the world who want to know how the platform even allowed such a significant data breach to happen in the first place.

Secondly, we've got no way of knowing whether the ads created by Cambridge Analytica *did* sway public opinion. But, as investigative journalist Carole Cadwalladr said at a 2019 TED Talk about her role in exposing Cambridge Analytica, we all need to take these tactics seriously:

'Democracy is not guaranteed, and it is not inevitable. And we have to fight. And we have to win. And we cannot let these tech companies have this unchecked power. It's up to us: you, me and all of us. We are the ones who have to take back control.'

Essentially, even though we can't know for sure what happened, it doesn't mean this isn't a pressing concern.

Finally, this could be just the beginning. Cambridge Analytica closed operations in 2018, and Facebook has made changes to its platform that mean other companies can't collect the same vast amounts of information. But there's a good chance similar companies, similar psychological profiles about users and similar highly personalised ads already exist.

The question is, what can we do to protect ourselves?

The less personal information you put online, the less it can be used against you in any way. The thing is, social media platforms know this. If you don't share things, you won't get the full experience, which is why many of us do continue to share so much about ourselves. I know it's unrealistic to suggest anyone would stop using many of the social media platforms and sites this applies to. If we want to keep using these platforms, we need to accept that many of them might run counter to what we'd consider privacy and security best practice.

So, there are other things you can do, like be cautious about quizzes, games and other third-party apps that want access to your social media platforms – as well as your emails and other accounts. Facebook has changed the amount of data people who create these apps and quizzes have access to, but it's still a good rule to follow online.

This means anytime an app asks you for permission to access your Facebook account (or any account for that matter), your friends list or anything else, ask yourself why it might need that information. If you can't think of a good reason, don't accept it.

Managing privacy is less about imposing rules and more about shifting your mindset. All of us should be critical about what we see online. You might be thinking you're not susceptible or that your Facebook information doesn't give away *that* much about you. But research about similar kinds of psychological profiling, which could be similar to the methods used by Cambridge Analytica, show specially tailored ads and photos can be highly persuasive.

One 2017 study matched the content of ads to each individual's psychological characteristics based on what they liked on Facebook. In one experiment, people were sorted depending on whether they were considered to be extroverts or introverts. Both groups were shown an ad for a line of make-up, but they were different. The first was aimed at extroverts and featured a woman dancing in a crowded nightclub with 'Dance like no one's watching (but they totally are)' written underneath. The ad for introverts instead featured a smiling woman on her own, looking into a mirror with the slogan: 'Beauty doesn't have to shout.'

The researchers found that showing people the ads that were tailored to their extraversion level resulted in up to 40 per cent more clicks and 50 per cent more purchases than ads that weren't personalised. This suggests that it might be possible to influence people by tailoring persuasive ads to their psychological needs. That might not seem all that surprising, but the important part is that in this particular study these were needs that had only been determined from a list of things they'd liked on Facebook. Liking things on social media platforms might seem trivial to you and I, but it's vitally important to companies that want to build a big picture of who you are, what you're interested in and the kinds of ads you'll click on. Understanding this is key to working out how much we want to share online in future, and will hopefully give us all pause for thought next time we give something a virtual thumbs-up.

We consume such vast amounts of media each day we can't question the nature of every single ad or photo we see. I don't want you to sit with a checklist and analyse every puppy video or fact-check every news article your controversial aunt insists on sharing – that would be a full-time job and probably quite enraging. But, hopefully, this has planted a seed to be a little more critical in future.

FACING UP TO THE FUTURE

Next time you're in a big shopping centre or major airport, give the cameras a wave. They might be looking *very* closely at your face.

Facial recognition is a way to identify people from a photo, video clip or live footage of their face. It uses an algorithm (in most instances this will be a machine learning algorithm) created to pinpoint details, like the shape of their features or the distances between them. These details are then turned into a mathematical representation, which is run through a database to see if it matches up with any faces that are on file.

Facial recognition is used to verify your identity. For example, we use our faces to open up our phones – or at least we did before Covid-19 meant masks became the norm. This method can also give people access to personal data, private spaces or get them through airport security with less hassle. But it isn't perfect. Some researchers claim they've managed to fool the facial recognition system in iPhones by creating fake faces, although that's just one of many issues with facial recognition. One I think we all need to be wary about is how this same technology can be used to scan people's faces in public spaces.

Since the mid-2010s, some police forces in England and Wales have been using facial recognition to identify people of interest or people who have committed crimes. Imagine a camera scanning a large group of people then using a facial recognition algorithm to compare the faces it spots in the crowd with a database of records to see if anyone is on a watch list. This technology has been used at several events in England, like Notting Hill Carnival and Download Festival. It's also been rolled out to more and more public spaces over the past few years, including some London streets and shopping centres, with plans to continue.

The official goal of this technology is to identify suspects, prevent crime and keep everyone safe. In theory, that sounds good. In practice, things aren't so simple.

The first problem is reliability, because facial recognition systems can get things wrong.

A study from The National Institute of Standards and Technology in the US wanted to put a number of facial recognition systems to the test to find out if they are biased towards certain genders and races. Researchers were looking for evidence of a false positive. This is when the facial recognition software wrongly thinks two photos of different people are the same person. Or a false negative, which is when it doesn't match two images up that do show the same person.

The team used more than 18 million photos of more than 8 million people to test 189 facial recognition algorithms from 99 different developers. They found that many of the same algorithms used by the police had the highest error rates and false positives for Black women. They were also ten to 100 times more likely to generate false positives for Asian and Black faces than Caucasian faces.

This is deeply concerning. We already know that algorithms can be biased. But when it comes to policing, this bias takes on an even greater significance because it could lead to racial discrimination, false accusations and unlawful arrests.

Facial recognition trials have shown mistakes do happen – even when a real person is checking to make sure they don't. In one of the Metropolitan Police Service's trials of facial recognition in London between 2018 and 2019, 42 matches were found. Out of those 42, 16 were rejected by the real person who double-checked what the software flagged up. Four people were subsequently lost in the crowd. Fourteen of those people were wrongly stopped. Only eight were correctly stopped.

You might think that having a real person on hand to check the matches would ensure everything goes smoothly and there's no discrimination. But if that's the case, then why were 14 people wrongly stopped? To be clear, we don't know the exact circumstances of this particular trial. But based on what we do know about how humans respond to algorithms, something called automation bias could be to blame. This is when the person checking to see if the facial recognition algorithm is correct believes the algorithm over their own judgement.

In a *New York Times* interview about the issues with facial recognition, Timnit Gebru, a computer scientist and the technical co-lead of Google's Ethical Artificial Intelligence Team, says: 'If your intuition tells you that an image doesn't look like Smith, but the computer model tells you that it is him with 99 per cent accuracy, you're more likely to believe that model.'

If we imagine a future in which there are zero errors and no algorithmic bias (I want to stress we're nowhere near that future yet), there are still questions about where facial recognition should be used – and if it should be used at all.

The most obvious issue is the risk it poses to our individual privacy. Think about it. Your face could be scanned at any time when you enter any space without your consent – you might not even find out it's happening. What's more, you probably wouldn't get away with just covering your face up or avoiding the cameras, in case you were wondering. According to a report in the *Financial Times*, a man was warned there was a facial recognition trial in his area and, because he didn't want his face to be seen, he pulled his jumper up over it. Police insisted they scan his face. He wasn't a target, but because he was forced to have his face scanned, he swore at the police and he ended up being fined.

A common argument in favour of more facial recognition being used in public spaces is that if you're not doing anything wrong, then you've got no reason to worry, right? Maybe. But this argument is a little naive considering we don't know how facial recognition might be used in the future or which companies might have access to recordings of our faces. What's more, we don't know whether the steps we're taking now to allow this kind of tech into our lives and spaces might pave the way to much broader and more invasive forms of surveillance in the future.

While I was writing this chapter, a number of steps were being taken to slow down the use of facial recognition in some countries. For example, several cities in the US have introduced bans on facial recognition in certain spaces – proof that it is and should be possible to apply the brakes while companies address some of facial recognition's most significant issues.

You might think there's little we (as in, you and I) can do about this kind of surveillance tech. This isn't the same as a personal choice about whether to hand your holiday snaps over to Facebook or not. While it's true we might not be able to stop anyone from using facial recognition technology on our own, what we can do is push for rules from leaders and policymakers about how it should be used, demand more openness from the companies that make it, as well as the property owners, councils and police forces that use it.

My recommendation to you is to pay attention to stories in the news, take time to work out what your personal views are and ask yourself: is it worth risking our privacy and potential errors if it means reducing crime in the long run? There are plenty of serious questions we need to ask about this kind of tech, but no clear answers.

Your privacy and security shopping list
A VPN

Short for virtual private network (VPN). Think of a VPN as a secure 'tunnel'. Whenever you're using a public network, like Wi-Fi in a cafe, it creates a way for you to keep your information and what you're looking at private. If you didn't use one, someone else in the cafe with know-how could see what you're doing or access anything sensitive, like your passwords. In this way, it protects your security and it protects your data. But it also protects your privacy – it blocks websites, companies and internet service providers from tracking your information and browser history. What's essential is picking a good VPN that's trusted and has reliable reviews. That's because your VPN can see what you do in your secure VPN tunnel. You want to be able to trust the company that you grant access to your online activity, which is why I recommend paying for a VPN as some of the free options could sell your data as part of their business model. Remember: if you're not paying for the product, you are the product – this doesn't just apply to social media platforms.

Anti-virus software

People who create malware and viruses to hack your tech are always developing new ways to access devices and important information. Luckily, lots of anti-virus software companies update security regularly to protect against all kinds of threats, including phishing scams. Once you've downloaded anti-virus software, you can tweak the settings so it runs regular scans and you can specify the level at which it'll keep you protected. You want to find one with good reviews that you find easy to use, with lots of updates.

A password manager

As mentioned earlier, a good place to start would be using a free trial of a paid service and adding a few less important passwords to the manager to see if you like how it works and, crucially, to check whether you remember your master password. Then sign up to the full version.

WATCH OUT FOR THE PRIVACY PARADOX

A privacy paradox is when people know what they *should* be doing and say they care about their privacy. Maybe they have a password manager, they stay up to date on privacy news and are always on the lookout for scams. But then, in the next breath, they do something that could put their personal information at risk.

I came across a privacy paradox myself when I was writing this chapter in 2020. I saw a lot of people on Twitter who were troubled that they had to download apps designed to track where they went and whom they were in contact with to control

Covid-19. But many of these same people had already down-loaded apps a few weeks before that changed their faces to look young, old or swap genders – and tweeted the proof. These same apps (at least allegedly) had lax privacy controls. This suggests to me that people are less likely to check the privacy of apps they desperately want.

There's no judgement here. Just like privacy fatigue, the privacy paradox makes sense. Many of us can appreciate the importance of these concerns, but putting them into practice every day isn't always easy. It can be exhausting to question every decision, to read every privacy policy and to school every friend on why you don't want your location shared. That's why I'm not surprised privacy researchers identified that this gap between privacy attitudes and behaviours stretches back long before smart technology too. What I'm saying is: it's completely normal to be inconsistent.

GOOD PRIVACY PRACTICE IS LIKE GARDENING

To avoid the privacy paradox, it helps to think of shoring up your online life like gardening. You need to pay attention to it often; otherwise, it's going to grow into an unmanageable mess. Here are ways you can tend to your privacy like you're tending to a hedge:

Keep everything updated

Update apps, the software that runs your devices and any other services often. Privacy and security experts always recommend this as the first port of call for keeping yourself safe. That's because if a company is hacked, or has identified a vulnerability, it will often quickly take steps to address the problems and roll them out in the next update. You might think not updating your tech just makes you lazy, but it can also make you vulnerable.

Prune apps that can access your social media accounts

Many apps want to access your social media accounts – often for a good reason. For example, if I go into my Twitter settings right now, my Spotify account is linked to it. That's helpful because I often tweet about playlists. But there are plenty of other apps you might have linked to your social media accounts over the years that you probably no longer use. Clear these out. If they're exploited, they can grab information from your account or worse.

Keep an eye on privacy and security settings

Whether it's Instagram or your emails, regularly check your settings. Social media platforms often change these settings, add new ones or rename different features. You don't want to find out too late that you're leaking information.

Weed old accounts you won't use again

If you tried an app and didn't like it or bought a new fitness tracker so don't need the app for your old one any more, get rid of it. Don't just delete the app. Go into the settings and find the option to delete your account completely first. This way if that company ever runs into problems, you're minimising your chances of being affected.

Back things up

Make sure you regularly back up everything you care about. This includes photos that you'd be upset to lose or conversations on WhatsApp you always want to keep. You can use an external hard drive, which you plug into a laptop or computer via USB, or a cloud service, like Dropbox.

Feed your password manager

Whichever method you choose to ensure your passwords are protected, keep it up. It's easy to have one productive day that begins with a lot of coffee when you sort everything out. But then you might find you can't be bothered to do it again when you sign up to something new. Add new accounts to your password manager regularly.

Checklist

Privacy fatigue is normal. But we need to make an effort to wake up from it before something goes wrong. These issues are important, and I'd bet we could all benefit from finding more balance.

Use different passwords. If one company is hacked, your password could be exposed. Regularly check to see if your details are included in a breach. Use a password manager to generate unique passwords and keep track of them all.

Set up two-factor authentication. This gives you another layer of protection. Add it to any account that allows you to, including your bank, emails, Amazon, Twitter, etc.

Anyone can be affected by scams. Familiarise yourself with the telltale signs and never let someone who calls you, emails you or sends you a text whip you into a panic. Take a few deep breaths and then always call the official number yourself to find out what's going on.

There's a trade-off between the benefits of tech and the risks. This is something we have to accept right now. You can either opt out and choose not to buy new devices or sign up to new accounts. Or take small steps to protect against risks. Aim for a mixture of both weighing up the pros and cons each time.

Regularly check your privacy and security settings. Think of this like an ongoing process and a good habit; that way you're less likely to be caught out.

Consider investing in products to add to your security and protect your privacy. A VPN, anti-virus software and a password manager are all good places to begin. Although I recommend buying them rather than using free versions, I promise it's money well spent.

BODY IMAGE

GETTING ENVY, ENDLESS EDITING AND INFINITE SCROLLING UNDER CONTROL

Several years ago, I was following what you might call an excessive number of Instagram accounts whose posts were focused solely on fitness and dieting, under the broad umbrella of spreading #wellness.

At the time, I had a sneaking suspicion I'd become swept up in Instagram circles using hashtags like #cleaneating and #detox due to my own past issues with food. But I plastered over those concerns with selfies of me posing with eye-wateringly expensive juice brands and posting status updates about completing the latest gruelling fitness challenge devised by whichever Insta-influencer was hot that week.

The irony is that I was losing hours out of every day drifting through photos of food on my phone – flat lays of smoothie bowls, zero-sugar brownie trays, protein shake recipes – while eating very little actual food myself (unless you count the occasional keto energy ball or paleo snack bar masquerading as food).

I began not eating for long periods of time, and then only allowing myself so-called 'clean' foods and exercising incessantly to make up for it. All the while, I was spending hours and hours thinking about food. Individually, these things might not sound too unusual, but when you put them all together they're the tell-tale signs of a more serious problem. Instead of any crystal-clear moment of clarity, I experienced a gradual, painful and sometimes embarrassing series of moments that showed me that the way I was feeling about myself and my body was very much at odds with the fake-smiling Lycra-clad me all over my Instagram grid.

I don't blame Instagram or my phone for my getting stuck inside a 'clean-eating' bubble, because even though these technologies enabled me, they also helped me get better. After several lifestyle reboots, multiple food-related therapy sessions and stricter rules about what I allow myself to look at online, my Instagram feed has been repopulated with a range of account types completely unrelated to health, eating and 'perfect' bodies. It's now full of space photography, tech news, people getting their hair done (this is so soothing), brutalist architecture, comic book artists, photographers and some very good dogs.

What's more, the spot on my phone's home screen where the calorie-counting app I used to open 15–20 times a day is now taken up by an app which measures my moods. I used to depend on Facebook groups for dieting advice and clean eating recipes. Now I visit Facebook groups to lend support to other people struggling with food issues. I used to use photo-editing apps to artificially smooth my skin and brighten my eyes. Now I noodle about with sci-fi filters that make me look like a cool robot or an alien. In the past, fitness trackers gave me hyper-accurate ways to track the number of calories I'd burned. Now I use my Fitbit every so often to keep tabs on walks I've taken or weightlifting sessions but have no idea how many calories I've used up in the process, and I'm not interested in guessing.

The point here is that now tech isn't the decider of how I treat my body and what goes into it – I am. I used my digital devices in the past to fan the flames of the problems I had with eating, fitness and how I felt about my body. Now I use those same digital devices to pour cold water on them.

WHY BODY IMAGE MATTERS

Body image is 'a person's perceptions, thoughts and feelings about his or her body'. That means poor body image is when we feel unhappy with our bodies in some way. This can lead to body dissatisfaction, which is 'a person's negative thoughts and feelings about his or her body'.

Body dissatisfaction doesn't necessarily lead to more serious problems with eating or mental health. Sometimes it's normal to feel negative thoughts about your body and how you look from time to time, but it is a risk factor for other mental health problems, including depression and eating disorders.

Important: Here, we're looking at body image concerns in general rather than focusing on eating disorders. Visit the resources on page 335 for more information and support.

Our body image can be determined by a huge range of factors. A few of these factors include the relationship we have with friends and family, the way people around us talk about bodies and appearance, as well as idealised images in the media.

Links have been found between body dissatisfaction and the media people look at – whether that's magazines, newspapers, TV or movies – for decades. Every person has a different experience. But experts believe images we see in the media affect us because they so often show one thin (usually white, usually able-bodied) ideal of what a body should look like. This makes us, the viewers or readers, think this thin ideal = normal, expected and central to attractiveness.

What we see with the help of digital technologies might be no different. But the links between what you see online and how you feel about your body are hotly debated and widely researched right now for several reasons:

1. Numerous studies have been published over the past few years that point to a (possible) connection between time spent on social media and body image issues – we'll look at these in more depth next.
2. There are concerns that the popularity of social media might be directly related to a rise in cases of eating disorders.
3. Many of us have our own anecdotal evidence that spending time on social media seems to negatively affect how we feel about ourselves and our bodies sometimes.

However, just like the links between time spent on screens and mental health, we can't say with certainty these things are connected – or at least connected as neatly as saying: 'this leads to this'.

DOES OUR TECH HAVE THE POWER TO INFLUENCE OUR BODY IMAGE?

Let's investigate what researchers have discovered to date. Whenever a tech-related body image story makes the news, it's covered in a way that tends to be both general and exaggerated. Like, edited selfies are the source of body image stress. Or, Instagram causes body dissatisfaction. Or, maybe, influencers are at the root of disordered eating. But in reality, there's much more subtlety. We need to understand that or we could end up outlawing certain apps and social media accounts when the real problems remain overlooked.

Depending on which study you read, you'll find a different set of theories. I've selected what I believe the key concerns are below:

There might be a link between social media use and negative body image – but it's small

One 2019 study examined a considerable amount of research about tech and body image links to identify patterns. The researchers found that, on the whole, there was a significant lack of consensus. They concluded that, yes, there is a link between spending time on social media and experiencing body dissatisfaction (the researchers call this body image disturbance). But it's small. It's still significant, especially considering how much time many of us spend online, but not as shocking or surprising as previously thought.

It could be that the more you use your digital devices, the more likely you are to encounter body dissatisfaction issues

A study of teenage men and women in 2017 found that there was a correlation between the time they spent on social media platforms and the likelihood that they'd have self-esteem and body image issues afterwards – in some cases, symptoms of an eating disorder. But, as we've explored before in the Mental Health chapter this might be because people who already experience these problems end up spending more time online as a result.

One of the most significant indicators of body dissatisfaction is social comparison

The adverse effects of social comparison on body image come up again and again in the research. The main (but not so surprising) finding is that one of the key reasons people are impacted by what they see online is because they compare many aspects of their lives, including the way they look, to other people.

Editing photos of ourselves can make us feel more unhappy

Research suggests that the more time people spend manipulating their images (like editing small details, tweaking filter settings or putting on a 'beauty mode'), the greater body-related and eating concerns they reported after.

A focus on photos might spell trouble

One 2017 study of 259 women aged between 18 and 29 years old found that those who engaged with more pictures on Facebook and followed accounts focused on appearance on Instagram experienced more body dissatisfaction than those who didn't look at photos or followed more accounts the researchers deemed neutral and not related to appearance. Interestingly though, the same study found that if you *don't* use social media in these ways – maybe you read status updates more than look at photos or follow more landscape, nature, craft and pet accounts than ones about humans – then there's no connection between social media use and body image whatsoever. Another study pitted Facebook and Instagram against each other, finding those who looked at Instagram reported more photo-based comparison and decreased body satisfaction than the Facebook group.

It's easy to point to these possible connections, but not to find any definite answers. Instead, we can use these studies to inform how we each choose to engage with our favourite apps and the digital habits that might be putting us at risk.

Many experts make the point that experiencing some degree of body dissatisfaction after looking at photos of other people is nothing new – magazines and TV had the same effect, right? But I can't help but feel the odds aren't stacked in our favour when it comes to digital technologies.

Here are some of the things I've personally found make social media spaces more challenging to navigate than more traditional forms of media:

- You can access photos of other people whenever you like and wherever you are. Rather than dealing with difficult emotions healthily, you can instantly address them in a way that might not be good for you. For example, you might be in a really unhelpful habit loop that looks something like this: I don't feel good. I'll look at Instagram to make myself feel worse. I don't feel good again. This is an example of an unhealthy emotional regulation strategy. Head to page 54 for a more in-depth reminder about how this works. Or, check out the guide to changing your habits, which begins on page 42.

- Image editing has become so advanced you don't need any skill to make changes to your photos and so anyone can do it with an app.

- There are built-in, real-time ways to assess faces and bodies, thanks to an algorithm that favours popular content, as well as likes and comments. This means you're more likely to see the things other people have already passed judgement on – with lots and lots of likes implying what the ideal might be.

- We know algorithms 'decide' what to show you based on what's popular and what you might like. However, there's mounting evidence to suggest that Instagram's algorithm might favour images of slim, white and able-bodied people, while censoring others. To be clear, we don't know with certainty how the algorithm works and whether it's solely to blame for instances of censorship – user reporting and human judgement could be responsible too. But reports of bias are important to keep at the forefront of your mind. Social media platforms might give you access to different views of the world and different bodies *sometimes*, but they might also censor and control what we see (and therefore our view of the world and our place in it), at other times. For more on algorithms and their power to shape our views and opinions, visit the Identity chapter on page 303.

- You can follow someone without them following you back. We can follow strangers on many social media platforms, which might make us less likely to prioritise connection. We've already learned that by not putting connection at the front and centre of our experiences and being passive can lead to more comparison and dissatisfaction.

- There's a two-way element. You're not just consuming something from a magazine, but you're looking with a profile that has photos of you and information about you on it too. People might be looking at you at the same time as you're looking at them, or someone else. This might mean you have more opportunity to make comparisons between how you look and how someone else does.

Technology might be a breeding ground for body dissatisfaction **by its very design**. Although we can't change how these social media platforms work, we can reduce the adverse effects now we know what to look out for.

LOOKING AT OTHER PEOPLE

None of us are immune to social comparison. It serves a function: we look at the lives of others to evaluate our place in the world. It's a natural part of using social media and, therefore, one of the reasons we're drawn to it.

Although we explored the effect social comparison has on our emotions in the Mental Health chapter, it's relevant here too. Several studies have linked our tendency to compare ourselves to others online with body dissatisfaction. This can happen on many different sites and social media platforms. But research suggests Instagram might lead to the most appearance-based comparison and, in the process, lower body satisfaction.

I think there are a few key features that set Instagram apart from the rest. One is the sheer volume of images that we see on Instagram. More than 100 million images are uploaded to the platform every day, and although they're not all of people's bodies – and you'll only see a tiny proportion of them – it's true that we're exposed to a vast amount of pictures of other people.

I checked, and I can comfortably look at just under 20 photos in a minute (that's taking the time to stop and read the captions and hit 'like' on most of them as well). Sure, you might not be able to keep up that pace, but the point is that if you spend 20, 30, 40 minutes on Instagram each time, you might be exposed to thousands of photos every day. That's a lot of opportunity for comparison.

Another reason why Instagram could be a hotbed for comparison is that many people (typically, but not always) use it to show the more positive aspects of their lives. Photos tend to be carefully curated, filtered, often staged and sometimes heavily edited. Social comparison might be a part of everyday life, but Instagram has never been a reflection of the ordinary.

What's more, the mechanics of Instagram might play a part in fuelling comparison as well. One study suggested that most of the comparison that takes place on social media is upwards comparison. This is when you compare yourself to people who seem to have more desirable qualities than you or whom you perceive to be more physically attractive than you. Upwards comparison has been linked to low mood and body dissatisfaction.

Researchers proposed that people might compare themselves upwards rather than downwards on Instagram because they can see the likes and positive comments from other users so easily. They suggest that this might reinforce how attractive and great someone seems – a recipe for hateful and harmful upward comparison.

Important: Studies show we all feel the effects of social comparison from time to time, but interestingly, we don't all feel social comparison when we log on to social media. One 2018 study found that some people felt happier when they saw positive posts on Instagram – the same ones that made others feel worse.

It isn't always easy to identify when you're comparing yourself to someone else. But don't be dissuaded from making changes to how you use Instagram, because this is important. We know social media platforms are designed to keep us coming back for more. We also know comparison is something many of us engage in and, sometimes, actively seek out. That means we must take steps ourselves to stop following people or engaging in comparison when we know it doesn't make us feel good – because Instagram isn't going to do it for us. Its priorities lie in keeping us looking.

We need to pay close attention to how we feel when we're on social media platforms, as well as any lasting feelings that stick around long after we've put down our phones. Here are some steps to better pinpoint the problem.

Identify your triggers

Pay close attention to who or what brings about feelings of envy and comparison. Is one person your trigger? Or maybe one type of image? You can mute words, block accounts and unfollow people to manage what you see.

Interrupt the comparing and despairing

When you notice you're weighing your body, life and whole identity up against someone else's, it's normal to feel shameful or embarrassed. But this is a perfect storm for sadness, low self-esteem and a shaken body image. Instead, realise that no, it might not be the best use of your time. But accept you've noticed your thinking pattern and move on – maybe mute or unfollow before you do.

Avoid knee-jerk reactions

I've read a lot of advice about dealing with comparison, and some people suggest you can assess the comparison and use it to achieve more yourself. Maybe you see someone doing perfect squats on Instagram – does that mean you should get to a squat rack, stat? I'm not so sure.

Comparison in some areas of our lives, like maybe professional achievements, could spur us on to achieve more. But when it comes to health, fitness and body image I don't think trying to improve ourselves off the back of comparison is good for us. Watch out for knee-jerk decisions that you think you're making for yourself that are, instead, fuelled by comparison. Some bad decisions I've made in the past after comparing myself to someone else include: buying loads of new skincare, spending money on weight loss products and signing up to a pricey online fitness program.

Get grateful

Interrupt comparison by doing the absolute opposite: focusing on how great *you* are. List your strengths, as well as what you're thankful for. When you're in a comparison spiral, it's like you're blinkered. You can see what everyone else has – or what one person has if you're fixating on someone in particular – and you ignore what else is going on with you in your own life.

You could create a compliments or strengths jar. Every time someone says something nice to you or something good happens, put a little note in the jar. Then, when you need cheering up, reach in and grab one out. Think the jar idea sounds too twee? Write them in a note-taking app on your phone instead.

UNDER THE INFLUENCE

An influencer is a broad term that means a lot of different things these days. A *Wired* guide to influencers explained that 'it is simultaneously an insult and an aspiration'. This likely sums up how many of us feel about influencers. At the same time, some of our favourite people to follow online are influencers and yet influencer culture might be what we like least about social media these days.

Put simply, an influencer is someone 'with the power to affect the buying habits or quantifiable actions of others by uploading some form of original – often sponsored – content to social media platforms'. Influencers tend to have a lot of followers or subscribers (whether we're talking about Instagram, Twitter, YouTube or any other social network). Some style their clothes, take photos of themselves and work with brands to post ads. Others might be considered influencers and are also models, make-up artists, bloggers, video editors and designers, which means they also post ads but maybe not as often. It might seem completely new, but being an influencer is a similar kind of role to a celebrity who has a string of endorsements. Or just the most popular person you know dictating what's hot and what's not. Whenever I think of how to sum up what an influencer does succinctly, I think of the scene in *Mean Girls* in which one of the high school students sincerely says to the camera: 'I saw Cady Heron wearing army pants and flip-flops, so I bought army pants and flip-flops.'

The main difference between a celeb endorsement and what influencers do is that the latter can have some say over the ads and sponsored content they create. Sure, they need to get paid by brands, but they also need to consider their followers and don't want to bombard them with advertisements that seem fake on their social media accounts.

Or at least most don't. Some influencers exploit people, push products followers don't need in a way that feels shady and come across as dishonest. But these are the people who give influencers a bad name – and the reason many people and media outlets tend to be hyper-critical of them. However, plenty of other influencers have buckets of integrity, use their large followings as a force for good, create great content and are super-talented in their own right. It's a mixed bag, which makes it hard to know whom to follow and when to stop.

There are a few reasons why I think it's essential we take a look at the relationship between influencers and body image.

Weight loss products

There's been some controversy about the number of influencers who make a living by selling products that promote dieting or an unhealthy focus on weight and exercise – like 'detox tea', which contains laxatives, or appetite suppressant lollipops.

Many of these products have little to no scientific backing; influencers often claim to use these products themselves and push them on to a young audience. You could argue that this is no different to similar products being sold in regular ads and that individuals should have the freedom to buy what they like. However, there's less regulation to call bullsh*t on them or repercussions for promoting products that might be dangerous.

Heavily edited images

There's evidence to suggest that exposure to heavily edited photos, in this case selfies that had been retouched and reshaped, can directly lead to lower body satisfaction in teen girls. Not all influencers post heavily edited photos, but cultivating a perfect, aspirational wardrobe, house, lifestyle, face and body is common.

Tip: Seek out influencers who make a point of *not* heavily editing their pictures. I enjoy following a handful of beauty influencers for their expert make-up advice and tutorials, as well as the fact they don't use filters or lots of image manipulation. One of my current favourites is make-up artist Katie Jane Hughes (@katiejanehughes on Instagram).

A seemingly perfect life

Deals with brands, perfect-looking images and houses that look like they're straight out of a glossy interiors magazine. If we're trying to avoid following accounts that might trigger comparison, influencers that show only highly aspirational content present a problem.

Again, I want to stress that this might only apply to a small handful of influencers – many are good at what they do and share an authentic look at their lives. But given the nature of Instagram these days, it pays for us to take steps to make sure we're not being duped and our body image isn't being eroded by comparison without us being fully aware of how we're feeling.

BE CRITICAL ABOUT WHAT YOU SEE

Research shows that if you don't think critically about the content you're looking at – especially commercially created content, so that's the kind of content influencers create to sell you things – then you might be at risk of experiencing body dissatisfaction.

Getting critical about the ads and sponsored posts you see, what their purpose is and what you're being sold is all part of something called social media literacy. Not only is looking at what you see online through a critical lens important for your body image, but it might also be necessary for the health of your bank balance.

Ask yourself these questions:

- What am I being sold?
- Do I have evidence this product/service is good?
- Does it look like this influencer has tried it themselves?
- Can I seek out more reviews to check some of the claims that are being made?

I'm not imposing a buying ban, but being critical about what you see and, therefore, more deliberate about what you buy, will make you feel happier, and not to mention more in control in the long run.

Question what's in it for you

There's nothing wrong with following lots of influencers because you want to. But if you're feeling the sting of comparison every time you touch your phone, it might be worth considering whether who you follow is to blame.

Some questions I ask myself when I'm unsure about whether I need to keep an influencer in my life and my feed are: Do they put up images I enjoy looking at? Do they give me tips about things that are helpful? Do they work with brands I'm interested in? These are only three starter questions, but they're essential.

If all you're feeding is your curiosity, following them feels habitual and looking at their photos makes you feel less than happy, you might need to reassess.

Important: If you're 'hate-following' an influencer, please do yourself (and them) a favour and unfollow. It's keeping you stuck, angry and fuelling hate and irritation every time you log on. You might think this is keeping you one step ahead of them, but you're only hurting yourself. This is the sign you've been waiting for to stop the hate-following and find some peace.

I think we could all do with being more critical about which influencers we follow, what messages they're putting across and how they're making us feel about our bodies and our lives.

HOW TO UNFOLLOW

We know that looking at an endless stream of images can fuel comparison. But this doesn't just happen to us. We can exercise control over whom we follow and what we see – so why don't we?

While I was researching this book, I came across other books, some blog posts and various news articles that gave some version of this advice: 'unfollow accounts that don't make you feel good!!'

It was the advice that accompanied most of the studies and research that I've cited in this chapter too, with various researchers and psychologists recommending we unfollow, mute and block others more regularly. But we all know it's not always that simple. Here's why:

We can't always tell what's good for us

I don't believe that any of us are intentionally trying to sow the seeds of body image dissatisfaction by who we follow. But, sometimes without us even realising it, that's the effect that following certain accounts has on us.

In the past, I've convinced myself that following fitness influencers would be suitable for motivation and workout tips. But I now know that this can lead to unnecessary body image stress when I should be filling my feeds with even more space news and puppies. Let's take the example of 'fitspiration' images. This has become a hugely popular way to share fitness-related posts and pictures, often with the hashtag #fitspiration or #fitspo. But it tends to be focused more on outcomes, gains and slimness than having fun while swimming or enjoying a run – the only kind of movement I'm interested in these days.

Although the goal of these images might genuinely be to inspire a healthy and active lifestyle (or at least that's what the people who post them say), they might have unintended negative consequences. Seeing images of bodies and fitness can make people feel unhappy about their bodies – regardless of their intentions.

What I'm saying is, it isn't easy to separate what we should be following from what we shouldn't – if it was, you probably wouldn't be reading this.

Remember: The people who engineer our social media platforms are switched on to what gets us checking, coming back for more and spending hours scrolling – including social comparison and FOMO. This doesn't mean to say we can't control our actions ourselves, but it's important to remember why doing something that causes us misery can, at the same time, feel impossibly enticing. It's not your fault, but you can do something about it.

Who we follow says a lot about who we are

I remember when I decided to unfollow most of the accounts I used to love (or think I loved) that were centred on fitness. As I unfollowed one after another, I started to question whether this was a good idea – I enjoyed fitness, and it felt like I was 'unfollowing' a part of myself.

I've heard this same worry from other people. They get concerned that unfollowing someone in their professional circle or an influencer their friends all admire might put them on the outside of their friendship group or affect what people think of them if they're not clued up on any new gossip – this is when muting and checking on your own terms can be a great option.

This is normal. Anyone who thinks a social media platform is trivial or unimportant for connecting with others hasn't spent any time on one. But it also means it's difficult to unpick who we are from our social media platforms – and vice versa.

Now we're clear about some of the problems we're up against, let's consider how we might make things better by (slowly and selectively) unfollowing. This is a simple invitation to get curious and begin to ask: is this person worth my time, my effort and, potentially, feeling bad about myself for?

If that question still feels tricky, don't worry. Let's break this down into five chunks that will shed more light on when to hit unfollow:

- **Does this account, person or brand make me feel bad?** Let's begin by weeding out the accounts you should have unfollowed a long time ago but haven't for whatever reason. Maybe it's someone you know through a friend, and you don't want to offend them. Or it could be a foodie account that you thought would serve as inspiration but is making you think about food every single time you log on. This is your permission to do something about it. You don't owe anyone a follow – and, if you can't decide, mute in the meantime. They will never know you've done it, and you won't have the added anxiety of an unfollow.
- **Does your behaviour feel unhealthy after looking at them?** Even if someone doesn't make you feel bad, their photos or captions might affect your behaviour.

Here's what I mean: I once spent time scrolling through a fitness influencer's Instagram account. I found some great kettlebell workouts – yay! – but also felt a strong urge to go to the gym afterwards, and ended up actually cancelling plans to go out. You might think that's a positive. I was motivated to work out, and I did, right? But if I'm honest about it, the decision to go to the gym wasn't about positive steps. It was fuelled by envy at how much better she looked than I did and fear that I should be doing kettlebell swings 24/7 from now on. It made me lose valuable time with a friend when I could have gone to the gym later that day as I'd planned.

This is an example of my behaviour being directly, and negatively, affected by something I'd seen on Instagram. So although it wasn't apparent to me that this influencer made me feel bad, paying attention to the feelings after made it clear. It was time to unfollow.

- **Have I learned something or taken away something good or positive?** No one has enough time. We love to talk about how busy we are. This is why I think that, unless you're getting something positive or worthwhile from whom you follow, they're just not worth your precious time.

Even if an account isn't making you feel bad now or even later, if it's not teaching you something, making you feel happy, relaxed, cheerful or just thoughtful about a big issue, then it's not worth it. Your feed doesn't need to be filled with puppies or flowers (although I bet that would make you feel exceptionally chill). But you need to get some small reward. If you don't, you know what the answer is: unfollow.

- **Do you know the person?** During my research for this chapter, I found it interesting (but not wholly surprising) to learn that one study suggested we might feel worse when we look at celebrities and distant peers compared to friends and family.

That means if you're following people on the periphery of your friendship circle, who you met years ago or just vaguely know, it might be best to admit they shouldn't be there.

Celebrities are tricky because they can be positive forces, teach us things and, if they're people we admire, just make us feel good. But I have unfollowed many over the years. After all, it's their job to look as prosperous and happy as possible. Some are great at showing us more authentic sides of their A-list lives, but many are all toned bodies, beautiful faces and super-fancy holidays. Also known as comparison fuel.

- **Do they talk a lot about weight loss?** This is a huge deal-breaker for me; even if it's an account that's about healthy weight loss or weight loss and fitness.

Anything to do with losing weight, posting about goal weights or before and after photos gets an immediate unfollow from me. If you follow people who only occasionally talk about weight loss, maybe you don't want to be quite so drastic. How about instead set a 'three strikes and they're out' policy? Three posts about weight loss or anything that makes you feel icky (it might be super-tricky yoga poses you know you'll never get into) and they're gone.

You might think these questions are too strict or prioritise the wrong things for you, in which case borrow bits of them or make your own. There's no one right way to do this. The point is to create a few guidelines in your head about what you do and don't want to see whenever you pick up your phone. Applying these questions now and again to accounts I feel iffy about has been extremely helpful for me. And I think it could make a massive difference to you in your quest for more balance too.

OUT WITH THE OLD, IN WITH THE NEW

Whenever I begin to change my behaviour, Indiana Jones swings into my mind. In the *Raiders of the Lost Ark* movie, Indiana Jones, an archaeologist, explorer and adventurer played by Harrison Ford, is faced with a critically important task. He enters an ancient chamber to retrieve the Golden Idol, a shining, priceless artefact about as big as his hand. It's right there in front of him, and all he needs to do is take it. But he (rightly) suspects that the treasure is on a weighted plinth. That means if he removes it, a trap will appear. A spike might fall from the sky; lava might fill the room, snakes might be set loose. The answer? He must replace the shining object with something of equal weight, in this case, a bag of sand. Which, spoiler alert, he almost manages.

The reason this scene resonates with me is because I've learned over the years that if I stop doing something, I need to find something else to take its place. This is the same thinking that underpins the process of rewiring our habit loops when we learned about the importance of The Golden Rule on page 42.

So if we're unfollowing people and accounts that we've decided *are not* good for us, we need to replace them with others that *are*.

How do we find what to follow instead? What should we replace our Golden Idols with? Consider this an opportunity to fill your social media feeds with inspiring, creative, fun, relaxing and genuine posts for a change.

After unfollowing a lot of accounts, I found myself worrying about what I like and what interests me. At first, I felt like a giant empty shell. But it turns out there are loads of things I love that I could intentionally seek out and look at regularly – all kinds of things that could lend themselves to a platform all about images.

You could look at art and architecture, feed your crafty hobbies or follow accounts about forest walks and seaside adventures. I also highly recommend you fill your feed with a diverse range of bodies, races and voices to better reflect your offline world. It's up to you. But the more variety, insights, fun, authenticity and less of a focus on things that might negatively affect your body image and your mood, the better.

Important: The good news about taking these steps now is that Instagram may actually 'learn' what you prefer to look at and could give your feed and 'discover' page a makeover in the process. That's because the algorithm that 'decides' what to show you when you open up Instagram will serve you more of the same content you've interacted with in the past. It can take a while to change, but means unfollowing, muting (and even blocking, if you're brave) accounts will stop you from seeing the things you don't want to see, like diet ads, and more of what you do want to see. For more on how this works, check out the Identity chapter.

EDITING OUR SELFIES OR EDITING OURSELVES?

I'm not going to present a case for or against selfies here. They're one of the many things on the bingo card of tech-related activities that are often misunderstood. What's more, research is conflicting. Some studies suggest selfies are a desperate plea for validation and the hallmark of sadness; others indicate they might be a sign of confidence and a channel for creative expression. I think we can safely say: selfies can mean different things to different people.

Instead, let's examine why we edit them and what tweaking photos of our faces says about what we think of ourselves – if anything.

Have you ever wondered what you'll look like in 50 years? Or if you'd prefer your face with a Hollywood-approved makeover, glowing white, perfectly straight teeth and baby-smooth skin? Luckily (or, not so luckily, depending on how you see it), there are hundreds of apps you can run your selfies through that promise to transform your face in a multitude of ways within minutes.

Last year I uploaded a selfie (okay, 12) to one of these apps, and I was presented with results that gave me a glimpse into alternate realities. Me as a man. Me as an 80-year-old, me as a considerably more attractive version of myself, me as some kind of doll-like child?

You've probably seen (and, likely, tried) a similar app yourself. There are a few that offer up the same options, and every couple of months they reappear with an even more believable take on what we'd all look like as pensioners. These apps are catnip for those of us who spend a lot of time online. Last time one of these apps was rereleased with promises of a smarter, better set of face-changing tools, my Twitter feed was full of gender-switched and octogenarian-ified selfies.

I'm never sure how I feel about seeing these different versions of myself. I think the whole thing is ridiculous, probably a ploy to get me to hand over my face to feed a machine learning algorithm somewhere, a colossal waste of time, a bit of fun and a source of creeping insecurity, all at once.

A small sample of the questions that ran through my head after seeing the results included: will I have that many wrinkles as I age? Should I be more aggressive about my skincare regimen now? And the indignant: why don't I look more like the hot version of me?

This was just one app. We all know there are many, many more that you can download right now. Similar ones are designed to show you what you might look like in the future. Others are created for precise editing, which includes a whole toolbox of features, from smoothing your skin to lengthening your legs, as well as lots of real-time filters on Snapchat or Instagram, which add dog ears, heart eyes, blurred-out skin, puffy filler-enhanced lips and so much more to your face. You don't need to work at a magazine and have a design qualification to change the way you look any more – you just need a smartphone, a selfie and a few spare minutes.

What's more, everyone else has access to these same kinds of quick-sharing, skin-smoothing, face-changing apps too. So you might be looking at other people's edited faces and bodies all day long without knowing what that's doing to your own body image – especially if you spend a lot of time on apps that are all about the images, like Instagram.

It's hard to know unless you quiz everyone you follow or keep a tally of the people who like to use the blurry, cute, heart-eye filter. But I'd bet most image editing isn't the drastic kind. Not the photos of us as great-grandparents and different genders. Not the dramatically edited photos celebs are always accused of upload-ing to Instagram in which their body parts are pushed smaller or pulled bigger. I think for the vast majority of us editing – if we do it at all – is to add a flattering filter, so our faces look a little less red, whiten our teeth or blur out a spot. We might all find overly edited images shocking and deceptive. But is there anything wrong with a little light editing?

I thought I was in the 'of course not!' camp, but after feeling a whole messy soup of feelings about the results from the face-changing app, I'm not so sure.

As you might expect, research about what editing our faces and seeing the edited images of others does to our body image and self-esteem doesn't reveal anything conclusive, but it does suggest excessive editing could be harmful to some of us. One 2015 study found that participants who engage more in manipulating their photos (editing them, adding filters to them) were more likely to experience greater body-related and eating concerns.

What's more, there's evidence that those of us who regularly edit our photos are feeling envious. But not towards other people, towards the edited versions of ourselves.

I tried an Instagram plastic surgery filter in the name of research for this chapter that made me look ridiculous. I hated it. But I also couldn't help but wonder if other people might think those hyper -inflated lips, sharp, defined cheekbones and eerie, blurred-out skin combine to create a Franken-face that's better than my real one? It's no wonder that Instagram banned some of the filters explicitly associated with cosmetic surgery. It's been suggested that this weird brand of envy we might feel towards our filtered selves might lead to us pursuing surgery in real life. It's hard to know how pervasive this problem is. Still, some plastic surgeons claim that people are entering their offices and asking to look not only more like their favourite Instagram stars, but their favourite Instagram filters.

I know that there's a strange disconnect between the me I see on the screen that's edited and me in real life. Fascinatingly, one of the reasons for this uncanny 'it's me but not me' feeling might be less to do with editing and more about your phone's camera. The short distance from the camera lens to your face when you hold it up to take a selfie can cause it to look distorted, which tends to make your nose look a little bigger and your ears look smaller. Most of the time this is barely noticeable but it could explain why you sometimes feel like you look different compared to your selfies when you look in the mirror or have a photo taken from more of a distance, but can't quite put your finger on the reason why.

I think the idea we would see an image of ourselves and immediately consider surgery might be overblown. But we also need to pause and think about whether our digital technologies are fuelling dissatisfaction we wouldn't have been switched on to otherwise. After all, how would you know you wanted a smooth, filtered, highly edited face unless you'd seen a glimpse into what that would look like over and over and over?

The obvious answer here is to take fewer photos of yourself or more that are unedited, unfiltered and possibly (if someone will help you out or you use the timer feature) further away. But that's easier said than done if editing has become second nature.

Remember: Be wary of what you read in news articles about selfies, editing and plastic surgery – especially those that sound sensational. Sometimes they will be highlighting a genuine concern and include research from a psychologist or scientist. Other times a photo editing app or a plastic surgeon might have come up with a story (or the quotes and stats within it) which the paper or website has decided to write up.

This means there might not be a new trend or a worrying rise in plastic surgery that's influenced by apps – but the headline makes it seem like there is. Get critical about what a news story is telling you. If the only person with a voice in the article is a plastic surgeon saying, 'Everyone wants plastic surgery because of Instagram!!', question why. To make people think they want it too? To get their name in the paper? This isn't an attack on plastic surgeons, it's just a made-up example to show you what to look out for. This can warp our perception more than an editing app could.

Cutting down on editing

It can be challenging to stop editing your photos if it's become the norm for you. As ever, start slowly and wean yourself off rather than imposing a ban. One 2018 study about selfies found that participants who weren't able to retouch or retake their selfies felt anxious and less physically attractive afterwards. By just saying, 'Don't edit again, ever,' we could be making ourselves, and others, feel more stress. Instead, normalising your unedited face might take time – don't be concerned if you don't instantly adjust.

I've never heavily relied on photo editing apps. But I did go through a stage of getting used to seeing my skin with a filter on it, so my cheeks were blurred and glowy, as well as settings that made the whites of my eyes a little brighter, so I looked healthier and well rested. I've gradually stopped using filters and editing my photos altogether, but it's taken a long time to be okay with a non-edited version of myself. I didn't expect to be suddenly delighted with my natural face overnight, but normalising completely ordinary things, like pores, has taken considerably more time than I'd have ever imagined it would.

We all need to move at our own pace here, so do what you can:

- Can you carry on as usual but take an unedited photo of yourself and look at it now and again? (You don't even need to share it with anyone, just get more used to unedited you.)
- Can you cut down to editing your photos just three times on each photo?
- Can you go for a week without editing?
- Can you go without editing from now on?

Getting real about your intentions

Like a lot of the topics we've examined in this book, a big part of how you feel might be dictated by your intentions for editing your photo, for sharing your selfie, for following people on social media.

So if you intend to make a couple of deliberate changes when you're editing a picture of yourself, I don't think you have anything to worry about, especially if editing your photos is a source of fun and creativity for you. Of course, it's impossible to interrogate your intentions constantly, but I think it's good to acknowledge the way filters, editing, heavy make-up, all these things we see as 'bad' for body image can be reframed as positive if they allow us to be more creative.

For example, 3D make-up creator Ines Alpha creates AR filters to allow people to play with different versions of beauty. She makes filters full of colour, light and abstract paintings – worlds away from the smooth skin, big sexy baby eyes and large lips that feature in plastic surgery-inspired and beautifying filters.

'I hope that my work helps people have a more open-minded attitude,' she tells *Wired*. 'You can experiment with filters and even if people think you look weird, you are expressing yourself. It's so important for people to feel like they can be different.'

I've started to seek out filters that are more in line with Alpha's views. Those that allow me to play with the way my face looks, but turn it into a shiny robot or colourful masterpiece rather than a smoothed and filtered face.

THE TRUTH ABOUT TRACKING

We have always tracked things. In official records, diaries and scribbled-on scraps of paper. Who owes us money, when our period is due, where we travel. Our devices make keeping tabs on these things even easier and give us tools to track more effectively. GPS creates maps of the places you visit. Food databases keep a detailed diary of what you eat and when. Algorithms to predict when your next period might be due based on information about you – and information from other people who use the app too.

There are many apps and devices engineered solely to help you track your life – especially with a health and fitness focus. A Fitbit to keep tabs on how many steps you take. A running watch from Garmin to clock up the time you spend pounding the pavement. A calorie-counting app to track the nutritional value of what you eat. It is nothing short of amazing to me that we can track so much about ourselves – and that this technology is advancing all the time.

For example, as I'm writing this chapter, Apple unveiled its newest smartwatch: the Apple Watch 6. This device can measure your sleep, detect when you're washing your hands, track your workouts (and the type of exercise you're doing), measure the oxygen saturation in your blood, follow the steps you take and elevation levels you scale, track how many calories you burn, measure your heart rate and much more.

Tracking these things gives those interested in fitness more accurate measurement tools. It provides people with health issues with options to take monitoring into their own hands. It's also a dream come true for gadget lovers who are curious to find out more about their health and their bodies.

However, the wealth of data our tracking devices and apps present us with at the push of a button (often, you don't even have to push a button, the screen comes on with the flick of your wrist) can feel overwhelming. This might lead to a not so healthy preoccupation with numbers, stats and optimisation. For me, that meant an obsession with hitting specific goals each day and a feeling of panic if I stopped tracking. For others, this can mean a constant pressure that they have to be always improving and optimising or they've failed. I think it's essential to take a closer look at how this kind of tech-enabled tracking could fuel body dissatisfaction.

Research about the effects that tracking tech can have on our body image is scarce. But a growing pile of evidence suggests I'm not alone in finding that tracking could lead to or exacerbate an unhealthy preoccupation with food, fitness and weight.

One 2018 study found that participants who reported using monitoring tools exercised more compulsively and had more problems with dietary restraint, concerns about weight and shape, exercising for weight control and purging behaviours – which in this case meant exercising to work off calories – than those who didn't.

Interestingly, the study also gives us some insight into how the intentions behind using apps and trackers play a role in how they make us feel. Those who were found to have higher levels of food and exercise-related concerns and behaviours were the ones who used apps and trackers to control their weight and shape – in comparison to those who used them for more general health reasons.

These findings don't necessarily mean apps and trackers designed to track calories, exercise or anything else to do with your health cause or trigger problems. Instead, people who already have issues with disordered eating or over-exercise tendencies might be more drawn to tracking what they do. This is the same as people who spend a lot of time online and tend to report more symptoms of depression and low self-esteem [page in mental health]. Did the tech they use *cause* these issues, or do they use tech more *because* of these issues? These are essential questions but, as of yet, we don't have any definitive answers.

It's the same story if we look at research that focuses on calorie-counting apps. One 2017 study put MyFitnessPal under the spotlight – an app with a huge food database that allows you to record everything you eat each day, giving you a breakdown of your calorie and nutrient intake. You can set up goals to help you hit a certain amount of nutrients or food groups or calories each day.

The participants who took part in the study had recently been discharged from an eating disorder clinic. Seventy-five per cent of them reported having used MyFitnessPal in the past. Seventy-three per cent of those said that they believe the app had 'at least some-what' contributed to their eating disorder. Thirty per cent said that it had 'very much' contributed to their eating disorder.

This was a study that relied heavily on the participants retro-spectively assessing their relationship with MyFitnessPal, which means we can afford to be cynical about the results. But other studies point to similar findings, as well as anecdotal evidence that it's easy to look for with a quick search online.

The lesson here isn't that using tech to track your runs, your heart rate, your food intake or even your weight is necessarily going to harm you. But that we are all different, and our rela-tionship with our bodies, our minds and our tech is complicated.

Before you begin tracking by using an app or fitness tracker, ask yourself these questions:

What's your reason?

The 2018 study about fitness tracking found those who were motivated to change their weight and shape were more likely to experience problems when they began tracking. Instead, goals should be health-focused, not weight-focused. Now, if I wear a fitness tracking device, I make sure any goals I set are about long-term happiness and health: not reaching a certain number on the scales.

Do you have a history of worrying about food and weight?

Tracking tools might exacerbate problems that you've had in the past, putting goals and numbers at the forefront of your mind. If you still want to try something, find a device that doesn't focus on weight and calories or one with settings that can be customised. For example, most Fitbit devices do track the calories you've burned, but you can customise the app's home screen so you don't see that information by default.

How do you want to use it?

A device you strap on for a purpose, whether that's to keep tabs on your sleep or track your runs, is much better than wearing one 24/7 or tracking every single bite of food you eat with an app. I've found wearing my favourite fitness tracker for a few days then intentionally leaving it off has been helpful. One of the ways I've changed my relationship with wearable devices has been by allowing myself to, ironically, not wear them all the time. Instead, there are days when I'm interested in what my fitness tracker can tell me and days when I'm not. I'm aware this goes against a lot of the marketing messages you'll find are used to sell these devices, which are often focused on always-on, all-the-time capabilities.

Remember: For every person who finds health-focused tech can exacerbate disordered eating behaviours, another might use the same app or device to set and healthily reach goals with no problems. A lot of research about behavioural change does suggest that monitoring what you do can be an effective way to make lasting changes. There's no right or wrong here. Instead, tracking everything is the right option for some of us – not all of us.

Checklist

Spending time on social media might impact how you feel about your body. Some people could experience significant body dissatisfaction after spending time on image-focused social media platforms, like Instagram. Others might not be affected at all. Experts believe this depends on your history, who you follow and how you use your favourite apps and social media platforms.

Comparing yourself to others can make you feel worse. Social comparison is both normal and why some of us feel sad, inadequate and envious when we spend time looking at images of other people. *Notice* when these feelings are triggered and take action – mute, unfollow or focus on what you're grateful for instead.

Assess the influencers you follow. Who makes you feel good, recommends products that you like and has an outlook that gels with yours? Unfollow anyone who doesn't tick the boxes for you. Remember: no matter how popular they are or how invested you feel in their lives, **you don't owe them your time and energy.**

Fill your feed with things that make you happy. Whether you want to feel creatively inspired, calm or energised, fill your social media feeds however you like. Space photography, hair, dogs: this is what I'm focusing on right now. Find what makes you feel good and unfollow anything that doesn't. Be strict about what you let into your life.

Cut down on selfie editing. Not all selfies are bad (far from it). Editing isn't terrible either. But there is evidence that a link exists between how much we edit our photos and how we feel. Experiment with what makes *you* feel good. Can you take pictures and edit them in a way that's fun, creative and not tied to a specific beauty ideal? Or give up on editing altogether? Or set yourself a three edits max rule?

Avoid tracking apps or wearables if you've had issues with eating in the past. Continually monitoring what you're eating, how you're moving and how many calories you've burned off might lead to problems with disordered eating and over-exercise. If you have any doubts, pass.

Important: If you want to find out more about where you can get help and support for disordered eating and body image issues, head to the resources on page 335.

RESPONSIBILITY

HOW SMALL TECH CHOICES CAN MAKE BIG DIFFERENCES

I have a robot vacuum cleaner. I call it HAL after the computer that tries to kill everyone in Stanley Kubrick's *2001: A Space Odyssey*. Except my robovac doesn't talk and hasn't (yet) tried to flush anyone out of an airlock. Instead, my HAL goes whizzing about the floor on little wheels, sucking up all the dust and dirt and crumbs on its scheduled daily clean before returning to its charging station. Before I bought it, I checked the reviews – all four or five stars. I made sure spare parts are available to buy – so I'm not lumbered with a whizz-less robot. Also, it was in a sale.

I bought it because I wanted something to help keep my flat clean, but I'm under no illusions about whether I actually *need* a robovac. My partner and I are both able-bodied, we own a regular vacuum cleaner and we live in a small flat which we could (and do) clean ourselves without any assistance. Like many of the devices we all buy, my little HAL is a convenience, not a necessity. It's healthy to question our tech-buying choices often and ask ourselves whether we really *need* another new device in our homes. Because new tech purchases can have an effect that goes further than our wallets.

Let's consider your smartphone for a moment. Many of the materials used to make it are mined from deep inside the earth, and workers might be putting their lives at risk right now to retrieve more of them. What's more, the rate we're all encouraged to upgrade our phones means we're adding to an already enormous amount of electronic waste (e-waste).

Now, the next device decision we make isn't going to solve these issues overnight. But this chapter is going to look at practical and effective ways we can each take more responsibility with our tech. Buying – and not buying – new devices, learning how to repair, reuse and recycle the ones we already own and reassessing our relationship with quick and convenient services.

To keep this chapter focused on practical and effective advice, I've included recommended reading on the topics I didn't have space to cover – including tech bias and bullying – in the resources section at the back of the book.

Don't worry – I'm not about to launch into an impassioned plea that you stop buying new technology and downgrade all the way back to a Nokia 3210 (although I'm sure you'd enjoy a game of Snake as much as I would). Our aim is to find our tech balance and to consider the small changes we can make that might stack up to create a positive impact.

WHY YOU KEEP BUYING NEW STUFF

We've already discovered that dopamine drives us to seek out new rewards – it's one of the reasons we're continually touching our phones. We've also learned that often the expectation (lots of exciting new messages) can feel better than the reality (an empty inbox). It's why George Washington University Professor and Psychiatrist Daniel Z. Lieberman MD and Georgetown University lecturer Michael E. Long describe it as 'the anticipation molecule' in their book *The Molecule of More,* which is all about dopamine. We look forward to the reward that new things will bring us, whether that's an email, the latest smartphone or any other shiny new piece of tech.

However, the ongoing pursuit of new things can become costly and exhausting. I like how Professor of Neuroscience Wolfram Schultz describes dopamine neurons as 'the "little devils" in our brain that drive us to rewards.' The problem is, they're never satisfied: 'The little devil not only drives us towards rewards, it drives us towards ever-increasing rewards.'

This is important because it explains why we might escalate our hunt for familiar rewards or constantly be on the lookout for brand new rewards and experiences – never satisfied with what we already have. We've learned this isn't the case with social media checking as the unpredictable reward schedule keeps us interested in the same dopamine circuit time and time again. It's why you're probably thinking about checking Instagram right now even though you just checked a few minutes ago. But what about when something becomes dull and predictable? Like a phone you've had for two years? You might want a new one simply because you're due an upgrade. But I'd bet that dopamine could also be playing a role in making you feel good about the anticipation of getting a brand new one – especially if persuasive advertising is at work to convince you this new phone is exciting, different and way more rewarding than your current one. What you have then is a craving for newness – regardless of whether you truly need anything new or not.

Research shows this novelty-seeking behaviour in action. Let's take a look at just a few studies. The first is from 2006 and suggested that we want to see what rewards we can get from new things – even when we know old things reward us already. The participants played a card game in which each card had a nice landscape on it. They had to pick a card and would get a reward. The aim was to make the most money. They soon learned that certain cards got them the best rewards time and time again. But then new cards were added. Rather than go with the sure thing, the cards they knew came with rewards, the participants picked the new cards.

This was a small study with only 20 participants, but it's a good example of showing how illogical our pursuit of newness can sometimes be – even when we have something good, and in itself rewarding, under our noses.

A more recent study from 2015 aimed to find out whether the placebo effect works in video games, but the findings might explain why we sometimes fall hard for bold tech claims. The researchers asked 21 participants to play an adventure game called Don't Starve. In it, the players had to collect objects to stay alive. In the first round, players were told the map of the game they were playing in was randomly generated. In the second round, they were told that an 'adaptive AI' had changed the map based on their skills.

At the end of each round, the participants filled out a survey and they rated the second game as better than the first – they said it was more immersive. However, the second round wasn't generated by an adaptive AI at all. It was also randomly generated, just like the first.

Again, I find the number of participants in this study rather small to start making big assumptions. But I think it's interesting that being told about an advanced tech claim (adaptive AI) seems to have altered the participants' perception of the game they played – even though it wasn't even there to begin with.

That we might all be hard-wired to look for novelty won't be a surprise to anyone who loves shopping – it might be comforting instead. But it can hopefully help us to see the truth behind why we crave new things – even when the things we have are, more often than not, perfectly fine. Our hard-wired craving for new things is a problem that affects all of our buying habits – it's why we're all being urged to cut down on everything from plastic to fast fashion and address our need for stuff head-on. For now, we're going to focus on new devices.

I want you to imagine a large elephant. It would be about 14 feet high and weigh about 6.8 metric tonnes. Now multiply that elephant by 8 million. According to the UN Global E-Waste Monitor 2020 Report, that's how much tech waste (also called e-waste) everyone around the world produced in 2019. This works out at about 53.6 million metric tonnes.

If that many elephants are hard for you to visualise, how about nearly 6,000 Eiffel Towers? What I'm saying is, that's a lot of old computers, phones, speakers, toasters, heating systems and lights to deal with. What's more, that number is expected to keep rising to reach 74.7 million metric tonnes by 2030. We've got a big tech waste problem – and that's only one reason why we need to get a better handle on our tech consumption.

MAKING AND BREAKING GADGETS

How many different materials do you think are needed to make your phone? The surprising answer is about 70, give or take a few. These materials have properties that mean they're essential for getting our devices to work – they create screens, help with conductivity and produce vibrations.

However, mining some of these all-important elements from the earth can cause problems. It can destroy natural habitats, as well as lead to air and water pollution that could affect local communities.

There's also widespread evidence of poor working conditions. Let's take mining for cobalt as an example. Cobalt is a silvery metal that's needed to make lithium-ion batteries – the batteries that power your phone and your laptop. There's already a high demand for cobalt, but because it's also needed to make the batteries in electric cars, that demand is likely to get even higher. The harsh conditions of cobalt mining have led to deaths, accidents and serious long-term health issues for miners, which is why cobalt is sometimes referred to as 'the blood diamond of batteries'. More than 60 per cent of cobalt originates from the Democratic Republic of Congo (DRC). According to an Amnesty International report, cobalt mines are often dug by hand and go into the ground for hundreds of metres. This means there's poor ventilation and no support. There's no official number on the amount of deaths and injuries from these mines, but workers told researchers that accidents are common, and tunnels have collapsed. What's more, many children carry out jobs in the mines. Back in 2014, it was estimated that 40,000 children were working in the mines of the DRC – we could assume that this number is likely to be higher today given the increasing demand for cobalt. Some of these children reportedly spend 12 to 24 hours down the mines.

Not only do these miners of all ages work in hazardous conditions for long hours and low pay, but there are long-term health risks to cobalt exposure. It can harm their eyes, skin, heart and lungs, as well as lead to life-threatening complications, including cancer.

I know what you're thinking. Why don't we just stop this from happening? Unfortunately, it's not that simple. A big problem is it's difficult to be sure which technology companies are obtaining their cobalt from these mines. The official line from many major brands is that they don't tolerate human rights abuses, like the ones I've outlined above. But supply chains are complicated, which means it's not always possible to say – at least with certainty – who gets what from where.

Luckily, several technology companies have committed to addressing problems in their supply chains in recent years. Some have taken more concrete steps, like Apple, which now buys cobalt from miners directly to ensure workplace standards are met. But it's still difficult to know for sure what's going on. What's more, even if tech companies ensure these resources are mined in more ethical ways, one day they will run out. Right now, research is being done to look for alternatives, but not everything can be replaced by something else – at least not yet.

One answer to the problem of our finite resources is recycling. But, as you might expect, that isn't without its share of problems either. For starters, most people are not doing it enough. Only 17.4 per cent of that vast 53.6 million metric tonnes of tech waste I told you about before was properly collected and recycled. The tech that was thrown away is now in a landfill somewhere and (over time) toxic metals, including lead, mercury, cadmium and chromium, can end up leaking into the soil and impacting the surrounding ecosystem.

So, the answer is to recycle, right? Yes, but in the correct way (more on that soon). Over the years, some tech waste has been intentionally exported to countries like Ghana, Pakistan, Thailand and Ukraine – often because refuse workers are cheaper there. These are countries that already have their own share of tech waste to deal with.

In poor working conditions, people are required to dismantle tech, picking at parts and burning some to find metals which can then be sold on. Exposure to some of the materials inside phones can be extremely harmful, and the tech that's not reused is often dumped, which again can leak toxic chemicals into the soil and affect communities.

What a mess. A massive 53.6 million metric tonnes of it. If you read the last few pages while side-eyeing your phone, you're not alone. But getting these hard-to-stomach truths on the table is essential to motivate us all to better understand what's going on and take action.

There are two things we can learn here. The first is that technology companies need to take responsibility for obtaining and using materials in a way that's safe and ethically sound, as well as helping to dispose of devices we no longer need. We might not have a say over this, but we can promise ourselves right now to stay informed about these issues and buy products from brands that are making solid efforts to ethically supply and recycle their tech – as well as call out and avoid those that aren't.

The second is that we're not unimportant in all of this. We can choose to buy less tech, slow down the process of buying new and throwing away not so new, and learn to repair, reuse and properly recycle our devices. These small changes, as well as a shift in mindset away from 'must buy new' to 'must make do', could stack up to have a big impact.

HOW TO BUY LESS

One way to reduce the impact your tech-buying habits have on the environment is to buy fewer devices less often and make do with what you have.

Luckily, the Marie Kondo effect of the last five years has encouraged many of us to make peace with our things and learn to question our motives before we buy more. When it comes to tech, there are some specific considerations, like what if your work laptop is slowing you down? Or what if your phone provider tells you that you're long overdue an upgrade? Whenever you feel the urge to buy a new device, you need to slow down and work through the following steps to establish whether it's a real need or one created by smart marketing and our own innate cravings for new things.

Look at what you've got

Ask yourself whether you need a new device or if you can use one you already have. For example, if you have the latest smartphone, do you need a separate camera? Unless you can think of a good reason, the answer is probably not. It's more likely that the idea of it appeals to you. Instead, learn about how to make the most of the camera on your phone or download an app to make photo editing easier (I'm a big fan of Snapseed). Your smartphone is packed with features you could buy a separate device to handle but don't need to – sleep tracking, audio recording, run mapping, to name just a few.

Switch on to advertising tactics

Throughout this book, I've encouraged you to be more critical about the advertising you see – whether that's in magazines, on social media platforms or in the form of sponsored content from influencers. Is it the device that you want or the life, style or promises it claims to bring you? For example, last week, I convinced myself I needed a hair drying and curling device from a top tech brand because an influencer had created a great video about her experience with it. It took some soul-searching and pulling myself back from the 'buy' button to realise I was sleepwalking into buying it because she'd made it sound so damn good when I absolutely did not need it. I already have both a hairdryer and curling tongs – combining them would add zero value for me other than less money, more guilt and a tiny bit less space in my drawers.

Escape the upgrade treadmill

There's no right answer as to when you need to upgrade your phone, but every year or two is a short amount of time for your pocket-sized computer. The same goes for most electronic devices. Make this your mantra: just because you're allowed to upgrade, doesn't mean you need to.

I've created this checklist to run through to help you decide whether it's time to upgrade your phone, trade in your laptop or get a new games console – and what else you could do instead – or whether you should just jazz up your current handset with a new case and wallpaper.

- **It's slow.** If the device is slow, emails and messages are taking a long time to load, and it's stopping you from getting things done, you need to do something about it. There are ways to combat this problem – deleting old apps and moving photos and videos to a cloud service or another device are steps worth taking before you get a new one.

- **It's damaged.** Sometimes you can repair damage (more on that soon), or you can live with a small crack in a laptop or phone. If it's affecting how you use it or it can't be replaced, it might be time to get a new one. But always check it can't be repaired first: phone repairers can do amazing things sometimes, fixing the seemingly unfixable in minutes.

- **It won't update.** Companies roll out updates that work across most devices, but as your phone, TV, tablet or e-Reader gets older, it might reach a point when updates no longer work. Check the website of the company that makes your device to see if updates are still being rolled out. If they're not, it could be time to upgrade. This is important, as being unable to update a device can make you vulnerable to security threats.

- **Its battery doesn't last long.** If it keeps running out of battery, that's going to be a pain. This defeats the point if the device in question is a phone because you can't take it out and about with you without worrying. Consider upgrading or check out the advice about repairs and replacing batteries in the next section.
- **It feels unsafe.** If you're concerned a lack of updates means your privacy or security is at risk, or maybe an appliance doesn't feel safe any more because it's broken, it's time to look for a new one.

Maybe after all of that, you *have* justified a new purchase for yourself. What you need to know now is that there's buying something and then there's smartly buying something – we want to do the latter.

HOW TO BUY SMART

You can buy clothes, cars and do your food shop in a way that's more considerate, deliberate and ethically sound. You can do the same with tech – there's just a little more to look out for. That's why I've written the ten tech-buying commandments that come from years of reviewing technology, testing devices at demos and recommending what and how other people should buy theirs.

Not all of these are easy or quick to do – make sure you have time to spend searching for answers before you buy. What's more, you don't need to tick off all of these, but the more, the better. I find keeping this list with me is particularly handy to refer back to when I'm considering buying two similar products from different brands. Work through each commandment, and one should (hopefully) stand out as the winner.

The important things we're looking for are **quality, repairability and longevity**. That way you won't need to buy as many new devices, you can get them repaired rather than bin them and use them for longer. If you remember just three things, it should be those.

1. I shall check if it can be repaired

Repairing our devices should be much more straightforward than it is. Some of the biggest technology companies make it difficult to repair their products, using screws and parts that are tricky to find. That means you either can't fix them or you have to go through their repair service, which often works out much more expensive than getting a device repaired at an independent company. What's more, some parts can be hard for even professionals to get to or fix and replace – some devices without a replaceable battery can become useless pretty quickly. An excellent place to start is on the website iFixit – a site all about repairs that rates products based on how easy they are to fix.

2. No patterns, colours or styles I will get bored of

This depends on your personal taste. I always go for the most straightforward, functional looks if there's any choice: neutral colours and no patterns. Otherwise, I'd have got bored of it by the time it arrives. If you're looking at a device online, make sure you've seen a few photos of it – lighting can make colours and materials look completely different – as well as from a few angles.

3. Durability is important

Don't worry. I don't mean every device you buy from now on needs to be wrapped in a military case and come with a guarantee that you could safely drop it from a waterfall or anything like that. What I mean is, if you try it in a shop, make sure it doesn't feel like it's going to snap. Read reviews about bits that might break, including hinges, awkward buttons or any other part that might wear away quickly. If it's not already durable, would it be easy to make it more durable? My MacBook lives in a shell case with cosmic designs on it, which makes it less likely to break if I drop it. I also have another carry case zipped around it when I take it out of the house. Cases that are truly durable and drop-proof aren't cheap, but they can save you an absolute fortune on repair bills in the long run.

4. I shall read reviews

Search online for the product you're looking for and the word 'review'. But don't click on the first result you see. The top few might be paid-for ads that won't be impartial, or they might be sponsored posts. Instead, look at reviews on sites that are trustworthy, like review website Which? or reputable technology sites, like TechRadar and CNET. Reviews on retailer websites are also worth checking, like Amazon. Just make sure you read a wide variety, as some can be unhelpful or might be fake. Good reviews will reveal things you can't always tell from a photo or description or even trying it in the shop for a few minutes. This should also give you an idea about how long the device will last and what kind of wear and tear to expect.

5. It must be easy to update

This is a consideration that's often ignored but is arguably one of the most important. Your devices run on software. But this software needs constant updates to keep it working, address security issues and iron out any bugs. If you're buying a brand new device, the company will, hopefully, allow you to update it for a long time. But if you're buying something that's been out for a while or buying a laptop, phone, printer or computer that's second-hand or has been refurbished, you need to check if you can still update it. Search online for the product and the company. You should be able to find a list of devices that are supported by updates. This point is well worth your time as some companies only guarantee support for a few years.

6. I will consider the price (a tricky one)

Everyone loves a bargain, but sometimes it makes much more sense to go for a device that's more expensive and from a reputable brand with great reviews than a discounted device from a brand you've never heard of before. You might wince now, but you won't regret it in the long run. However, just to confuse things, don't assume expensive always equals quality or that lots of features are what you need by default. For example, I wanted to get my dad one of the Amazon Echo smart home devices for Christmas a few years ago, but couldn't decide between an Echo Plus (expensive) or a Dot (cheaper). I took a good look at the specifications (the list of everything you need to know about the device) and decided to get the Dot. It was more than enough for what he wanted it for – he still considers it his most helpful device to this day and the Echo Plus would have been overkill.

7. It will play nice with my other devices

This is called compatibility. In other words: will this device work with the others I have? Will these headphones pair with my phone? Will a new smart bulb play nicely with my smart assistant? This is one of the reasons people often buy lots of devices from the same brand – there's none of this worry, as everything communicates seamlessly with everything else. I recommend that sometimes, but I also don't like thinking anyone is being pressured into choosing a device just because it's easy. Search online for the product you want and the device – you have to find out if they'll work well together.

8. I shall buy refurbished tech (when possible)

Refurbished generally means a device has been restored to a condition that's close to new, whereas second-hand means it comes straight to you after someone has stopped using it – it usually hasn't been repaired. Refurbished devices can save you money, as they're cheaper than buying new and mean you'll keep a device in circulation for a bit longer before it's sent off to be recycled. It's normal to have reservations about refurbished tech (and if you'd rather buy new, that's fine) but if you put in the research, you can end up getting yourself a great (almost) new device. If you're at all concerned, purchasing a refurbished product from its original manufacturer is an excellent way to ensure you get a good deal. The manufacturer will have standards to meet and access to materials needed for repairs. Before buying refurbished, you need to find out as much as you can about the device. How new is it? What condition is it in? Does it have a warranty from the company that refurbished it? Does it come with original documentation and accessories? There are different grades for some refurbished devices, where A is the best and will be almost like new, B will show a little more wear and tear and C might look worn or be missing accessories. Second-hand is also an option. It can be riskier because you're usually getting the device from the existing owner, it might be more worn and won't have a warranty, but you *might* also get a fantastic deal.

9. Eco-credentials are important

If you're buying a home appliance, check if it has an energy efficiency rating or whether there's any other consideration that could set one product apart from another. I needed a printer last year but didn't feel great about buying ink cartridges and paper regularly. I decided to buy one from Epson's EcoTank range, which has tanks that you fill with big bottles of ink instead of small cartridges that produce more waste. Some keywords to look out for are renewable materials, sustainability, as well as low power consumption. Before buying a device, you can also check if it's on the Electronic Product Environmental Assessment Tool (EPEAT) online registry – a list of sustainable products from manufacturers. It's a way for you to evaluate the effect a product has on the environment.

10. I shall try and find one to touch

This isn't always possible, but I've been shocked over the years at how many devices I've been sent to review that ended up feeling and fitting nothing like I expected them to from the photos and even the descriptions of what they're made from. Sometimes this is a pleasant surprise – a heart rate chest strap that was much comfier than I was expecting. Other times, it's not. Like the fitness tracker designed for 24/7 wearing I had to take off after it made my skin itch just 15 minutes after strapping it to my wrist. If you have the opportunity to see the device you want in real life, go for it. Press the buttons, feel the materials against your skin and pick it up to check the weight too.

> **Tip:** If you need a new phone but want to break free of the upgrade cycle, check out Fairphone, a sustainably produced smartphone.

BORN TO DIE

Whenever I tell someone about buying less tech, they ask me some variation of: 'But isn't the battery/software/device made to stop working after a few years anyway?' This is an excellent question. What they're referring to is called planned obsolescence.

Obsolescence is when something doesn't work and needs to be replaced. Planned obsolescence is when a device is produced that quickly becomes obsolete on purpose. We all know technology moves fast, but this term is used to describe the way companies create products knowing they'll last only a few years or intentionally making a device with a short lifespan – maybe to coincide with a new product launch, so you'll buy the next one.

We can't say for sure which devices have been engineered to stop working after a certain amount of time – household appliances and phones tend to be the ones people suspect the most – and plenty of companies have been accused of planned obsolescence over the years.

For example, a few years ago, Apple was accused of reducing the battery life of its older iPhones to force users to upgrade. But back in 2017, Apple said this was true, but it wasn't to make people upgrade. Instead, the company claimed it was an effort to reduce the demand on the phones that had weak battery performance – this would prevent the phones from shutting down. France's Competition and Fraud Body (DGCCRF) fined Apple millions, and the company agreed to pay the fine.

Because people know that their devices might be engineered to become obsolete, they're sometimes resigned to the fact they'll pack in after a year or two regardless of what they do, and they don't interrogate the buying process for something new as much as they should. This doesn't need to be the case. As well as buying smart, we can also learn how to repair, recycle and reuse our devices.

HOW TO REPAIR, RECYCLE AND REUSE

We can keep devices in use, working well and out of landfills by repairing them, recycling parts in an environmentally responsible way, reselling them or giving them away to someone else – we just need to learn how.

Repair

Uh-oh, your device is broken. It's tempting to get a new one and not deal with the hassle. Repairing your devices isn't always possible, easy or safe. But it might be much more straightforward than you expect.

You have a few options: You can search online, and chances are you'll find several independent tech repair businesses in your area. Or, you could go to the company you bought the device from. Many have their own repair services. This might work out easier because some companies make it difficult for anyone else to repair their devices, whether that means the screws and spare bits aren't widely available, or parts are glued in. However, they tend to charge a premium. If this sounds confusing, it's intentionally that way. After all, companies would rather you either turn to them for repairs or buy new products instead of learning how to fix things yourself or relying on a local tech repair team to help you.

Luckily, the Right to Repair movement is gaining steam. This is a movement that believes people should be able to fix the technology they buy. It calls for products to be designed for repair as well as support for repairers of all kinds.

Online communities, like iFixit, are helping to drive this movement and provide people with ratings about a device's 'repairability', as well as details about how you can fix them yourself and connect with communities of repair experts.

Make it a priority to buy tech that can be fixed, create a list of local places that can help you fix your tech and, if you're feeling up to the challenge, start researching how you can fix your devices yourself – the guides on iFixit are a great place to begin. Thinking about repairing rather than buying new might feel daunting. But shifting our focus to sustainability rather than production could have significant benefits in the long term, not only reducing the impact on the environment and workers, but giving us more power and control where it feels like we have none. I know it might seem more intimidating to fix a fitness tracker or speaker than it would to take up a hem on a skirt or add a button to a shirt, but with the right tools and know-how, you might be able to do more than you think you can.

Recycle

There are a few different ways you can recycle your old devices. Some areas have recycling schemes – check your local council's website to see if there are any collections or special places for old tech at recycling centres near you. Many major tech companies and retailers also have their own trade-in schemes – sometimes offering you money off your next phone or purchase if you hand over your old tech.

Other services ask you to send products that can be refurbished or reused, others recycle the bits of your devices that can be used again. You can also sell your phone to a recycling company and (if it ticks all the boxes) make some money from it too. Try sites like Music Magpie and SellMyMobile.

Reuse

One of the easiest things to do with devices you no longer want is to sell them so someone else can use them (eBay is a good option) or give them to friends and family.

Over the years, I've given my old phones and Kindles to my family. Before you hand them over, check whether updates still support the device or if it's become obsolete. There might still be some ways to use obsolete devices, but you will want to give friends and family a heads-up and ensure there aren't security risks when you pass them on.

There are also services that aim to reuse your old devices and give them to people who really need them, like children, the elderly or refugees. I've added a list of these services to the resources on page 336.

> **Important:** If you're going to give your devices away or send them off to be recycled, you'll need to make sure you've securely removed everything important from them. Back up any files, photos, messages or anything else that's important. You can put these on an external hard drive, in cloud storage (like Dropbox, iCloud or Google Drive) or transfer them to your new device. Double-check they've been backed up before you get rid of your old device.

Right before you send it off, do a factory reset, which you should find in the settings of the device itself or its app. To be extra safe, you might also want to consider removing the hard drive. Search online for the best options for your device. Also, check out the tips on page 125 for advice about backing things up and taking the risk out of relying on your tech.

PAYING THE PRICE FOR SUPER-FAST DELIVERY

A theme that's come up again and again in this book is convenience, mainly whether the convenience our devices bring to our lives is worth the trade-off that often comes with them.

For example, do you want a new phone once every 18 months, knowing it can have an environmental impact? Or do you really need a smart assistant to make things easier at home if it's capable of tracking what you're doing, recording everything you say and learning everything there is to know about you? Finally, do you want facial recognition tech in every public space to catch criminals when we also know it might falsely accuse someone else of being one in the process?

The last five to ten years has seen a massive rise in services that we arrange, use and pay for with our phones and devices that are the ultimate in convenience, bringing us products, taxis and pizzas to our doors quickly and efficiently – often with added bonuses, like too-good-to-be-true deals, real-time tracking and premium delivery services that get you the stuff you want quicker than you can imagine. But do we pay the price for this convenience too? The answer is: someone else probably does.

The people who produce and distribute all of these things to us might do so in poor conditions. Think about it. To get a pizza to you in under an hour or a table lamp to you tomorrow morning, workers need to be running flat out in warehouses, kitchens and on the roads to hit the high delivery expectations we all demand. What's more, many of the companies in question hire independent contractors or gig workers. This means they might have more flexibility, but equally don't have the same rights a full-time employee would. That's why it's hardly surprising that many of the companies that put convenience and speed at the front and centre of their business offerings are often called out for workers' rights issues.

For example, at the time of writing this book, Uber is attempting to overturn an appeal in the UK that ruled drivers are workers – which means they're entitled to workers' rights and holiday pay. Uber claims its drivers are self-employed and use the platform only to connect with customers.

Deliveroo has faced similar criticism over the years. Even though it has allegedly improved its conditions, there are still many stories of riders and drivers who work long hours for little pay. What's more, details about Amazon's drivers and warehouse workers often make news headlines due to poor working conditions. Admittedly, many of these issues appear to have been addressed, but during the pandemic, Amazon came under fire again for its treatment of workers in the US. It's hard for us to know whether these problems are getting better when we're seeing things from the outside and being fed statements from spokespeople.

There are plenty of other concerns too, like the effect companies that offer super-cheap, super-fast and super-convenient services have on other companies. Any business that doesn't push its workers as hard and bring you things at breakneck speed ends up missing out. This could put many businesses, especially smaller, local ones, at risk because it's impossible for them to compete.

That's not to mention the environmental impact of all of those deliveries, including the transportation involved, the packaging and the cardboard that adds to landfill sites. This puts us in a tight spot – should we stop using the apps that champion convenience because they're not treating workers well? Or will that put more people out of work? Let's aim for something in the middle. We don't have to swear off these services forever. But, instead, understand the impact of the choices we make when we hand over our money to them.

Slow down your expectations

In the days of pressing 'buy' and expecting things to turn up at your doorstep within a few minutes, hours or, at the most, a day, asking you to expect slower times might seem like a step backwards. But how often do you really *need* another book to add to your reading pile this afternoon or a new bath mat within 24 hours? Unless there's a legitimate emergency, wean yourself off deliveries within a day. This will open up scope for you to shop at a broader range of places and make you less dependent on major online shopping hubs.

Do your (local) research

Big online retailers have become so widely used because they make everything quick and easy. If you want to rely on them less, you'll have to find where else you can buy the other things you want. Is there a local delivery service you can rely on instead? You won't know which businesses offer deliveries unless you take the time to research and explore. Usually, a search online will serve up information about where you can buy local produce, cakes, groceries and books.

Support workers when you can

If you want to continue to use services that have courted controversy in the past, make an effort to stay switched on to strikes and movements that are going on, like when Amazon workers went on strike during Amazon Prime Day in the US. You might not be able to boycott businesses all the time, but you can support workers when they need it or ask us all to.

Make problematic companies your backup plans

Cut down your reliance on big companies by only using them when you absolutely must. If there's a big delay on something you need or you can't find it on any other service, it's your call: maybe you can make an exception. Remember: if we want independent bookshops and local food retailers to stay in business, we have to continue to shop with them – even if it means we sacrifice some convenience.

Checklist

Buy less tech. Question whether you need new tech or if a device you already have could serve a similar purpose. Don't fall for shiny new gadgets and bold marketing claims. Question why it is you *really* want something – will it make things better? What purpose will it serve?

Find tech that can be fixed. You might not be able to ensure every purchase is repairable. But know what to look out for: batteries that can be taken out, strong hinges, reviews that are full of positive experiences. Find a new device that's able to be fixed or built to last.

Read reviews. Do your research. Not all reviews are trustworthy, but bookmark sites that rate and review devices, as well as iFixit for important information about how to repair them.

Super-fast delivery should be a backup plan. Consider services that champion convenience and fast delivery as backup places for your tech, books, food and anything else. Research local and independent retailers that you can buy similar products from.

IDENTITY

HOW OUR LIKES AND BELIEFS ARE INFLUENCED BY TECH

During a recent Twitter check-in, I saw lots of people I follow tweeting about a list of the most influential indie songs they grew up with. Everyone was reposting the list along with memories of what was going on in their lives when their favourite track was released. Of the 50 songs on the list, I recognised only five and can hum (badly) only two of them.

It might not sound like a big deal, but it seemed to me that a bunch of people I feel I have a lot in common with, and that I'm the same age as, were sharing experiences I couldn't relate to. It seemed that when my Twitter followers were listening to The Futureheads, The Automatic, The Pigeon Detectives and every other band beginning with 'The', I was rocking out to Queens of the Stone Age, Deftones and Incubus.

As I scrolled through their musically inspired memories, a familiar feeling of not fitting in started to rise to the surface. Being picked on at school for being the only girl who liked *Star Trek* and for not eating meat (for five years, anyway). But instead of letting that feeling swallow my mood, I looked closer.

I discovered only two of the accounts tweeting about the indie list belonged to people I know for a fact are the same age as me. I've no idea about the rest, and the difference of a couple of years in either direction can account for all kinds of taste differences. Also, anyone like me who had a head full of Queens of the Stone Age, Deftones and Incubus wasn't going to be tweeting about the indie bands – they'd have nothing to say – and so I wasn't going to see 'my people' showing up in this topic. But this didn't occur to me straight away. I had to dig for it.

We tend to look to our communities – both online and offline – for the sense of belonging we need in order to function in society. For a minute there, my corner of the internet seemed to be rejecting me through the sharing of familiar experiences that I simply couldn't relate to. In reality, though, this was really just a small sample of the people I follow.

This reminded me how we're all continually weighing our views, interests and opinions against everybody else's – and we're doing it with blinkers on. That what we see online at any given moment is always a segment of a segment of a segment – just a tiny piece of everything there is to see. For example, the number of people I saw tweeting about the list (about 20) is barely representative of a neighbourhood, much less 'my generation'. When a news announcer says something like 'Twitter reacted with outrage to this announcement' they're talking about people commenting on a current trending topic, these can peak at around 11,000 tweets. If we say every tweet is one person, that's the equivalent of a packed-out No. 1 Court at Wimbledon, or the entire population of Ardrossan – a small town on the North Ayrshire coast.

Not only is what we see a small fraction, it is, in many ways, a view that is entirely unique to each of us. Let's stay with Twitter as our example. By default, you don't see the most recent tweets as they're being shared – unless you've changed some settings. Instead, the algorithm running your timeline makes decisions about what you probably want to see, based on the tweets you've replied to, retweeted and liked, as well as things you've searched, profiles you've clicked through to, trending topics you've opened up and so on.

This is going on everywhere you look, whether it's Twitter, Facebook and Instagram, or Netflix, Google and Amazon. We've stopped seeing what's out there and started seeing – due to the algorithms powering all these platforms – more of what we've seen already. The reason for this makes practical sense. Who has time to read everything that's going on? Or sift through it all to find the stuff that's actually interesting? But if something else is doing all of the deciding for us, is there a danger that our view of the world, and ourselves, can become distorted?

When people's shared attitudes and opinions online, ranging from 'who should run the country' to 'the best song of 2007', can influence how we feel about ourselves, it's super-important that we take that control back into our own hands and preserve our sense of perspective. That's why, in this chapter, we're going to look at the ways we allow what we do online to shape our identity and how technology is able to influence the ways in which we see ourselves.

YOUR APPS SHAPE YOUR TASTES

To better understand the pros and cons of technology that decides what to show us and what not to show us, let's look at Spotify.

When I was writing this book, I listened to a playlist on Spotify called Deep Focus over and over and over. It was full of tracks that were soothing, rhythmic and, admittedly, forgettable – the perfect combination to work to. The more I listened to this playlist, the more I noticed my other playlists, the ones Spotify creates regularly for its users, like Discover Weekly (a selection of song suggestions I haven't listened to yet that updates every Monday), started to resemble the Deep Focus playlist. I had a library bursting with similar, simple and soothing tracks to work to – perfect. Or so I thought.

What about when I wanted music to work out to, to cook to or when I wasn't in the mood to write to something soothing and rhythmic but craved tracks that have a lot of bass to whip me up into a productivity frenzy instead? Yes, I could just search for these songs. But the point is, Spotify was learning from what I was listening to – and learning fast – but it was only learning from one small part of my identity: a part that I didn't want to make any bigger. If all my tastes and interests are a restaurant, Spotify was serving only one dish. But I don't need to tell you that what makes us, well, us, is made up of lots of different parts.

This endless supply of Deep Focus-inspired tracks was all thanks to a recommendation algorithm (check out the algorithm explainer on page 84). These are designed to 'map our preferences against others, suggesting new or forgotten bits of culture for us to encounter'. The one that powers the Discover Weekly playlists is complex and involves what Spotify refers to as 'magical filtering' of what it knows you like and what other users like you have added to their own playlists. Similar systems are at play guessing and shaping your interests in different places, and are easier to dissect.

Here are a few of the most popular ones: Netflix uses a similar algorithm to suggest TV shows and movies you might want to watch based on what you've watched before and what people with interests like yours have enjoyed. As does Pinterest, which recommends photos, designs and boards that might be relevant to what you've looked at and interacted with before. YouTube's algorithm works in the same way to bring you the videos in the Up Next sidebar, which suggests similar videos to watch next based on what you're watching right now. The algorithm behind TikTok decides what you want to see next in the For You feed by analysing what you've watched before, as well as which videos other users have watched all the way through. The Instagram Explore tab is filled with new accounts and photos and people to follow based on what you tend to like, interact with and spend your time looking at.

There are more examples dotted all over the internet, and each algorithm is different – some are much more complex and accurate than others. These algorithms allow apps, sites and services to easily say: if you liked this thing, then you'll love this thing.

This sounds good, right? I like to think of it as if I'm being served a selection of only the best bits of food on a shiny plate rather than trying to elbow someone out of the way to get sad leftovers at a huge buffet. It takes the stress away from us *and* saves us a lot of time. What's more, these algorithms often (okay, most of the time) do a good job and accurately predict what we want to watch, pin and like next. I opened my Instagram Explore tab while writing this paragraph to prove my point. Yep, it's a constellation of photos of space, people getting their hair done and the sea – me to a tee.

But there are problems. The main one is that these algorithms can end up nudging our interests and tastes into a corner. Like me listening to nothing but Deep Focus-influenced music all day long. Maybe you know what you like, you enjoy your corner and you're happy with the same things being served day in and day out – like eating your favourite meal all the time. But is that how you want to live? As much as I'd love to eat pizza for breakfast, lunch and dinner, it's at least worth taking a look at what else is on the menu from time to time.

What's more, if we sit back and let our apps decide what's coming next, we lessen the opportunity for new things to land at our feet, and serendipitous discoveries are out of the window for good. Yes, we can still make decisions. But, often without realising it, those decisions are confined to the range of options we're presented with because the things that are surfaced are still a small selection of everything that exists.

We also lose control of our tastes. What I mean by that is we are all a glorious, messy mixture of different likes and dislikes. My tastes might be similar to yours, but each of us is unique. However, the algorithms that underpin all of our favourite apps can never fully account for this. Instead, they put us into categories that flatten all the different parts of us into one – or decide we're a particular type of person. But I'm not a Deep Focus person all the time, despite what Spotify might think. Sometimes I like shallow faffing about, working out, relaxing, thumpy tracks that make my head hurt. What worries me is the thought that, over time, we will start to believe that we are (and even unconsciously become), the one-dimensional people our apps tell us we are.

Eli Pariser, activist and author of *The Filter Bubble,* says that algorithms can lead to 'self-fulfilling identities'. Unlike a self-fulfilling prophecy, which happens when your expectation about something becomes real, this is about what an algorithm thinks you'll like: 'the Internet's distorted picture of us becomes who we really are'.

Spotify's assumptions about our tastes and interests are part of a broader problem. All of the recommendation algorithms we looked at above are working in tandem with data about your browsing history: what you buy, what you click on, what you search for, even what you linger on longer on your screen before continuing to scroll. All of this information then surfaces different news stories, what you see in your feeds, what products you're shown and what Google results you'll get – this vast web of data is used to show you a completely different online world from the one that I see.

It's just like looking at the world through a filter that's personalised to you. This is what Eli Pariser calls a filter bubble. He explains: 'The basic code at the heart of the new Internet is pretty simple. The new generation of Internet filters looks at the things you seem to like – the actual things you've done, or the things people like you like – and tries to extrapolate. They are prediction engines, constantly creating and refining a theory of who you are and what you'll do and want next. Together, these engines create a unique universe of information for each of us – what I've come to call a filter bubble – which fundamentally alters the way we encounter ideas and information.'

PUSHING US TO EXTREMES

The problem with filter bubbles can be bigger than having lots of samey playlists to wade through. Similar recommendation systems can also suggest blog posts, videos and news articles that could influence your views about the world – and even your place in it.

To understand this, let's take a look at a piece in the *New York Times* called 'YouTube, The Great Radicalizer' written by sociologist and writer Zeynep Tufekci in 2018. In it, she looks specifically at YouTube and argues that it has become a space that can breed extreme views – even for people who didn't go looking for them. She found that the YouTube algorithm takes an interest you have – that's something you've searched for – then recommends something else. That makes sense and is what we've come to expect from our experiences online. The problem is that, sometimes, the recommendation pushes you one step further into a topic or subject area than you wanted to go.

Tufekci gives the example of searching for jogging and being shown videos about ultra marathons. Showing an interest in vegetarianism to then be recommended videos about veganism. And, most worryingly, watching videos about politics to be pushed towards videos about conspiracy theories, Holocaust denial and white supremacy. 'It seems as if you are never "hard core" enough for YouTube's recommendation algorithm,' she writes. 'It promotes, recommends and disseminates videos in a manner that appears to constantly up the stakes. Given its billion or so users, YouTube may be one of the most powerful radicalizing instruments of the 21st century.'

To be clear here, this isn't *always* how YouTube works. Every time you search for an innocuous video, you are not recommended something shocking to watch next. But there are examples of research that does spot these escalating recommendations, which are sometimes called 'radicalisation pathways'. And there's anecdotal evidence from other people to suggest that views can become more and more extreme the more you watch YouTube.

Some of this evidence comes from a man called Caleb Cain, who believes he was 'brainwashed' by YouTube videos. Journalist Kevin Roose wrote a story about Cain for the *New York Times* and explained that he had 'gotten sucked into a vortex' of far-right political videos on YouTube. Roose writes: 'Over years of reporting on internet culture, I've heard countless versions of Mr Cain's story: an aimless young man – usually white, frequently interested in video games – visits YouTube looking for direction or distraction and is seduced by a community of far-right creators.'

He acknowledges that there are many factors at play when someone is radicalised – we could never blame something as complex as that on videos alone. But he believes that YouTube and its recommendation algorithm have created 'a dangerous on-ramp to extremism'.

If you have a lot of questions right now, don't worry. I did too. The main one being: but why would YouTube want to radicalise people intentionally? The answer is simple: it doesn't. Tufekci does not believe it's YouTube's mission to push people to such extremes, but instead suggests it's a by-product of wanting more and more of our attention. Google (the company that owns YouTube) is an advertising broker, which means the longer you stick around and watch videos on YouTube, the more money can be made from you looking at ads.

A highly effective tactic to ensure you stick around and don't get drawn elsewhere is to create an algorithm that's specially designed to do just that – keep you watching. According to reports, 70 per cent of the time people spend on YouTube is thanks to a chain of recommendations suggested by the algorithm behind the video platform. And how does it get you to stick around? It shows you increasingly more extreme videos. 'As we click and click, we are carried along by the exciting sensation of uncovering more secrets and deeper truths,' Tufekci writes. 'YouTube leads viewers down a rabbit hole of extremism, while Google racks up the ad sales.'

Guillaume Chaslot, a former YouTube engineer, has spoken out about the recommendation algorithm in the past. He said the same thing as Tufekci – this isn't intentional, it's part of a plan to grab and hold on to your attention: 'someone could be completely radicalized through viewing hours of YouTube videos on end – and from the perspective of the algorithm, that's actually jackpot.'

When I first read this, I couldn't get my head around why anyone would keep watching videos without alarm bells ringing that each one is getting progressively more extreme. But we've already learned about our innate drives for new experiences and different things, our insatiable curiosity and how often we mindlessly stay tuned into bottomless experiences.

To understand this in food terms, Tufekci likens YouTube to a restaurant where we're gradually fed more and more sugary and fatty foods. That means after a while we come to expect the most sugar and calorie-laden food and the restaurant of YouTube brings it to us. This means we are slowly conditioned to want extreme content, and the responsibility no longer lies with YouTube but with our appetites. 'When confronted about this by the health department and concerned citizens, the restaurant managers reply that they are merely serving us what we want.'

In early 2019, YouTube published a blog post about how its recommendations system is always being updated, and one of the most recent updates reduced the number of recommendations for what it calls 'borderline content'. These are videos YouTube believes could misinform people in ways that might prove harmful. The examples given included flat earth conspiracies and miracle cures for serious illnesses. This is a step in the right direction, but tech companies are extremely secretive about how algorithms work. This means we have no way of knowing what these changes look like for each of us and our own personalised recommendations.

If you look at this content deliberately, aware that the videos are getting more and more extreme, it might not have the same impact. But this isn't obvious, and we're accustomed to not only mindlessly watching things, but clicking on links that are recommended to us. In short, we put too much trust in our tech. That means, unknowingly, our tastes and views might be distorted. When it comes to dieting, politics and beliefs, it's not hard to imagine how we might become more accustomed to videos that nudge us into a particular direction. If we let them, the consequences could have a significant impact on our own health and well-being – as well as the health and well-being of others.

I've focused on YouTube here but pushing people to extremes to get them to spend more time on a particular platform isn't unique. Another example comes from the way some reports have found Facebook users can be nudged towards conspiracy theory groups. This is something Facebook, at the time of writing, appears to be actively addressing by removing certain groups and content.

How to push back

How can we enjoy our apps, search for things we genuinely want to see and not fall victim to being nudged by algorithms? One answer comes from an unlikely place. At a keynote speech in 2019, CEO of Apple Tim Cook said: 'Today, certain algorithms pull towards you things that you already know, believe or like. And they push away everything else. Push back! It shouldn't be this way.'

The problem with Cook's advice is it's not always easy to 'push back' when we're already subject to a power imbalance. The reason that many researchers and journalists are worried about algorithms that fuel our favourite apps, sites and social media platforms is we don't know much about how they work. This is why they're sometimes referred to as 'black box' algorithms or systems. This is a reference to data monitoring systems, like a black box on a plane. But it's also used to describe their mysterious working – we know what the Spotify or YouTube algorithms need to do their thing and what they give us at the end, but we don't know what happens in the middle.

Here are steps we can all take to step outside of these recommendation algorithms. Or at least how to remind ourselves to use the internet with more awareness about their presence.

- **Notice what you're shown.** The simple act of noticing what you're recommended on different sites and social media platforms can give you more control over whether you follow them or not – especially on YouTube. This doesn't always work. After all, the point is that your recommendations are (mostly) seamless. But since I began making a conscious effort to spot recommendations, I feel like I've been given a new way to look at the internet and a new (much more cautious) attitude to the way I move around it.

- **Choose what you want to engage with.** The more awareness you have about when you're being pushed in a particular direction versus searching for something, the more you can make a habit of not clicking on what Amazon recommends you buy next or start working your way through YouTube's Up Next sidebar. This is hard. After all, the whole architecture of your apps – of most of the internet – is built to derail you. But reminding yourself why you visited a platform and intentionally bypassing the recommendations completely will keep you focused.

- **Avoid bottomless experiences.** If you know you're a sucker for more, more, more then avoid bottomless experiences altogether. Don't look at the Instagram Explore tab. Don't look at the sidebar in YouTube. I know for some of us that's near-impossible. But luckily there are tools to help us. Some plug-ins can block bottomless news feeds, recommendations and trending topics completely – check the resources at the back of the book for examples.

- **Change recommendation settings.** Different apps, sites and services will have different ways of changing your recommendation settings or deleting your history and starting afresh. Make it a priority to find them. Turning them off or changing them will enable you to have an experience in which you feel more in control. But be warned, this could make your experience different – it might feel less personal because, well, it is. But if you don't like the idea of being nudged to buy, click and share, it's a good option. Search for the platform you're using and 'clear recommendations' or 'delete history' to get started.

- **Game the system.** You can't go in and tinker with the algorithm, but some apps allow you to have more control over what you see. One good example here is Instagram. In the Instagram Explore tab, you can click on a post you're not interested in and don't want to see more of, then you'll see three dots in a row (horizontal in iOS and vertical in Android) above the post. Click this and then click 'Not interested'. This should 'train' the algorithm to show you fewer posts like that – although it might take a while for you to notice a difference.

PUTTING ON A SHOW

We've considered how our technology might shape who we are and what we like. But this isn't one-sided. We assert our identities online too. However, anyone who's agonised over how to word a tweet or worried about whether a photo is right to share with everyone on Facebook will know that being yourself online isn't always straightforward.

In the 1950s, Canadian sociologist Erving Goffman suggested a theory of identity all to do with performing. This was before scrolling through social media platforms became the norm, but I think it's still relevant to the different roles we play both offline and online today.

Goffman encouraged us to see our identity, and the ways we present ourselves to others, as a performance – the same as getting on stage and taking part in a play. In his book, *The Presentation of Self in Everyday Life*, he explains we are all 'performing' much of the time. Sometimes we are completely taken in by our own act – we believe our own performance. Other times we know we are play-acting. There's a spectrum in between. We might know our act is a sham, but we might put on a sincere show – Goffman gives the example of a doctor who provides a patient with a placebo to help them recover.

Goffman expands on the performance metaphor throughout an entire book. But the bits I think are essential for us to know about who we are online are that our performances have a stage when we're among other people – that's where we perform and give off certain impressions. And there's also a backstage area. This is where we relax and step out of character, which might mean returning home after a day at work.

If you're thinking: wait, so am I always performing in this metaphor? Then the answer is: mostly, yes. Referring to the famous quote from Shakespeare's *As You Like It*: 'All the world's a stage, and all the men and women merely players,' Goffman writes: 'All the world is not, of course, a stage, but the crucial ways in which it isn't are not easy to specify.'

Many researchers have extended this same thinking to the internet, social media, emails, games and any other spaces our devices allow us to virtually occupy. But it's not as clear when we transport Goffman's metaphor from the real to the virtual who we're performing for, where the stage is and whether there's even a backstage where we can take a metaphorical breather. Which begs the question: is every screen a stage?

HOW WE ALL ACT THE PART

If we take Goffman's performance metaphor online, then one of the key things we need to consider is different audiences – which is his way of saying the different groups of people you're in touch with. This could be your close family, your extended family, your friends, your work colleagues or anyone else.

Now, this is obviously a consideration offline too. You act differently at a job interview than a dinner with your close family or a bar with friends. But in the real world, it's obvious to us who our audiences are in those situations: interviewer, family, friends. Easy. Making these distinctions online can be tricky because, unless we're sending a private message to only one other person, we can't always guarantee the audience is who we think it is – even then they could forward it on or take a screenshot to share with others.

For example, when I tweet, I assume it's going to be seen by my Twitter followers. Even then, it's likely to be only the followers who interact with me regularly, right? Wrong. Because my Twitter profile is public, technically, anyone could see that tweet from across a broad spectrum of audiences. There's no distinct audience online – they are all one.

Researcher danah boyd explains that these are 'collapsed contexts'. She writes that even when we think we understand whom we're writing to or performing for online, the potential audience can be much broader and drawn from lots of different contexts.

What this means is it can be challenging to show different sides of yourself online and keep them completely separated. For me, this isn't a big deal because my personal and professional lives already merge a lot across my social media accounts. But for someone keen to 'perform' one identity on LinkedIn and another on, let's say, Instagram, it requires more consideration – or an acceptance that someone, anyone, could, potentially, see both sides of you.

Is the idea that we can be different people online impossible? I remember reading this quote from Facebook co-founder and CEO Mark Zuckerberg years ago and it's stuck with me ever since: 'You have one identity,' he said. 'The days of you having a different image for your work friends or co-workers and for the other people you know are probably coming to an end pretty quickly [. . .] Having two identities for yourself is an example of a lack of integrity.'

He should be an expert on this – he controls the most popular social network. But even though that's what he might want, not everyone is ready to collapse different groups of people into the same space, and we shouldn't have to be.

A study carried out in 2017 found that participants change what they do and say online, as well as which profile photo they use, depending on how formal or informal they consider the platform they're using. The researchers looked at the way 116,998 About.me users (an online service that lets you create a simple landing page with your details on it) filled out information online on Facebook, Twitter, LinkedIn and Instagram. Results showed that there are different conventions for different platforms and they fall on a spectrum of more formal – which covers About.me and LinkedIn – and more informal – Facebook and Instagram.

Research has found determining what information we should share in different virtual spaces isn't always easy and there's friction between social networks. One 2016 study found participants had a strong desire to both set up boundaries between platforms and break them down too, depending on what they wanted to share. There were examples of participants saying they don't want people in a professional setting to see their Facebook page – they work on their LinkedIn and have it in their email signature but delete it when they're looking for a place to live – and others who wanted to strictly keep one type of profile private.

The researchers think this shows what's known as a social-technical gap – when there's a disconnect between what we know we want to do socially (share with some people and set boundaries with others) and what we can do technically (we're constrained by what each platform allows). In other words, communicating face to face is (mostly) more fluid and natural. But trying to code that same ease of communication into our tech – even today – isn't easy or even possible. We're all doing the best with what we have.

Setting virtual boundaries

It's not easy to separate your different 'audiences' and 'perform' different sides of yourself for them online. But there are tools and features we can all take advantage of to help us put up some virtual boundaries:

- **Create groups to share with.** Back when Facebook first introduced settings to allow users to create friend lists, I created some and then rarely used them. However, these tools can be useful. Building lists on the social media platforms that allow you to create them means you can make certain people VIPs – that way, you can decide to only share things with them. I like the way Instagram allows you to make a close friends group and then only share Instagram Stories with them. This is great if you want a public Instagram account that anyone can see, but also a more intimate way to show your close friends or family what you've been up to each day.

- **Consider your employer.** This will depend on the role you're in – or the one you want. If you're applying for jobs at a company that has strict policies, consider taking steps to tone down what you do, delete old tweets or make content private – that way, you don't have to worry about anything.

It's worth considering that if you have to censor yourself a lot to get a job, that company might not be a good fit for you. But I realise it's not possible for some of us to rule out employers – tread carefully and do your research.

- **Decide what's personal and what's professional.** If you don't want to merge your personal and professional lives, you need to make some decisions. Choose which platform will be for personal use, which will be for professional use and then be deliberate about what you upload to each. Some people create separate accounts – one where they share photos of their kids and another for professional news. Or maybe LinkedIn and Twitter are where you're professional, and Instagram is where you have fun and you keep your profile private. It doesn't matter, and for some of us it might not be a concern at all. But if you're one of those people who's conscious of a clash of audiences – or you're self-conscious about one particular audience – make a plan about what you'll share where and stick to it, always keeping up to date with privacy settings, which might affect this plan if they change.
- **Different email signatures.** Some email service providers allow you to create multiple email signatures. This means you can switch your signature depending on who you're contacting. Search online for your email provider and 'different signatures' to figure out if it's possible and how to get set up.
- **Go private.** If you don't need to have an online public presence for work, consider whether you should set your social media accounts to private – especially if you're concerned about someone checking up on them. Alternatively, pick one that'll be personal, where you only chat with people you're close to, and make that private instead. There's such a lot of advice online about personal branding and curating perfect social media accounts, but unless that's your job you don't have to feel pressured to share things publicly, ever.

If you're used to having public accounts, this might seem drastic. But it's a simple way to stop potential employers (and anyone else) from seeing photos, status updates, tweets, friends lists and any other personal information you'd rather they didn't see. However, this isn't a sure-fire way to stop things from getting out. Remember networked privacy? Anyone who follows you could, technically, share what you publish. That means you should think twice before you upload anything you think could put your job at risk – even if your account is private.

WELCOME TO THE ECHO CHAMBER

Goffman's performance metaphor can get confusing online, because we are not only performing for our audiences but what our audiences do and say can influence us. Many of the people we connect with in virtual spaces, like Facebook, Twitter, TikTok and Instagram, can shape our views, opinions and interests in the same way algorithms can.

This is to be expected from any group setting – online or offline. But although it might be normal, that doesn't mean we don't need to pay closer attention to how these group dynamics play out, because you might find yourself in an echo chamber.

An echo chamber is exactly what it sounds like. A virtual space in which our views are continually reinforced by other people who share the same views and opinions as us – they are echoes of what we already think and believe. This happens because most of us, often without being aware that we're doing it, follow and engage with people who have the same (or similar) views to us.

Being drawn to people like you is, for the most part, expected. It has a name: homophily, which means you're more likely to be connected to people like you than people who are not like you. Or, more simply: birds of a feather flock together. It might not seem like there's anything wrong with this. After all, if you were only following and interacting with people online whom you disagreed with, you'd be extremely stressed out most of the time.

But there are some issues with echo chambers and flocking together with other humans just like you. The very nature of these communities means you see the same opinions and views again and again – and they're just like your own. This might make you feel validated, but you're not seeing the bigger picture or how the world really is outside your one loud chamber. This works to reinforce our views, which means we don't think critically about issues, we're less likely to be able to empathise with others who are different to us and we're never challenged on our beliefs. This can lead to problems with intolerance, misinformation and conspiracy theories – the same people are sharing the same things and no one is questioning any of it.

Echo chambers exist, in part, because of some common biases. Let's quickly cover these so we know what to look out for. There's confirmation bias, which is the tendency to believe things that support what we already think and dismiss everything else. This keeps the echo chambers going – we don't have a reason to question anything because the views and opinions are playing into our own biases. There's also in-group bias, which describes our natural tendency to favour someone from our own group. In another context you might not take someone's opinions and views as trustworthy, but if they're part of your community, you might be looking at them through rose-coloured glasses.

As well as reinforcing beliefs, echo chambers can also give us a distorted view of what things are like on the outside of them. For example, I know a few people who still, to this day, can't believe Donald Trump became president in the US or that so many people voted for Brexit in the UK because they believed everyone they knew considered both of those things impossible and ludicrous. Plenty of people outside of their echo chambers, clearly, did not.

It's worth mentioning here that some experts believe echo chambers don't present a problem – at least not a significant one. They suggest that people are open to information that contradicts their own world views. Maybe it's because I've seen first-hand how much misinformation and conspiracy theories have spread online throughout 2020, but call me cynical – I think it pays to be cautious here rather than assume the best of everyone.

Whether echo chambers are impenetrable or not, what's most important to us is realising we *might* be in a community that reinforces our beliefs – so how do we challenge them? The answer is: slowly. I don't think you should immediately go and follow a bunch of people you're going to disagree with – I'd worry about what that would do to your blood pressure.

What's more, going against the grain and feeling like you don't belong to a group or having differing opinions isn't always good. It can lead to a feeling of disconnection and ostracism – something which we, as humans, fundamentally do all we can to avoid. Research shows that ostracism, which means feeling excluded, can threaten our fundamental needs of belonging, self-esteem, control and even a meaningful existence.

When someone feels threatened by ostracism, they will do what they can to repair their threatened needs. Might this explain my freak out at not knowing many indie bands among my Twitter peers? So instead of breaking free of the communities we all find ourselves in, whether they're 'good for us' groups, echo chambers or something in between, we can all be more deliberate about stepping outside to hear different perspectives.

Getting a fresh perspective

It's important to seek out different views and opinions that challenge us – not tell us what we already know. Do this gradually, and in the spaces you want to. For example, I made an effort to follow a broader range of people on Twitter, but I'm keeping Pinterest exactly how it is because I like it that way – pick and choose where you'll challenge yourself.

- **Be critical of what you see.** Don't assume every tweet, news article or even photo is accurate, current or hasn't been tampered with – especially if it makes you feel a strong emotion.
- **Choose your news.** News sites can be biased towards a certain political agenda or set of beliefs. Seeking out a broad range of news sites helps ensure you're not being nudged down one particular path.
- **Click, like and share with awareness.** You're not only in an echo chamber – you're part of what keeps others from breaking out of theirs. Now you know more about the nature of echo chambers, are there things you can say and share that might invite others to think critically too?
- **Look beyond social media for news**. The news that's shared on social media could favour the more extreme, clickbaity headlines and news stories. Remember algorithms are likely to favour the things that get people riled up and sharing furiously. Visit sites directly instead or use a news aggregator, like Feedly. This allows you to add multiple sites, which means that the most recent stories are then presented back to you in one stream.
- **Mute, mute, mute.** I don't think we talk about how great it is to mute people enough. Muting on Twitter, unfollowing

on Facebook, muting on Instagram. These are ways to keep people in your friends list but keep them out of your daily feeds. If you're serious about addressing your echo chamber but not sure where to begin, start by muting people to let more diverse voices through the noise.

Checklist

Remember the power of algorithms to shape your experiences. Recommendation algorithms power many of our favourite apps and services. They're complex but work on the assumption that if you like one thing you'll like something else that's similar.

Take control of recommendations. Either make a conscious choice not to fall down a recommendation algorithm rabbit hole, change your settings or use a plug-in that will strip some sites and services of them.

We all 'perform' online. This is a way of thinking and talking about the different 'roles' we play when we talk to other people. This happens offline too, but online it can be trickier to manage.

Consider your personal and professional lives. One way to manage different audiences online is to consider where your personal and professional lives can be separate or should be merged. Could you have a private Instagram for close friends? Do you need to have a professional Twitter account?

We are all living in echo chambers. Similar people talk to similar people. This is often how we make friends – it's normal. But it also means our views can be restricted and we have our own views and opinions echoed back to us without critically engaging in them.

Find different news sources. Break free of the echo chamber by not relying on social media for news. Find differing news sites and use a news aggregator like Feedly to read them.

THE FUTURE

WHY IT'S NEVER TOO LATE TO CHANGE
WHAT HAPPENS NEXT

'The past is written but the future is left for us to write.'
– Jean-Luc Picard, *Star Trek: Picard*

When you picture the world five, ten, even 50 years from now – what do you see?

Until recently, I would've laid the blame on science fiction movies for causing most of us to visualise the future as some kind of battered landscape presided over by a dead-eyed dictator or a bunch of nasty robots. Lately, however, the news has been doing a bang-up job of painting that picture for us. But seriously, who wants that?

That's why, when my mind fast-forwards into the future, it always looks like *Star Trek*. Its many incarnations on TV and in movies offer one of the most life-affirming and optimistic visions of the future you'll find anywhere. For a lifelong tech-lover like me, it's always had plenty to love – wireless gizmos with flashing lights that can diagnose and treat exotic maladies, warp engines that light up like fireworks before sending wide-eyed explorers across the galaxy. And it was busy being socially inclusive long before everyone realised that's a good and healthy thing to do. Back in 1968, Lt. Uhura (Nichelle Nichols) and Captain Kirk (William Shatner) shared the first interracial kiss on American television in the episode 'Plato's Stepchildren'.

Science fiction obviously isn't trying to predict the future. It's a representation and commentary on the problems and preoccupations of the time that it's made in. But it can inspire the future. Don't believe me? Go and take a look at the communicators they used on the show in the 1960s and tell me they aren't clamshell mobile phones. Or the wireless touchscreen Personal Access Display Devices (PADDs) Captain Picard and his crew were using in the late 1980s. You think it's a coincidence Apple called its own version the iPad?

Inclusivity, curiosity and optimism were hard-wired into the show's DNA by its creator Gene Roddenberry. That's why *Star Trek* always inspires me (and why *Star Trek* fans are, by and large, very nice people).

This chapter isn't about *Star Trek* or even science fiction. It's about the kind of world we want to make for ourselves and where we can look for the inspiration to guide us. Everything we've explored in this book has been about what each of us chooses to do next. How we take more control of our time. How we see beyond clickbait headlines and tech alarmism. How we spot the tactics of unscrupulous tech companies designed to pull us deeper into their data webs. As soon as we put any of these changes into action, we're affecting our future.

It's not about being fed up with our phones (although that's part of it). We need to decide the direction we're going in so that the future is a destination we want for ourselves, not just a place we find ourselves in.

In this final chapter, we're going to take a peek over the horizon to consider what's coming next, reframe our expectations and equip ourselves with the energy and impetus to look ahead with clarity and calm.

WE TIME TRAVEL ALL THE TIME

Before we move forward, let's look back. Humans have been thinking about the future, planning for it and guessing what might be just around the corner (or paying others to) for millennia. Whether that involved consulting with religious leaders or those who claimed to have mystic connections or turning to tarot cards and learning how to read tea leaves. Nowadays, we might consult the predictions of futurists, consume the imagined futures of science fiction stories or download an astrology app.

You wouldn't call yourself an oracle, a fortune teller or a superforecaster. But most of us are thinking about the future all the time. Each of us has an innate ability not only to consider what might happen in the future but imagine ourselves in it. This is called mental time travel – and there's no DeLorean or other type of time machine required.

According to psychologists Thomas Suddendorf and Michael C. Corballis, mental time travel can be best described as 'the mental reconstruction of personal events from the past (episodic memory) and the mental construction of possible events in the future.'

Remember at the start of this chapter when I invited you to imagine the future? This was an exercise in mental time travel. You were projecting yourself into a future you dreamed up – or, like me, borrowed from Gene Roddenberry. If that felt too distant, try something a little simpler. Imagine what will happen when you wake up tomorrow morning. What do you do? How do you feel? What can you see?

You can also use this ability to mentally travel into the past. Think back to a particularly memorable birthday. Imagine where you were, who else was there, how you felt. Can you take a trip back to that moment?

Experts believe our capacity to project ourselves into the past, as well as possible futures, has had a distinct evolutionary advantage. We can plan ahead, anticipate danger and learn from mistakes we've made.

There's still much we don't know about mental time travel. For example, experts are still trying to figure out if animals – like crows and apes – can project themselves into the future like we can too. They think it might be possible, but it's not like they can ask them.

What we do know is that research suggests mental time travel can make us feel good. One 2009 study found that participants who were asked to think about positive things happening in their futures were significantly happier than they were two weeks before in comparison to those who dreamed up only neutral or negative future events for themselves. Though what's interesting here is that those who engaged in neutral mental time travel into the future weren't happier, but were less stressed at the end of the study.

This suggests that considering what the future might look like – as long as it's good or neutral – could benefit us. Conversely, thinking about the future in a negative way might not. Other studies have suggested that mentally time travelling and imagining negative experiences is prevalent in people with anxiety and depression – this will come as absolutely no surprise to anyone who has experienced anxiety and the whirlpool of thoughts about the future that often accompanies it.

However, to confuse matters a little, thinking about the negative things that might happen in the future won't necessarily cause anxiety or lead to problems for everyone. In some cases, imagining the worst-case scenario might actually prepare people for the future and help people who are suffering from anxiety to cope better. In positive psychology, these are known as defensive pessimists. These people perform better when they lower their expectations and imagine how everything could go wrong. Ask these people to be more positive and it can impair their performance at a task.

We might have different ways of thinking about the future, but the important thing is we can all consider it, imagine it and project ourselves into whatever future we've dreamed up. This gives us the tools we need to eventually build a better future for ourselves – and others.

TENETS FOR TOMORROW

To help us stay focused on what we want for ourselves today, tomorrow and beyond, we need to get clear what a life of tech balance truly looks like – a state of balance I like to refer to as techquilibrium. What that looks like for me might be different for you. But I think there are some useful tenets that pull out the key themes we've explored that you can – literally or metaphorically – carry around with you. Reminders to help you make more conscious decisions and take a more active role in the ways you use technology – and stop technology from using you:

- **I choose how my free time is spent.**
- **I make the improvements that work for me.**
- **I value having the choice to switch on or off.**
- **I watch for my feelings being pushed.**
- **I don't need extreme changes, I need balance.**

A BRIGHTER FUTURE?

We also have a responsibility to think bigger than us. We can begin to imagine how the problems with our technology today, as well as the structures that shape it, might be improved upon tomorrow.

Our role in questioning the status quo might seem small. But we can commit to staying informed, calling for greater regulation and new policies, demanding more transparency and speaking out for those who are actively oppressed by the tech that shapes our world today.

Put simply, we can advocate for technology that is built with good intentions, and for all of us. This will give us the best chance of creating the future we truly want to be part of.

A future where technology is not put on a pedestal but created for and by everyone. Where tech entrepreneurs are not held up as gods and given unimaginable wealth, power and autonomy.

A future where our devices aren't demonised, and we can feel confident about working with them, having fun with them, using them to connect and relying on them to give us gateways to other people, places and experiences.

Thinking about the future doesn't have to make you starry-eyed or blindly hopeful. I'm not asking you to believe the future will be good, easy or anything like *Star Trek*. But I am asking you to believe that you can play a part in creating it, changing it and making it better for yourself and for others too.

RESOURCES

Timekeeping and content blocking:
Forest: forestapp.cc
Freedom: freedom.to
LeechBlock: proginosko.com/leechblock/
Moment: app.inthemoment.io
OFFTIME: offtime.app
Rescue Time: rescuetime.com
StayFocusd: search 'stayfocusd' in the Google Chrome web store
Toggl: toggl.com

Mental health:
Anxiety UK: anxietyuk.org.uk
CALM: thecalmzone.net
Counselling Directory: counselling-directory.org.uk
Mental Health Matters: mhm.org.uk
Mind: mind.org.uk
Rethink Mental Illness: rethink.org
Samaritans: samaritans.org.uk

Mood-tracking and CBT:
Catch it: liverpool.ac.uk/csd/app-directory/catch-it
Daylio: daylio.net
MoodKit: thriveport.com/products/moodkit
Moodfit: getmoodfit.com
Moodily: search 'moodily – mood tracker' in your app store
MoodMission: moodmission.com

Meditation:
Buddhify: buddhify.com
Calm: calm.com
Headspace: headspace.com
Insight Timer: insighttimer.com
Waking Up: wakingup.com

Tech bias:
Algorithms of Oppression: How Search Engines Reinforce Racism by Safiya Umoja Noble
Hello World: Being Human in the Age of Algorithms by Hannah Fry
Math Destruction: How Big Data Increases Inequality and Threatens Democracy by Cathy O'Neil
Race After Technology: Abolitionist Tools for the New Jim Code by Ruha Benjamin
Weapons of

Relationships:
Clinic to End Tech Abuse: ceta.tech.cornell.edu
ManKind Initiative: mankind.org.uk
Refuge Charity: refuge.org.uk
SafeLives: safelives.org.uk/
Women's Aid: womensaid.org.uk

Scheduling:
Asana: asana.com/apps/asana
Evernote: evernote.com
Remember the Milk: rememberthemilk.com
Things: culturedcode.com/things
TickTick: ticktick.com
Todoist: todoist.com

Sleep:
Calm: calm.com
Dohm Classic sound machine: yogasleep.uk
f.lux: justgetflux.com
Noisli: noisli.com
Philips Hue smart lights: meethue.com
Sleepio: sleepio.com

Tech time-out:
How to Break Up With Your Phone by Catherine Price
How to Do Nothing by Jenny Odell
Off. Your Digital Detox For a Better Life by Tanya Goodin

Body image and eating disorders:
Beat: beateatingdisorders.org.uk
National Centre for Eating Disorders: eating-disorders.org.uk
NHS – Eating Disorders: nhs.uk/conditions/Eating-disorders/
Overeaters Anonymous: oagb.org.uk

Password management:
1Password: 1password.com
Dashlane password manager: dashlane.com
LastPass: lastpass.com
NordPass: nordpass.com

RESOURCES

VPNs:
ExpressVPN: expressvpn.com
NordVPN: nordvpn.com
Surfshark: surfshark.com
Windscribe: windscribe.com

Virus protection:
Bitdefender: bitdefender.co.uk
Kaspersky: kaspersky.co.uk
Norton: uk.norton.com
Sophos Home: home.sophos.com

Scams:
ActionFraud: actionfraud.police.uk
Citizens Advice: citizensadvice.org.uk
Take Five: takefive-stopfraud.org.uk

Online harassment:
Bullying UK: bullying.co.uk/cyberbullying
Facebook Bullying Prevention Hub: facebook.com/safety/bullying
How to report abuse on Snapchat: support.snapchat.com/en-gb/a/report-abuse-in-app
How to report harassment and bullying on Instagram: help.instagram.com/contact/584460464982589
How to report inappropriate content on YouTube: support.google.com/youtube/answer/2802027
National Bullying Helpline: nationalbullyinghelpline.co.uk
TikTok Safety Center: tiktok.com/safety/resources/anti-bully
Twitter Help Center: help.twitter.com/en/safety-and-security/cyber-bullying-and-online-abuse

Recycling:
Government Recycling Collections: gov.uk/recycling-collections
Local Recycling Collections: recyclenow.com/local-recycling
Recycling for Good Causes: recyclingforgoodcauses.org
Reuse Network: reuse-network.org.uk
Solidaritech: solidaritech.com
WEEE Charity: weeecharity.co.uk

Getting rid of content:
Search online for: Distraction Free for YouTube
Search online for: News Feed Eradicator for Facebook
Search online for: Remove YouTube Recommended Videos, Comments
Search online for: UnDistracted – Hide Facebook, YouTube Feeds

News
Feedly: feedly.com
Fipboard: flipboard.com
Pocket: getpocket.com

REFERENCES

Introduction

'Technology'. Lexico.com. Oxford University Press (OUP). 2020. https://www.lexico.com/definition/technology

'The dubious practice of detox'. *Harvard Women's Health Watch*. 2008. https://www.health.harvard.edu/staying-healthy/the-dubious-practice-of-detox

'Texting Isn't the First New Technology Thought to Impair Social Skills'. Thompson, Clive. *Smithsonian Magazine*. 2016. https://www.smithsonianmag.com/innovation/texting-isnt-first-new-technology-thought-impair-social-skills-180958091/

'Women And Children First: Technology And Moral Panic'. Rooney, Ben. *The Wall Street Journal*. 2011. https://www.wsj.com/articles/BL-TEB-2814

'Bottomless bowls: why visual cues of portion size may influence intake'. Painter, J.E.; North, J.; Wansink, B. *Obes Res*. 2005;13(1):93–100. doi:10.1038/oby.2005.12

Addiction

'Survey: 1 In 4 Adults Checks Phone Less Than A Minute After Waking Up'. Study Finds. 2018. https://www.studyfinds.org/survey-quarter-checks-phones-less-than-minute-after-waking/

'Screen time stats 2019: Here's how much you use your phone during the workday'. Jory Mackay. RescueTime Blog. 2019. https://blog.rescuetime.com/screen-time-stats-2018/

Online Nation. OfCom 2020 Summary Report. https://www.ofcom.org.uk/research-and-data/internet-and-on-demand-research/online-nation/narrative

'The Relationship between Excessive Internet Use and Depression: A Questionnaire-Based Study of 1,319 Young People and Adults'. C.M. Morrison, H. Gore. Psychopathology 2010; 43:121–126. doi: 10.1159/000277001

'Problematic smartphone use associated with greater alcohol consumption, mental health issues, poorer academic performance, and impulsivity'. Chamberlain, S.R.; Grant, J.E.; Lust, K. *Journal of Behavioral Addictions J Behav Addict*, 2019, *8*(2), 335–342. Retrieved 17 May 2020, from https://akjournals.com/view/journals/2006/8/2/article-p335.xml

REFERENCES

'No More FOMO: Limiting Social Media Decreases Loneliness and Depression'. Hunt, Melissa G.; Lipson, Courtney; Marx, Rachel and Young, Jordyn. *Journal of Social and Clinical Psychology* 2018: Vol. 37, No. 10, pp. 751–768. https://doi.org/10.1521/jscp.2018.37.10.751

'Adolescent Sleep and the Impact of Technology Use Before Sleep on Daytime Function'. Chasens, Eileen R., PhD; Johansson, Ann E.E.; Petrisko, Maria A. *J Pediatr Nurs*, 2016; 31(5): 498–504. doi:10.1016/j.pedn.2016.04.004.

23 Hours to Kill. Jerry Seinfeld. Netflix. 2020. https://www.netflix.com/title/80170847

'Addiction'. *Psychology Today*: https://www.psychologytoday.com/gb/basics/addiction

'Does Internet and Computer "Addiction" Exist? Some Case Study Evidence'. Griffiths, Mark. *Cyberpsychology & Behavior*. Vol 3. No. 2. 2000. http://pdfs.semanticscholar.org/4d3e/28db-77fa52dab9a4461e5185f9a2dacac706.pdf

The Science of Addiction. Carlton, K., Erickson, W.W., Norton & Company, 2007, p. 2.

'Just Click No'. Wallis, David. *The New Yorker*. 1997 https://www.newyorker.com/magazine/1997/01/13/just-click-no

Internet Addiction Test. Young, Kimberly. Stoelting. 2016.

Caught in the Net: How to recognise signs of internet addiction. Young, Kimberley, 1998. John Wiley & Sons, Inc., 1998.

'Electronic Heroin': China's boot camps get tough on internet addicts. Phillips, Tom. *Guardian* Online. 2017. https://www.theguardian.com/world/2017/aug/28/electronic-heroin-china-boot-camps-internet-addicts

'Why it's too soon to classify gaming addiction as a mental disorder'. Orben, Amy and Przybylski, Andy. *Guardian*, 2018. https://www.theguardian.com/science/head-quarters/2018/feb/14/gaming-addiction-as-a-mental-disorder-its-premature-to-pathologise-players

'The benefits of playing video games'. Granic, I.; Lobel, A. R.C.M.E., 2014. *American Psychologist, 69*(1), (2014) 66–78. https://doi.org/10.1037/a0034857

'Examining common information technology addictions and their relationships with non-technology-related addictions'. Cheng, Cecelia; Cheung, Mike W.L.; Li, Angel Y.-L.; Sigerson, Leif. *Computers in Human Behaviour*. Volume 75. October 2017. Pp 520–526. https://doi.org/10.1016/j.chb.2017.05.041

'Internet addiction: Reappraisal of an increasingly inadequate concept'. Aboujaoude, Elias and Starcevic, Vladan, *CNS Spectrums*. 2016. -1. 1-7. 10.1017/S1092852915000863.

'Misunderstanding dopamine: Why the language of addiction matters'. McCandless, Cyrus. 2018. https://www.youtube.com/watch?v=aqXmOb_fuN4

Smartphone Compulsion Test. The Centre For Internet and Technology Addiction. https://virtual-addiction.com/smartphone-compulsion-test/

Flow: The Psychology of Optimal Performance. Csikszentmihalyi, Mihaly. Harper Perennial Modern Classics, 2008.

Habits of a Happy Brain. Breuning, Loretta Graziano. Adams Media, 2015.

'The Rewarding Nature of Social Interactions'. Bodden, Maren; Kircher, Tilo; Krach, Sören; Paulus, M. *Front Behav Neurosci*. 2010; 4: 22. doi: 10.3389/fnbeh.2010.00022

'Dopamine, Smartphones & You: A battle for your time'. Haynes, Trevor. Harvard University Blog, 2018. http://sitn.hms.harvard.edu/flash/2018/dopamine-smartphones-battle-time/

'Hypernatural Monitoring: A Social Rehearsal Account of Smartphone Addiction'. SPL Veissière M Stendel. *Front Psychol*, 2018. Feb 20; 9:141. doi: 10.3389/fpsyg.2018.00141. Erratum in: *Front Psychol*, 2018. Jul 03; 9:1118. PMID: 29515480; PMCID: PMC5826267.

Are cupcakes as addictive as 'cocaine'? Sloan, Jenna. *The Sun*. 2011. https://www.thesun.co.uk/archives/health/884925/are-cupcakes-as-addictive-as-cocaine/

Sean Parker Unloads on Facebook: 'God Only Knows What It's Doing To Our Children's Brains'. Allen, Mike, 2017. https://www.axios.com/sean-parker-unloads-on-facebook-god-only-knows-what-its-doing-to-our-childrens-brains-1513306792-f855e7b4-4e99-4d60-8d51-2775559c2671.html

'How a Handful of Tech Companies Control Billions of Minds Every Day'. Harris, Tristan, 2017. https://www.ted.com/talks/tristan_harris_how_a_handful_of_tech_companies_control_billions_of_minds_every_day?language=en

The Social Dilemma. Netflix, 2020.

Irresistible. Alter, Adam, Penguin Press, 2017.

'It's Not You. Phones Are Designed To Be Addicting'. Vox, 2018. https://www.youtube.com/watch?v=NUMa0QkPzns

What Is Technology Doing to 'Us'? Harris, Sam and Harris, Tristan. https://samharris.org/podcasts/what-is-technology-doing-to-us/

Schedules of Reinforcement. Ferster, C.B.; Skinner, B.F. Skinner Foundation Reprint Series. Original Copyright 1957 Prentice-Hall, Inc. Reprint: 1997, 2014.

'Use Unpredictable Rewards to Keep Behavior Going'. Weinschenk, Susan. *Psychology Today*, 2013. https://www.psychologytoday.com/gb/blog/brain-wise/201311/use-unpredictable-rewards-keep-behavior-going

'Skinner – operant conditioning'. McLeod, S.A. *Simply Psychology*. 2018. https://www.simplypsychology.org/operant-conditioning.html

'Hypernatural Monitoring: A Social Rehearsal Account of Smartphone Addiction'. Stendel, Moriah and Veissièr, Samuel P.L., *Frontiers in Psychology*, 2018. https://doi.org/10.3389/fpsyg.2018.00141

'Digital addiction: how technology keeps us hooked.' Ali, Raian; Arden-Close, Emily; McAlaney, John. *The Conversation*, 2018. https://theconversation.com/digital-addiction-how-technology-keeps-us-hooked-97499

'Motivational, Emotional, and Behavioral Correlates of Fear of Missing Out'. DeHaan, Cody; Gladwell, Valerie; Murayama, Kou; Przybylski, Andrew. *Computers in Human Behavior*. 2018. 29. 1841–1848. 10.1016/j.chb.2013.02.014.

'How the Instagram Algorithm Works'. Cooper, Paige. Hootsuite, 2020. https://blog.hootsuite.com/instagram-algorithm/

'Our minds can be hijacked': the tech insiders who fear a smartphone dystopia'. Lewis, Paul. *Guardian*, 2017. https://www.theguardian.com/technology/2017/oct/05/smartphone-addiction-silicon-valley-dystopia

'Tame Reactive Emotions By Naming Them'. Abblett, Mitch. Mindful.org, 2019. https://www.mindful.org/labels-help-tame-reactive-emotions-naming/

'Putting Feelings Into Words'. Lieberman, Matthew, et al. *Psychological Science*. May 1, 2007. Volume: 18 issue: 5, pp. 421–428. https://journals.sagepub.com/doi/abs/10.1111/j.1467-9280.2007.01916.x

REFERENCES

'A proposal for including nomophobia in the new DSM-V.' Bragazzi, Nicola Luigi and Del Puente, Giovanni. *Psychology Research and Behavior Management* Vol. 7, pp. 155–60. 16 May 2014, doi:10.2147/PRBM.S41386

'Is smartphone addiction really an addiction?', Carbonell, X. and Panova, T.T. *Journal of Behavioral Addictions*, 2018. 7(2), 252–259. Retrieved 19 May 2020, from https://akjournals.com/view/journals/2006/7/2/article-p252.xml

'Beyond Self-Report: Tools to Compare Estimated and Real-World Smartphone use.' Andrews, Sally; Ellis, David A.; Piwek, Lukasz; Shaw, Heather. Plos One. 2015 https://doi.org/10.1371/journal.pone.0139004

'No More FOMO: Limiting social media decreases loneliness and depression.' Hunt, Melissa G.; Lipson, Courtney; Marx, Rachel; Young, Jordyn. *Journal of Social and Clinical Psychology*, Vol. 37. No. 10. 2018. Pp 751–768. Accessed May 2020. [https://guilfordjournals.com/doi/pdf/10.1521/jscp.2018.37.10.751]

'Facebook's emotional consequences: Why Facebook causes a decrease in mood and why people still use it.' Greitemeyer, Tobias; Sagioglou, Christiana. *Computers in Human Behaviour*. Vol. 35, June 2014. Pages 359–363. https://doi.org/10.1016/j.chb.2014.03.003

'The Pomodoro Technique.' Cirillo, Francesco. https://francescocirillo.com/pages/pomodoro-technique

'What You Need To Know About Internet Addiction.' Young, Kimberly, 2015. https://www.youtube.com/watch?v=vOSYmLER664

'Media Use Is Linked to Lower Psychological Well-Being: Evidence from Three Datasets.' Campbell, W.K.; Twenge, J.M. *Psychiatry Q* **90**, 311–331 (2019). https://doi.org/10.1007/s11126-019-09630-7

'Less Facebook use – More well-being and a healthier lifestyle? An experimental intervention study.' Brailovskaia, Julia; Margraf; Jürgen; Schillack, Holger; Ströse, Fabienne. *Computers in Human Behavior*, 2020. 108. 106332. 10.1016/j.chb.2020.106332.

'More Time on Technology, Less Happiness? Associations Between Digital-Media Use and Psychological Well-Being.' Twenge, J. M. *Current Directions in Psychological Science*, 2019, 28(4), 372–379. https://doi.org/10.1177/0963721419838244

The Power of Habit. Duhigg, Charles. Random House Books. 2013

Tiny Habits. Fogg, B.J. Virgin Books, 2020

Mental Health

'Age, period, and cohort trends in mood disorder indicators and suicide-related outcomes in a nationally representative dataset, 2005–2017.' Binau, Sarah G.; Twenge, Cooper; Joiner, Duffy. *Journal of Abnormal Psychology*, 2019.

'Social media's enduring effect on adolescent life satisfaction.' Dienlin, Tobias; Orben, Amy; Przybylski, Andrew K. *Proceedings of the National Academy of Sciences*, May 2019, 116 (21) 10226–10228; DOI: 10.1073/pnas.1902058116

'A large-scale test of the Goldilocks hypothesis: Quantifying the relations between digital-screen use and the mental well-being of adolescents.' Przybylski, A.K.; Weinstein, N. *Psychological Science, 28*(2), 2017, 204–215. https://doi.org/10.1177/0956797616678438

'Are smartphones really that bad? Improving the psychological measurement of technology-related behaviors.' Ellis, D.A. *Computers in Human Behavior*, 2019, *97*, 60–66. https://doi.org/10.1016/j.chb.2019.03.006

'Emerging Field of Emotion Regulation: An Integrative Review'. Gross, J.J., *The Review of General Psychology*, *2*(3), 1998, pp. 271–299. https://doi.org/10.1037/1089-2680.2.3.271

'Emotions: how humans regulate them and why some people can't'. Rowlands, Leanne. *The Conversation*. 2018. https://theconversation.com/emotions-how-humans-regulate-them-and-why-some-people-cant-104713

Digital Emotion Regulation. Gross, J.J.; Koval, P.; Smith, W.; Wadley, G. *Current Directions in Psychological Science*. 2020. https://doi.org/10.1177/0963721420920592

'Just think: The challenges of the disengaged mind'. Brown, Casey; Ellerbeck, Nicole; Gilbert, Daniel; Hahn, Cheryle; Reinhard, David; Shaked, Adi. *Science*. 2014. 345. 75–7. 10.1126/science.1250830.

'Self-inflicted pain out of boredom'. Claes, Laurence; Havermans, Remco; Nederkoorn, Chantal; Vancleef, Linda; Wilkenhoner, Alexandra. *Psychiatry Research*, 2016. 237. 10.1016/j.psychres.2016.01.063.

Hjelm-Lidholm, Sara; Radon, Anita; Sundstrom, Malin. *Journal of Retailing and Consumer Services*. Vol. 47, March 2019, pp. 150–156. https://www.sciencedirect.com/science/article/pii/S096969891830167 X?via%3Dihub

'Characteristics of internet addiction/pathological internet use in U.S. university students: a qualitative-method investigation'. Howard, M.O.; Li, W.; O'Brien, J.E.; Snyder, S.M. *PLoS One*, 2015;10(2):e0117372. Published 3 February 2015. doi:10.1371/journal.pone.0117372

Out of My Skull. Danckert, James and Eastwood, John D., 2020.

'Does Being Bored Make Us More Creative?'. Cadman, Rebekah; Mann, Sandi *Creativity Research Journal*, 2014, 26:2, 165–173, DOI: 10.1080/10400419.2014.901073

'In Defense of Boredom: 200 Years of Ideas on the Virtues of Not-Doing from Some of Humanity's Greatest Minds'. Popova, Maria, 2015. https://www.brainpickings.org/2015/03/16/boredom/

'Induced Boredom Constrains Mindfulness: An Online Demonstration'. Koval, Samuel; Todman, Mcwelling. *Psychology and Cognitive Sciences – Open Journal*. 2015. 1. 1–9. 10.17140/PCSOJ-1-101

'Mobile Mindfulness Meditation: a Randomised Controlled Trial of the Effect of Two Popular Apps on Mental Health'. Flett, J.A.M.; Hayne, H.; Riordan, B.C., et al. *Mindfulness* 10, 863–876 (2019). https://doi.org/10.1007/s12671-018-1050-9

'Stressed nation: 74% of UK "overwhelmed or unable to cope" at some point in the past year'. Mental Health Foundation, 2018. https://www.mentalhealth.org.uk/news/stressed-nation-74-uk-overwhelmed-or-unable-cope-some-point-past-year

'Emerging evidence on COVID-19's impact on mental health and health inequalities'. Abbs, Isabel; Bibby, Jo; Marshall, Louise. The Health Foundation. 2020. https://www.health.org.uk/news-and-comment/blogs/emerging-evidence-on-covid-19s-impact-on-mental-health-and-health

'You're Doomscrolling Again. Here's How to Snap Out of It'. Chen, Brian X. *New York Times*, 2020. https://www.nytimes.com/2020/07/15/technology/personaltech/youre-doomscrolling-again-heres-how-to-snap-out-of-it.html

'The effectiveness of casual video games in improving mood and decreasing stress'. Parks, J.M.; Kevin, O'Brien; Russoniello, Carmen. *Journal of Cyber Therapy and Rehabilitation*. 2009. 2. 53–66.

'Searching for Affective and Cognitive Restoration: Examining the Restorative Effects of Casual Video Game Play'. McConnell, Daniel S.; Rupp, Michael, A.; Smither, Janan A.; Sweetman, Richard. *Human Factors*, 2017; 001872081771536 DOI: 10.1177/0018720817715360

Creating Electronic Learning Environments: Games, Flow, and the User Interface. Jones, M.G. 1998.

REFERENCES

'The Guilty Couch Potato: The Role of Ego Depletion in Reducing Recovery Through Media Use'. Eden, Allison; Hartmann, Tilo; Reinecke, Leonard. *Journal of Communication*, 2014. 64. 10.1111/jcom.12107.

'Rethinking Rumination'. Nolen-Hoeksema, Susan et al. *Perspectives on Psychological Science*, Vol. 3, No. 5, Sept. 2008, pp. 400–424, doi:10.1111/j.1745-6924.2008.00088.x

'Negative social comparison on Facebook and depressive symptoms: Rumination as a mechanism'. Bhatia, V.; Davila, J.; Feinstein, B.A.; Hershenberg, R.; Latack, J.A.; Meuwly, J. *Psychology of Popular Media Culture*, 2013, 2(3), 161–170. https://doi.org/10.1037/a0033111

'A Theory of Social Comparison Processes'. Festinger, L. *Human Relations*, 1954. 7(2), 117–140. https://doi.org/10.1177/001872675400700202

'Social comparison: Motives, standards, and mechanisms'. Corcoran, K. Crusius; J. Mussweiler, T. *Theories in Social Psychology*. 2011. (pp. 119–139).

'Correlates of Facebook usage patterns: The relationship between passive Facebook use, social anxiety symptoms, and brooding'. Joormann, Jutta; Shaw, Ashley M.; Timpano, Kiara R.; Tran, Tanya B. *Computers in Human Behavior*. Volume 48, July 2015, pp. 575–580.

'"It's complicated": Facebook's relationship with the need to belong and depression'. Steers, M.L-N. *Current Opinion in Psychology*, 2016. 9, 22–26. https://doi.org/10.1016/j.copsyc.2015.10.007

'How Does Online Social Networking Enhance Life Satisfaction? The Relationships Among Online Supportive Interaction, Affect, Perceived Social Support, Sense of Community, and Life Satisfaction'. Larose, Robert; Oh, Hyun Jung; Ozkaya, Elif. *Computers in Human Behavior*, 2014. 30. 69–78. 10.1016/j.chb.2013.07.053.

'The Contribution of Mobile Social Media to Social Capital and Psychological Well-Being: Examining the Role of Communicative Use, Friending and Self-Disclosure'. Chen, Hsuan-Ting; Xueqing, Xueqing Li. *Computers in Human Behavior*. 75. 10.1016/j.chb.2017.06.011.

The Relationship Cure. DeClaire, Joan and Gottman, John M., Harmony Books. 2001.

The Seven Principles for Making a Marriage Work. Gottman, John M. and Silver, Nan. 1999

'Primitive emotional contagion'. Cacioppo, John; Hatfield, Elaine; Rapson, Richard. *Review of Personality and Social Psychology*. 1992. 14. 151–177.

'New Perspectives on Emotional Contagion: A Review of Classic and Recent Research on Facial Mimicry and Contagion'. Bensman, L.; Hatfield, E.; Rapson, R.L.; Thornton, P.D. *Interpersona: An International Journal on Personal Relationships*, 2014; 8(2), 159–179. https://doi.org/10.5964/ijpr.v8i2.162

Communicating Emotion: Social, Moral, and Cultural Processes. Planalp, Sally. Cambridge University Press, 1999

The Age of Empathy. De Waal, Frances. Souvenir Press, 2019.

'Digital Emotion Contagion'. Goldenberg, Amit; Gross, James J. *Trends in Cognitive Sciences* 24, No. 4 (April 2020): 316–328

'Experimental Evidence of Massive-Scale Emotional Contagion Through Social Networks'. Guillory, Jamie; Hancock, Jeffrey; Kramer, Adam. Proceedings of the National Academy of Sciences of the United States of America, 2014. 111. 10.1073/pnas.1320040111.

'Measuring Emotional Contagion in Social Media'. Ferrara, Emilio; Zeyao, Yang. *PloS* one vol. 10,11 e0142390. 6 November 2015, doi:10.1371/journal.pone.0142390

'Multilevel Emotion Transfer on YouTube: Disentangling the Effects of Emotional Contagion and Homophily on Video Audiences.' Hannes Rosenbusch, Hannes, *Social Psychological and Personality Science*, Vol. 10, No. 8, Nov. 2019, pp. 1028–1035, doi:10.1177/1948550618820309.

'Susceptibility to emotional contagion for negative emotions improves detection of smile authenticity.' Manera, Valerie. *Frontiers in Human Neuroscience*, Vol. 7 6. 18 March 2013, doi:10.3389/fnhum.2013.00006

'The Emotional Contagion Scale: A measure of Individual Differences.' Doherty, R.W. *Journal of Nonverbal Behavior*. 1997. 21, pp. 131–154.

'The Ripple Effect: Emotional Contagion and its Influence on Group Behavior.' Barsade, S.G. *Administrative Science Quarterly*. 2002. 47(4), 644–675, https://doi.org/10.2307/3094912

'Untangling research and practice: What Facebook's "emotional contagion" study teaches us.' Barsade, S.G. *Research Ethics*, 2002. 12(1), 4–13. https://doi.org/10.1177/1747016115583379

Hello World. Fry, Hannah. W. W. Norton & Company. 2018.

Algorithms of Oppression. Noble, Safiya. NYU Press. 2018.

'Code-Dependent: Pros and Cons of the Algorithm Age'. Anderson, Janna and Rainee, Lee. Pew Research Center. 2017. https://www.pewresearch.org/internet/2017/02/08/code-dependent-pros-and-cons-of-the-algorithm-age/

'Facebook told advertisers it can identify teens feeling "insecure" and "worthless"'. Levin, Sam. *Guardian*, 2017. https://www.theguardian.com/technology/2017/may/01/facebook-advertising-data-insecure-teens

Focus

The Principles of Psychology. James, William, 1890. https://psychclassics.yorku.ca/James/Principles/prin11.htm

'A Cognitive Paradigm to Investigate Interference in Working Memory by Distractions and Interruptions.' Janowich, Jacki. *Journal of visualized experiments : JoVE* ,101 e52226. 16 July 2015, doi:10.3791/52226

Stand Out of Our Light. Williams, James. Cambridge University Press, 31 May 2018.

'Smartphones and Cognition: A Review of Research Exploring the Links between Mobile Technology Habits and Cognitive Functioning'. Chein, J.M.; Sherman, L.E.; Wilmer, H.H. *Frontiers in psychology*, 2017. 8, 605. https://doi.org/10.3389/fpsyg.2017.00605

'Back to the app: the costs of mobile application interruptions,' Bohmer, M.; Gehring, S.; Kruger, A; Leiva, L., in *Proceedings of the 14th International Conference on Human-Computer Interaction with Mobile Devices and Services–Mobile HCI*, Vol. 12, San Francisco, CA: 291–294. 10.1145/2371574.2371617

'Momentary interruptions can derail the train of thought'. Altmann, E.M.; Hambrick, D.Z.; Trafton, J.G. *J Exp Psychol Gen*. 2014; 143(1): 215–226. doi:10.1037/a0030986 https://interruptions.net/literature/Altmann-JExpPsycholGen14.pdf

'The attentional cost of receiving a cell phone notification.' Cary, Stothart et al. *Journal of Experimental Psychology*. Human perception and performance 41 4 (2015): 893–897.

'Brain Drain: The Mere Presence of One's Own Smartphone Reduces Available Cognitive Capacity'. Bos, Maarten W.; Duke, Kristen; Gneezy, Ayelet; Ward, Adrian F.

Journal of the Association for Consumer Research. 2017. 2:2, 140–154

REFERENCES

'The Extended iSelf: The Impact of iPhone Separation on Cognition, Emotion, and Physiology'. Almond, Anthony; Clayton, Russel B.; Leshner, Glenn. *Journal of Computer-Mediated Communication*, Vol. 20, Issue 2, 1 March 2015, pp. 119–135, https://doi.org/10.1111/jcc4.12109

'Neuroplasticity'. Moheb Costandi. *The MIT Press Essential Knowledge Series*. 2016.

'Second-language learning and changes in the brain'. Inoue, K.; Osterhout, L.; Poliakov, A., et al. *J Neurolinguistics* 2008, 21:509–21. https://www.sciencedirect.com/science/article/abs/pii/S091160440800002X

'Neuroplasticity: changes in grey matter induced by training'. Busch, V.; Draganski, B.; Gaser, C., et al. *Nature* 2004; 427:311. DOI: http://dbm.neuro.uni-jena.de/pdf-files/Draganski-Nature.pdf

'Sleep improves memory: the effect of sleep on long term memory in early adolescence.' Bunney, William E. Jr.; Potkin, Katya Trudeau. *PloS one* vol. 7,8 (2012): e42191. doi:10.1371/journal.pone.0042191

'Physical activity, fitness, and gray matter volume.' Erickson, Kirk I. et al. *Neurobiology of Aging*, Vol. 35 Suppl 2 (2014): S20–8. doi:10.1016/j.neurobiolaging.2014.03.034

'Meditation experience is associated with increased cortical thickness.' Lazar, Sara W., et al. *Neuroreport*, Vol. 16,17 (2005): 1893–7. doi:10.1097/01.wnr.0000186598.66243.19

'Cognitive control in media multitaskers'. Nass, Clifford; Ophir, Eyal; Wagner, Anthony D. *Proceedings of the National Academy of Sciences*, Sep 2009, 106 (37) 15583–15587; DOI: 10.1073/pnas.0903620106

'Does media multitasking always hurt? A positive correlation between multitasking and multisensory integration'. K.F.H. Lui, K.F.H., Wong, A.C. *Psychon Bull Rev* 19, 647–653 (2012). https://doi.org/10.3758/s13423-012-0245-7

'Unexpected dual task benefits on cycling in Parkinson disease and healthy adults: a neuro-behavioral model.' Altmann, Lori J.P. et al. *PloS one* vol. 10,5 e0125470. 13 May. 2015, doi:10.1371/journal.pone.0125470

'Supertaskers: Profiles in extraordinary multitasking ability'. Strayer, D.L.; Watson, J.M. *Psychonomic Bulletin & Review* 17, 479–485 (2010). https://doi.org/10.3758/PBR.17.4.479

'Who multi-tasks and why? Multi-tasking ability, perceived multi-tasking ability, impulsivity, and sensation seeking'. Sanbonmatsu, David M. *PloS one* vol. 8,1 (2013): e54402. doi:10.1371/journal.pone.0054402

The distracted mind: Ancient brains in a high-tech world. Gazzaley, A.; Rosen, L.D., 2016

'Why is it so Hard to do My Work? The Challenge of Attention Residue when Switching Between Work Tasks'. Leroy, Sophie. *Organizational Behavior and Human Decision Processes*. 2009. 109. 168–181. 10.1016/j.obhdp.2009.04.002

'About the Distinction between Working Memory and Short-Term Memory.' Aben, Bart et al. *Frontiers in Psychology*, Vol. 3 301. 23 August 2012, doi:10.3389/fpsyg.2012.00301

'Seven Isn't the Magic Number for Short-Term Memory'. Jacobson, Roni. *New York Times*. 2013. https://www.nytimes.com/2013/09/10/science/seven-isnt-the-magic-number-for-short-term-memory.html

'Working memory'. Baddeley, Alan David, 1983. *Philosophical Transactions of the Royal Society of London*. Series B, Biological Sciences. Vol. 302, No. 1110, Functional Aspects of Human Memory 11 August 1983, 311–324.

'Working Memory Capacity: Limits on the Bandwidth of Cognition.' Buschman, Timothy J.; Miller, Earl K., *Daedalus 144*, No. 1 (January 2015): 112–122. © 2015 American Academy of Arts & Sciences

'Too many tabs – why some people can multitask online and others can't'. Peggy Alexopoulou, Peggy. *The Conversation*, 2017. https://theconversation.com/too-many-tabs-why-some-people-can-multitask-online-and-others-cant-70722

'What are the differences between long-term, short-term, and working memory?'. Cowan, N. Prog Brain Res. 2008; 169:323-338. doi:10.1016/S0079-6123(07)00020-9. https://pubmed.ncbi.nlm.nih.gov/18394484/

'Implicit Memory: History and Current Status'. Schacter, Daniel. *Journal of Experimental Psychology: Learning, Memory, and Cognition*. 1987. 13. 501–518. 10.1037/0278-7393.13.3.501.

'Semantic Memory'. Chrysikou, Evangelina G.; Thompson-Schill, Sharon L.; Yee, Eiling. *The Oxford Handbook of Cognitive Neuroscience, Volume 1: Core Topics*

Episodic Memory. Fujii, T., Suzuki, M. *Encyclopedia of Neuroscience.*

The Memory Illusion. Shaw, J., Random House Books. 2016.

'Interactions between attention and memory'. Chun, Marvin M.; Turk-Browne, Nicholas B. *Current Opinion in Neurobiology*, vol. 17,2 (2007): 177–84. doi:10.1016/j.conb.2007.03.005

'The relationship between attention and working memory'. Fougnie, D. In N. B. Johansen (Ed.), *New research on short-term memory*. Nova Science Publishers. 2009.

'Point-and-Shoot Memories: The Influence of Taking Photos on Memory for a Museum Tour'. Henkel, L.A. *Psychological Science*. 2014. 25(2), 396–402. https://doi.org/10.1177/0956797613504438

'Photographic Memory: The Effects of Volitional Photo Taking on Memory for Visual and Auditory Aspects of an Experience'. Barasch, A.; Diehl, K.; Silverman, J.; Zauberman, G. *Psychol Sci.* 2017; 28(8):1056–1066. doi:10.1177/0956797617694868

'How the Intention to Share Can Undermine Enjoyment: Photo-Taking Goals and Evaluation of Experiences'. Barasch, A,; Diehl, K.; Zauberman, G. *Journal of Consumer Research*, Volume 44, Issue 6, April 2018, pp. 1220–1237, https://doi.org/10.1093/jcr/ucx112

'Cognitive Offloading'. Gilbert, S.J.; Risko, E.F., *Trends Cogn Sci.* 2016; 20(9):676-688. doi:10.1016/j.tics.2016.07.002

'Google effects on memory: Cognitive consequences of having information at our fingertips'. Gilbert, S.J.; Risko, E.F. Science, 5 August 2011:Vol. 333, Issue 6043, pp. 776–778. 10.1126/science.1207745

'Transactive Memory: A Contemporary Analysis of the Group Mind'. Wegner, D.M. In: B. Mullen, G.R. Goethals (eds) *Theories of Group Behavior*. Springer Series in Social Psychology. Springer, 1987. https://doi.org/10.1007/978-1-4612-4634-3_9

'Supernormal: How the Internet Is Changing Our Memories and Our Minds'. Ward, Adrian F. *Psychological Inquiry*. 2013. 24:4, 341–348, DOI: 10.1080/1047840X.2013.850148

You Are Not So Smart. McRaney, David. OneWorld. 2012.

'Searching for explanations: How the internet inflates estimates of internal knowledge'. Fisher, Matthew; Goddu, Mariel; Keil, Frank. *Journal of Experimental Psychology*: General, Vol. 144(3), Jun 2015, 674–687

Connection

'The Need to Belong: Desire for Interpersonal Attachments as a Fundamental Human Motivation'. Baumeister, Roy; Leary, Mark. *Psychological Bulletin*.1995. 117. 497–529. 10.1037/0033-2909.117.3.497.

'A theory of human motivation'. Maslow, A.H. *Psychological Review, 50* 1943 (4), 370–396. https://doi.org/10.1037/h0054346

REFERENCES

'Our Hierarchy of Needs'. Burton, Neel. *Psychology Today*. 2012 https://www.psychologytoday.com/gb/blog/hide-and-seek/201205/our-hierarchy-needs

'From the Outside Looking In: Sense of Belonging, Depression, and Suicide Risk'. Braden, A.; Fisher, Lauren B.; Overholser, James C.; Ridley, J.; Rosoff, C. *Psychiatry*. 2015. 78:1, 29–41, DOI: 10.1080/00332747.2015.1015867

'Social relationships and mortality risk: a meta-analytic review'. Holt-Lunstad, J.; Layton, J.B.; Smith, T.B. *PLoS Med*. 2010;7(7):e1000316. Published 2010 Jul 27. doi:10.1371/journal.pmed.1000316

'The "online brain": how the Internet may be changing our cognition'. Firth, Joseph et al. *World Psychiatry: Official Journal of the World Psychiatric Association* (WPA), Vol. 18,2 (2019): 119–129. doi:10.1002/wps.20617

'Relationship Formation on the Internet: What's the Big Attraction?'. Gleason, M.E.J.; Green, A.S.; McKenna, K.Y.A. *Journal of Social Issues*, 2002. 58: 9–31. doi:10.1111/1540-4560.00246

'Loneliness and Social Internet Use: Pathways to Reconnection in a Digital World?'. Cacioppo, J.T.; Necka, E.A.; Nowland, R. *Perspectives on Psychological Science*, 2018. 13(1), 70–87. https://doi.org/10.1177/1745691617713052

How Many Friends Does One Person Need? Dunbar, Robin. Faber & Faber. 2010.

'Ambient intimacy on Twitter'. Levordashka, Ana; Lin, Ruoyun; Sonja, Utz. *Cyberpsychology: Journal of Psychosocial Research on Cyberspace*. 2016. 10. 10.5817/CP2016-1-6.

'Passive and Active Social Media Use and Depressive Symptoms Among United States Adults'. Bowman, Nicholas; Escobar-Viera, César; James, A.; Knight, Jennifer; Primack, Brian; Sidani, Jaime. *Cyberpsychology, Behavior, and Social Networking*. 2018. 21. 437–443. 10.1089/cyber.2017.0668.

'The Relationship Between Facebook Use and Well-Being Depends on Communication Type and Tie Strength'. Burke, Moira; Kraut, Robin E. *Journal of Computer-Mediated Communication*, Volume 21, Issue 4, 1 July 2016, pp. 265–281, https://doi.org/10.1111/jcc4.12162

'Do social network sites enhance or undermine subjective well-being?' Jonides, J.; Kross, E.; Résibois, M.; Verduyn, P.; Ybarra, O. *Social Issues and Policy Review*. 2017. 11(1), 274–302. https://doi.org/10.1111/sipr.12033

Motivational, Emotional, and Behavioral Correlates of Fear of Missing Out. DeHaan, Cody; Gladwell, Valerie; Murayama, Kou; Przybylski, Andrew. (2013). Computers in Human Behavior. 29. 1841–1848. 10.1016/j.chb.2013.02.014.

'Extraversion, neuroticism, attachment style and fear of missing out as predictors of social media use and addiction'. Blackwell, David; Leaman, Carrie; Liss, Miriam; Osborne, Ciera; Tramposch, Rose. (2017). *Personality and Individual Differences*. 116. 69–72. 10.1016/j.paid.2017.04.039

'Disintermediating your friends: How online dating in the United States displaces other ways of meeting'. Hausen, Sonia; Rosenfeld, Michael J.; Thomas, Reuben J. Proceedings of the National Academy of Sciences September 2019, 116 (36) 17753–17758; DOI: 10.1073/pnas.1908630116

'A Rejection Mind-Set: Choice Overload in Online Dating'. Denissen, J.J.A.; Pronk, T.M., (2020). Social Psychological and Personality Science, 11(3), 388–396. https://doi.org/10.1177/1948550619866189

'There Are Plenty of Fish in the Sea: The Effects of Choice Overload and Reversibility on Online Daters' Satisfaction With Selected Partners'. D'Angelo, Jonathan; Toma, Catalina. (2016). Media Psychology. 20. 1–27. 10.1080/15213269.2015.1121827.

'Attached: Are you Anxious, Avoidant or Secure? Heller, Rachel; Levine, Amir. 2011. How the science of adult attachment can help you find – and keep – love.' Bluebird; Main Market edition (3 Jun. 2011)

'Romantic love conceptualized as an attachment process.' Hazan, C. and P. Shaver. *Journal of Personality and Social Psychology* 52 3 (1987): 511–24.

'Smartphone use undermines enjoyment of face-to-face social interactions.' Dunn, Elizabeth; Dwyer, Ryan; Kushlev, Kostadi. *Journal of Experimental Social Psychology.* 2017. 78. 10.1016/j.jesp.2017.10.007.

'Smartphones distract parents from cultivating feelings of connection when spending time with their children.' Dunn, Elizabeth; Kushlev, Kostadin. *Journal of Social and Personal Relationships*, 2018. 36. 026540751876938. 10.1177/0265407518769387

'Managing Expectations: Technology Tensions among Parents and Teens.' Blackwell, Lindsay; Gardiner, Emma; Schoenebeck, Sarita. *Proceedings of the 19th ACM Conference on Computer-Supported Cooperative Work & Social Computing*, 2016. (CSCW '16). 10.1145/2818048.2819928

'Emotional and aesthetic attachment to digital artefacts.' Turner, P.; Turner, S. *Cognition, Technology & Work, 15*(4), 403–414. https://doi.org/10.1007/s10111-012-0231-x

'NOMOPHOBIA: NO MObile PHone PhoBIA.' Bhattacharya, Sudip et al. *Journal of Family Medicine and Primary Care*, Vol. 8,4. 2019. 1297–1300. doi:10.4103/jfmpc.jfmpc_71_19

'Humans' attachment to their mobile phones and its relationship with interpersonal attachment style.' Bereczky, Boróka; Gigler, Dóra; Konok, Veronika; Miklosi, Adam. *Computers in Human Behavior*, 2016. 61. 537–547. 10.1016/j.chb.2016.03.062.

Work

'How to handle stress at work.' LeBlanc, Nicole J.; Marques, Luana. *Harvard Health Publishing.* Harvard Medical School. https://www.health.harvard.edu/blog/how-to-handle-stress-at-work-2019041716436

'Reversing burnout: How to rekindle your passion for your work.' Leiter, Michael; Maslach, Christina. Stanford Social Innovation Review. 2005. 3. 42–49.

'Employee Burnout, Part 1: The 5 Main Causes.' Agrawal, Sangeeta; Wigert, Ben. Gallup. 2018. https://www.gallup.com/workplace/237059/employee-burnout-part-main-causes.aspx

'Staff Burn-Out.' Freudenberger, H.J. *Journal of Social Issues*, 1974. 30: 159–165. doi:10.1111/j.1540-4560.1974.tb00706.x

'How Millennials Became The Burnout Generation.' Petersen, Anne Helen. BuzzFeed. 2019. https://www.buzzfeednews.com/article/annehelenpetersen/millennials-burnout-generation-debt-work

'Smartphone Use and Daily Recovery.' Bakker, A.B.; Derks, D. *Applied Psychology.* 2014. 63: 411–440. doi:10.1111/j.1464-0597.2012.00530.x

'Doing the Things We Do: A Grounded Theory of Academic Procrastination.' Olafson, Lori; Schraw, Gregory; Wadkins, Theresa. *Journal of Educational Psychology*, 2007. 99. 12–25. 10.1037/0022-0663.99.1.12

'Inside the mind of a master procrastinator.' Urban, Tim. YouTube. https://www.youtube.com/watch?v=arj7oStGLkU

Procrastination, Emotion Regulation, and Well-being. Pychyl, T.A.; Sirois, F.M. (Eds.), Elsevier Academic Press. https://doi.org/10.1016/B978-0-12-802862-9.00008-6

Procrastination and Stress: Exploring the Role of Self-compassion, Self and Identity. Sirois, Fuschia M., 2014 13:2, 128–145, DOI: 10.1080/15298868.2013.763404

'Your Desire to Get Things Done Can Undermine Your Effectiveness.' Francesca Gino and Bradley Staats. *Harvard Business Review.* 2016. https://hbr.org/2016/03/your-desire-to-get-things-done-can-undermine-your-effectiveness?

REFERENCES

'The Planning Fallacy: Cognitive, Motivational and Social Origins'. Buehler, Roger; Griffin, Dale; Peetz, Johanna. *Advances in Experimental Social Psychology*. Vol. 43, pp. 3–62. https://www.sciencedirect.com/science/article/pii/S0065260110430014

'Exploring the "Planning Fallacy": Why People Underestimate Their Task Completion Times'. Buehler, Roger; Griffin, Dale; Ross, Michael. *Journal of Personality and Social Psychology*, 1994. 67. 366–381. 10.1037/0022-3514.67.3.366

'Time Pressure, Performance, and Productivity'. Moore, Don, Tenney, Elizabeth. *Research on Managing Groups and Teams*. 2012. 15. 305–326. 10.1108/S1534-0856(2012)0000015015.

'Email Duration, Batching and Self-interruption: Patterns of Email Use on Productivity and Stress'. Czerwinski, Mary; Iqbal, Shamsi T.; Johns, Paul; Lutchyn, Yuliya; Mark, Gloria; Sano, Akane. Proceedings of the 2016 CHI Conference on Human Factors in Computing Systems (CHI '16). Association for Computing Machinery, New York, NY, USA, 1717–1728. DOI:https://doi.org/10.1145/2858036.2858262

Indistractable. *Eyal, Nir.* BenBella Books. 2019.

'Zoom Burnout is Real'. Angela Lashbrook. 2020. OneZero. https://onezero.medium.com/zoom-burnout-is-real-27e6938d0e1f

'Defining Mobile Tech Posture: Prevalence and Position Among Millennials'. Cool, Alex; Delay, Ariana; Lannom, Ali; Mays, Michelle; O'Donnell, Laryn; Stuber, Ruth. *The Open Journal of Occupational Therapy*. 2020. 8. 1–10. 10.15453/2168-6408.1640.

'Decreases in self-reported sleep duration among U.S. adolescents 2009–2015 and links to new media screen time'. Hisler, Garrett; Krizan, Zlatan; Twenge, Jean. *Sleep Medicine*. 2017. 39. 10.1016/j.sleep.2017.08.013.

'Teenage sleep and technology engagement across the week.' Orben, Amy; Przybylski, Andrew K., *PeerJ*, Vol. 8 e8427. 28 Jan. 2020, doi:10.7717/peerj.8427

Why We Sleep. Walker, Matthew. Penguin, 2017.

'Differential effects of light wavelength in phase advancing the melatonin rhythm'. Kennaway, D.J.; Lack, L.C.; Wright, H.R. *Journal of Pineal Research*, 2014, 36: 140–144. doi:10.1046/j.1600-079X.2003.00108.x

'Orthosomnia: Are Some Patients Taking the Quantified Self Too Far?.' Baron, Glazer et al. *Journal of Clinical Sleep Medicine*: JCSM : official publication of the American Academy of Sleep Medicine, Vol. 13,2 351–354. 15 February 2017, doi:10.5664/jcsm.6472

Privacy and Security

'The role of privacy fatigue in online privacy behavior', Choi; Hanbyul; Jung, Yoonhyuk; Park, Jonghwa. *Computers in Human Behavior*. 2017. doi: 10.1016/j.chb.2017.12.001

'It wouldn't happen to me': Privacy concerns and perspectives following the Cambridge Analytica scandal. Hinds, Joanne; Joinson, Adam; Williams, Emma. *International Journal of Human-Computer Studies*. 2020 102498. 10.1016/j.ijhcs.2020.102498.

'Using Fingerprint Authentication to Reduce System Security: An Empirical Study'. Liebrock, L.M.; Wimberly, H. 2011 IEEE Symposium on Security and Privacy. Berkeley, CA. pp. 32–46, doi: 10.1109/SP.2011.35.

'What Are "Data Brokers," and Why Are They Scooping Up Information About You?' Gruer, Yael. *Vice.* 2018, https://www.vice.com/en_us/article/bjpx3w/what-are-data-brokers-and-how-to-stop-my-private-data-collection

'Forget Facebook, mysterious data brokers are facing GDPR trouble'. Katwala, Amit, 2018. Wired UK. 2018. https://www.wired.co.uk/article/gdpr-acxiom-experian-privacy-international-data-brokers

'Privacy policies are read by an aging few'. Hart, Kim, 2019. https://www.axios.com/few-people-read-privacy-policies-survey-fec3a29e-2e3a-4767-a05c-2cacdcbaecc8.html

'We Read 150 Privacy Policies. They Were an Incomprehensible Disaster'. Litman-Navarro, Kevin, *New York Times*, 2019. https://www.nytimes.com/interactive/2019/06/12/opinion/facebook-google-privacy-policies.html

'The Average Reading Level of a Privacy Policy'. Sobers, Rob. *Varonis*. 2020. https://www.varonis.com/blog/gdpr-privacy-policy/

'"What Can I Really Do?": Explaining the Privacy Paradox with Online Apathy'. Hargittai, Eszter; Marwick, Alice. *International Journal of Communication*. 2016.

Privacy is Power. Veliz, Carissa. Transworld Digital. 2020.

'Revealed: 50 million Facebook profiles harvested for Cambridge Analytica in major data breach'. Cadwalladr, Carole and Graham-Harrison, Emma. *Guardian*, 2018. https://www.theguardian.com/news/2018/mar/17/cambridge-analytica-facebook-influence-us-election

'The Cambridge Analytica scandal affected nearly 40 million more people than we thought'. Kozlowska, Hanna. *Quartz*. 2018. https://qz.com/1245049/the-cambridge-analytica-scandal-affected-87-million-people-facebook-says/

'Cambridge Analytica: how did it turn clicks into votes?' Hern, Alex. *Guardian*. 2018. https://www.theguardian.com/news/2018/may/06/cambridge-analytica-how-turn-clicks-into-votes-christopher-wylie

'Hearing before the United States Senate Committee on the Judiciary and the United States Senate Committee on Commerce, Science and Transportation'. Zuckerberg, Mark. 2018. https://www.judiciary.senate.gov/imo/media/doc/04-10-18%20Zuckerberg%20Testimony.pdf

'Social media is a threat to democracy'. Carole Cadwalladr speaks at TED2019. https://blog.ted.com/social-media-is-a-threat-to-our-democracy-carole-cadwalladr-speaks-at-ted2019/

'Psychological targeting in digital mass persuasion'. Kosinski, M.; Matz, S.C.; Nave, G.; Stillwell, D.J. *Proceedings of the National Academy of Sciences* Nov 2017, 114 (48) 12714–12719; DOI: 10.1073/pnas.1710966114

'Many Facial-Recognition Systems Are Biased, Says U.S. Study'. Metz, Cade; Singer, Natasha. *The New York Times*. 2019 https://www.nytimes.com/2019/12/19/technology/facial-recognition-bias.html

'Facial recognition: ten reasons you should be worried about the technology'. Schippers, Birgit. *The Conversation*, 2019. https://theconversation.com/facial-recognition-ten-reasons-you-should-be-worried-about-the-technology-122137

'A Case for Banning Facial Recognition'. Timnit Gebru interviewed by Shira Ovide. *The New York Times*. 2020. https://www.nytimes.com/2020/06/09/technology/facial-recognition-software.html

'How London became a test case for using facial recognition in democracies'. Madhumita Murgia. FT.com. 2019. https://www.ft.com/content/f4779de6-b1e0-11e9-bec9-fdcab53d6959

'Portland's Radical Facial Recognition Proposal Bans the Tech From Airbnbs, Restaurants, Stores, and More'. Kaye, Kate. *OneZero*. 2020 https://onezero.medium.com/portlands-radical-facial-recogni-tion-proposal-bans-the-tech-from-airbnbs-restaurants-stores-and-32ada95430b6

'The Privacy Paradox: Personal Information Disclosure Intentions versus Behaviors'. Horne, D.A.; Horne, D.R.; Norberg, P.A. *Journal of Consumer Affairs*. 2007. 41: 100–126. doi:10.1111/j.1745-6606.2006.00070.x

REFERENCES

Body Image

Body Image. Grogan, Sarah. Routledge. 1999.

'The role of the media in body image concerns among women: a meta-analysis of experimental and correlational studies.' Grabe, Shelly et al. *Psychological bulletin* 134 3 (2008): 460–76.

'A meta-analytic review of the relationship between social media use and body image disturbance.' Saiphoo, Alyssa; Vahedi, Zahra. *Computers in Human Behavior*. 2019. 10.1016/j.chb.2019.07.028.

'#SocialMedia: Exploring the Relationship of Social Networking Sites on Body Image, Self-Esteem, and Eating Disorders.' Santarossa, Sara; Woodruff, Sarah J. *Social Media + Society*, Apr. 2017, doi:10.1177/2056305117704407.

'Photoshopping the selfie: Self photo editing and photo investment are associated with body dissatisfaction in adolescent girls.' McLean, Siân A. et al. *The International Journal of Eating Disorders*, Vol. 48,8 (2015): 1132–40. doi:10.1002/eat.22449 https://www.ncbi.nlm.nih.gov/pubmed/26311205

'Compared to Facebook, Instagram use causes more appearance comparison and lower body satisfaction in college women.' Engeln, Renee; Imundo, Megan; Loach, Ryan; Zola, Anne. *Body Image*. 2020. 34. 38–45. 10.1016/j.bodyim.2020.04.007.

'A Theory of Social Comparison Processes.' Festinger, L. *Human Relations*. 1954;7(2):117–140. doi:10.1177/001872675400700202

'The impact of appearance comparisons made through social media, traditional media, and in person in women's everyday lives.' Fardouly, Jasmine; Pinkus, Rebecca; Vartanian, Lenny. *Body Image*. 2017. 20. 31–39. 10.1016/j.bodyim.2016.11.002.

'Social Comparison as the Thief of Joy: Emotional Consequences of Viewing Strangers' Instagram Posts.' Anniek, W.; Eigenraam, S.; Hamelink, Kirsten. Möller, Marthe A.; de Vries, Dian A.; Wieringa. *Media Psychology*. 2018. 21:2, 222–245, DOI:10.1080/15213269.2016.1267647

'A Brief History of Instagram's Trouble With 'Weight-Loss Tea'. Grey Ellis, Emma. Wired.com. 2020. https://www.wired.com/story/brief-history-instagram-fitness-tea-ftc-complaint/

'Picture Perfect: The Direct Effect of Manipulated Instagram Photos on Body Image in Adolescent Girls', Anschütz, Doeschka; Carbaat, Ilana; Daalmans, Serena; Kleemans, Mariska. *Media Psychology*. 2018. 21:1, 93–110, DOI: 10.1080/15213269.2016.1257392

'Social media literacy protects against the negative impact of exposure to appearance ideal social media images in young adult women but not men'. McLean, S.A.; Paxton, S.J.; Tamplin, N.C. *Body Image*. 2018; 26:29–37. doi:10.1016/j.bodyim.2018.05.003

'"Strong Is the New Skinny": A Content Analysis of #fitspiration Images on Instagram.' Tiggemann, Marika; Zaccardo, Mia. *Journal of Health Psychology*, Vol. 23, No. 8, July 2018, pp. 1003–1011, doi:10.1177/1359105316639436. https://www.ncbi.nlm.nih.gov/pubmed/26176993 https://journals.sagepub.com/doi/10.1177/1359105316639436

'Negative comparisons about one's appearance mediate the relationship between Facebook usage and body image concerns.' Fardouly, J.; Vartanian, L. *Body Image*. 2015: 82–8.

'Faking it: how selfie dysmorphia is driving people to seek surgery'. Hunt, Elle. *Guardian*. 2019. https://www.theguardian.com/lifeandstyle/2019/jan/23/faking-it-how-selfie-dysmorphia-is-driving-people-to-seek-surgery

'"Selfie" harm: Effects on mood and body image in young women.' Musto, Sarah; Tiggeman, Marika; Williams, Lindsay. *Body Image*, 2018. 27. 86–92. 10.1016/j.bodyim.2018.08.007.

'This AR designer turns Instagram and Snapchat filters into fine art'. Behrmann, Anna, 2019 https://www.wired.co.uk/article/ines-alpha-digital-makeup

'Monitoring eating and activity: Links with disordered eating, compulsive exercise, and general wellbeing among young adults'. Bone, S.; Lanning, E.; Meyer, C.; Plateau, C.R. *Int J Eat Disord.* 2018; 51: 1270– 1276. https://doi.org/10.1002/eat.22966

'My Fitness Pal calorie tracker usage in the eating disorders'. Brosof, L.C.; Fewell, L.; Levinson, C.A. *Eat Behav*, 2017; 27:14–16. doi:10.1016/j.eatbeh.2017.08.003

'Effective behaviour change techniques for physical activity and healthy eating in overweight and obese adults; systematic review and meta-regression analyses'. Barth, T.; Eide, G.E.; Meland, E.; Samdal, G.B.; Williams, G. *Int J Behav Nutr Phys Act.* 2017;14(1):42. Published 2017 Mar 28. doi:10.1186/s12966-017-0494-y

Responsibility

'The Global E-waste Monitor 2020: Quantities, flows and the circular economy potential'. Baldé, C.P.; Bel, G.; Forti, V.; Kuehr, R. United Nations University (UNU)/United Nations Institute for Training and Research (UNITAR) – co-hosted SCYCLE Programme, International Telecommunication Union (ITU) & International Solid Waste Association (ISWA), Bonn/Geneva/Rotterdam.

The Molecule of More. Lieberman, Daniel Z. and Long, Michael E. BenBella Books. 2018.

'Dopamine reward prediction error coding'. Schultz, Wolfram. *Dialogues in Clinical Neuroscience.* 2016. 18. 23–32.

'Striatal Activity Underlies Novelty-Based Choice in Humans'. Daw, Nathaniel; Dolan, Raymond; Seymour, Ben; Wittman, Bianca. *Neuron.* 2008. 58. 967–73. 10.1016/j.neuron.2008.04.027.

'One Thing You Can Do: Keep Your Old Gadgets Out Of The Trash'. Garcia, Eduardo and Schwartz, John. *New York Times*, 2019. https://www.nytimes.com/2019/04/03/climate/nyt-climate-fwd-newsletter.html

'Planned obsolescence: the outrage of our electronic waste mountain'. Harris, John. *Guardian*, 2020. https://www.theguardian.com/technology/2020/apr/15/the-right-to-repair-planned-obsolescence-electronic-waste-mountain

'France fines Apple $27 million for slowing down iPhones'. Cooper, Daniel. Engadget. 2020. https://www.engadget.com/2020-02-07-france-apple-ios-slowdown-fine.html

'Why Europe's New Efforts to Tackle Unfixable Gadgets Are So Important'. Proctor, Nathan. OneZero. 2019. https://onezero.medium.com/why-europes-new-efforts-to-tackle-unfixable-gadgets-are-so-important-814781f6e107

'Uber drivers' fight for workers' rights reaches UK supreme court'. Booth, Robert. *The Guardian.* 2020. https://www.theguardian.com/technology/2020/jul/21/uber-drivers-fight-for-workers-rights-reaches-supreme-court

'"I don't even go to the toilet": Deliveroo riders will fight to be recognised as workers'. Chakelian, Anoosh. *New Statesman*, 2018. https://www.newstatesman.com/politics/economy/2018/06/i-don-t-even-go-toilet-deliveroo-riders-will-fight-be-recognised-workers

'Amazon accused of "intolerable conditions" at Scottish warehouse'. Osborne, Hilary. *Guardian*, 2016. https://www.theguardian.com/technology/2016/dec/11/amazon-accused-of-intolerable-conditions-at-scottish-warehouse

REFERENCES

'The real cost of Amazon'. Del Ray, Jason and Ghaffary, Shirin. *Vox*, 2020. https://www.vox.com/recode/2020/6/29/21303643/amazon-coronavirus-warehouse-workers-protest-jeff-bezos-chris-smalls-boycott-pandemic

'The Hidden Environmental Cost of Amazon Prime's Free, Fast Shipping'. Nguyen, Nicole. BuzzFeed, 2018. https://www.buzzfeednews.com/article/nicolenguyen/environmental-impact-of-amazon-prime

'"Beat the machine": Amazon warehouse workers strike to protest inhumane conditions'. Dzieza, Josh. *The Verge*, 2019. https://www.theverge.com/2019/7/16/20696154/amazon-prime-day-2019-strike-warehouse-workers-inhumane-conditions-the-rate-productivity

Identity

'The relevance of algorithms'. Gillespie, Boczkowski, P.J.; Foo, K.A.; Gillespie, T. (eds), *Media Technologies: Essays on Communication, Materiality, and Society*.

'The magic that makes Spotify's Discover Weekly playlists so damn good'. Pasick, Adam. *Quartz*, 2015. https://qz.com/571007/the-magic-that-makes-spotifys-discover-weekly-playlists-so-damn-good/.

The Filter Bubble. Eli Pariser. Penguin 2011.

'YouTube, the Great Radicalizer'. Tufekci, Zeynep. *New York Times*, 2018. https://www.nytimes.com/2018/03/10/opinion/sunday/youtube-politics-radical.html

'YouTube recommendation algorithm audit uncovers paths to radicalization'. Johnson, Khari. *Venture Beat*. 2019. https://venturebeat.com/2019/08/28/youtube-recommendation-algorithm-audit-uncovers-paths-to-radicalization/

'The Making of a YouTube Radical'. Roose, Kevin. *New York Times*, 2019. https://www.nytimes.com/interactive/2019/06/08/technology/youtube-radical.html

'YouTube's AI is the puppet master over most of what you watch'. Solsman, John E. *Cnet*, 2018. https://www.cnet.com/news/youtube-ces-2018-neal-mohan/

'Ex-Google engineer: Extreme content? No, it's algorithms that radicalize people'. Leprince-Ringuet, Daphne. *Cnet*, 2019. https://www.zdnet.com/article/ex-youtube-engineer-extreme-content-no-its-algorithms-that-radicalize-people/

'Continuing our work to improve recommendations on YouTube'. YouTube Team. YouTube Official Blog. 2019. https://blog.youtube/news-and-events/continuing-our-work-to-improve

'Down the rabbit hole: how QAnon conspiracies thrive on Facebook'. Carrie Wong, Julia. *Guardian*, 2020. https://www.theguardian.com/technology/2020/jun/25/qanon-facebook-conspiracy-theories-algorithm

'Apple CEO Tim Cook's Message to 2019 Graduates: "My Generation Has Failed You"'. Cao, Sissi. *Observer*, 2019. https://observer.com/2019/05/apple-ceo-tim-cook-tulane-2019-commencement-speech-climate-change/

The Black Box Society. Pasquale, Frank. Harvard University Press. 2015.

The Presentation of Self in Everyday Life. Goffman, Erving. Penguin. 1959.

'Social Network Sites as Networked Publics: Affordances, Dynamics, and Implications.' boyd, dannah. In *Networked Self: Identity, Community, and Culture on Social Network Sites* (ed. Zizi Papacharissi), pp. 39–58.

The Facebook Effect: The Real Inside Story of Mark Zuckerberg and the World's Fastest Growing Company. Fitzpatrick, David. Virgin Books. 2011.

'Wearing many (social) hats: How different are your different social network personae?'. Chang, H.W.; Karamshuk, D.; Lee, D.; Sastry, N.; Zhong, C. *In Proceedings of the 11th International Conference on Web and Social Media, ICWSM 2017* (pp. 397–406). (Proceedings of the 11th International Conference on Web and Social Media, ICWSM 2017). AAAI press.

'The Social Media Ecology: User Perceptions, Strategies and Challenges.' Zhao, Xuan et al. Proceedings of the 2016 CHI Conference on Human Factors in Computing Systems (2016)

'The Intellectual Challenge of CSCW: The Gap Between Social Requirements and Technical Feasibility.' Ackerman, M. *Human–Computer Interaction* 15 (2000): 179–203.

'Political Discourse on Social Media: Echo Chambers, Gatekeepers, and the Price of Bipartisanship'. Garimella, Kiran; Gionis, Aristides; Mathioudakis, Michael; Morales, Gianmarco WWW '18: Proceedings of the 2018 World Wide Web Conference. 913–922. 10.1145/3178876.3186139.

'Birds of a Feather: Homophily in Social Networks'. Cook, James M.; McPherson, Miller; Smith-Lovin, Lynn. *Annual Review of Sociology* 2001 27:1, 415–444.

'12 Common Biases That Affect How We Make Everyday Decisions'. Dwyer, Christopher. *Psychology Today*. 2018. https://www.psychologytoday.com/gb/blog/thoughts-thinking/201809/12-common-biases-affect-how-we-make-everyday-decisions

'Do digital echo chambers exist?' Amol Rajan. BBC News, 2019. https://www.bbc.com/news/entertainment-arts-47447633

'Cyberostracism: Effects of Being Ignored Over the Internet'. Cheung, Christopher K.T.; Choi, Wilma; Williams, Kipling D. *Journal of Personality and Social Psychology*, 2000, Vol. 79, No. 5, 748–762.

The Future

'Mental Time Travel and the Evolution of the Human Mind'. Corballis, Michael; Suddendorf, Thomas. *Genetic Social and General Psychology Monographs*. 123. 133–167.

'Back to the future: the effect of daily practice of mental time travel into the future on happiness and anxiety'. Hansenne, Michel; Quoidbach, Jordi; Wood, Alex M. *The Journal of Positive Psychology*. 2009. 4:5, 349–355

'Anxiety, Depression, and the Anticipation of Future Positive and Negative Experiences.' Byrne, Angela; MacLeod, Andrew K. *Journal of Abnormal Psychology* 105.2 (1996): 286–289.

'The positive psychology of negative thinking'. Chang, Edward C.; Norem, Julie K. *Journal of Clinical Psychology*. 2002. Vol. 58(9), 993–1001.

ACKNOWLEDGMENTS

This book took six months to write, but it's taken me 20 years to get to this point. That's how long it's been since my first column was published in the Scarborough Evening News, my local newspaper growing up. Clearly starting as I meant to go on, in that column I sought to find answers to the bigger questions of the day: who is best – Britney Spears, Christina Aguilera or Pink?

With that long journey in mind, I'd like to thank a few of the people who helped me to get here.

To my secondary school English teacher Mr (Gary) Futcher, thank you for showing me that I wanted to make my life all about words.

My first bosses, Stuart Bruce and Chris Norton, thanks for taking a gamble on a graduate fresh out of university and, more importantly, teaching me how to tweet.

Cate Sevilla, thank you for entrusting me with my first tech column at BitchBuzz and remaining a source of inspiration ever since.

To the many other editors and people who commissioned me and sent work opportunities my way over the years, thank you. Especially Sophie Charara, Michael Sawh, James Stables and the

Wareable team. James Peckham, Gareth Beavis and the lovely bunch at TechRadar. Marc Chacksfield, Jemima Kiss, Tom Pritchard, Matthew Bolton and, of course, Ashley Norris and Chris Price – I am so grateful to you for the ShinyShiny years (both sets of them).

A big socially-distanced wave to all of my wonderful friends. A special shout-out to Susie Freeman (and Tony!), your friendship has been a constant comfort since the Scalby School Drama days. Lauren Bravo for your writing wisdom and for answering my incessant questions, soothing me during freakouts, and our many brunches over the years – you've been a writing role model to me. Catherine Allen, thank you for your guidance and friendship – the tech industry is far, far better for you being in it. Rochelle Bugg, I'm incredibly proud of you and so glad we got to be book buddies. James O'Malley, thank you for reading bits of the book before they were bits of the book. And my Team ShinyShiny veterans, Elisabeth Edvardsen and Gerald Lynch, thanks for always having my back.

To Jemima Forrester, thank you for giving me the confidence to believe I could be published.

Thank you to Hayley Steed at Madeleine Milburn Agency for replying to my DM on Twitter asking about representation (I was shaking as I hit send!) and helping me navigate my very first book deal during a global pandemic.

To my agent Catherine Cho for believing in me and my writing from the first time we met. Thank you for throwing around so many ideas with me (Robots! The future!) before we settled on my first love: screens.

Enormous thanks to my editor Susannah Otter. Your passion for my idea from the get-go, as well as your guidance, insights, and encouragement, helped make what could have been a gruelling first-book marathon feel like a leisurely walk through the park. If I could create the perfect editor using a fancy people-making machine, it'd be you.

A massive thank you to the team at Bonnier Books for your hard work and support in pulling Screen Time together at break-neck speed. Especially Nikki Mander and Ali Nazari for getting the book out into the world. Your enthusiasm and energy was very much appreciated.

To Jenny, Mia and Ruby, thank you for keeping me fully up-to-speed with what the young people of today are tapping away at on their screens.

To my brother Robert, you're the best. Thank you for being a constant voice of encouragement. I'm grateful for every phone call and infinitely proud of you.

To my brilliant Dad for igniting my love for technology with big TVs, shiny new phones and Star Wars. To my incredible Mum for teaching me about resilience, motivation and for watching Star Trek with me for hours on end when I was small and starry-eyed. This book is for you both and I'm so glad you can finally hold my words in your hands.

The biggest thank you goes to my partner Steve. I feel incredibly lucky that we found each other through our screens and the long list of reasons why I couldn't have written this book without you include creating the perfect workspace for me, ordering regular motivational treat deliveries, impromptu brainstorming sessions, not letting me take second naps, and a lot more. But more than anything, for your unwavering belief in me. As often as I might doubt myself, you never do.

Finally, thank you to anyone who has read, liked, commented on, retweeted and shared my work. I've spent a huge part of my life staring into screens and it remains a fun and fulfilling way to work because of you.

ABOUT THE AUTHOR

As a technology journalist, Becca Caddy is at the forefront of digital innovation. She has written for publications like *New Scientist, Wired, T3, Metro*, the *Guardian* and the *Sunday Times*.